WELCOME TO THI
WITH YOUR HORSE!

To Our Directory Users:

Congratulations on your purchase of the 2003 ***Nationwide Overnight Stabling Directory &*** *Equestrian Vacation Guide.* Equine Travelers of America, has published the directory yearly since 1982. We welcome you to the thousands of other users and hope you find it useful and carry it with you always.

A note of explanation about the facilities that are listed in the Directory. ETA gathers listing information, puts it into directory form and sells the directory to traveling horsemen. The listing information printed in this directory has been provided to ETA by the host stabler. If you have any questions about exactly what is offered at each facility, ask any and all questions you have when you call to make reservations. Tell them what you are looking for and ask what size the stalls are, ask what type of fencing is used, ask about water, feed, bedding, etc. At the same time, you should ask what their requirements are - do they have a specific time for you to be there, do you need to call an hour or so before arrival, what arrangements can be made if the host is not there to meet you? As you can see, many questions need to be asked and answered at the time you call for reservations.

We do not ordinarily list prices in the Directory because hosts can change their prices at any time, adjust their price in anyway that they want and also, it gives the traveler the added incentive to call first and find out what the prices are. The incentive to call and make reservations is also the reason we do not usually give directions right to a host's driveway. Travelers need to call and make reservations first, and at that time get specific directions and find out what the prices are.

As to why every fairgrounds, arena, sale barn, etc. in the country is not listed in the Directory - Host stablers pay to be listed in our Directory; in other words, they are serious about offering overnight stabling. Although other places are available for overnight stabling, they don't necessarily want to advertise that fact and they don't want to pay to advertise. Also, many of these other types of places have no security at all. We want the best possible places we can get and encourage all users of this Directory to let us know of great overnight facilities they come across so we can add them to the next Directory.

REMEMBER TRAVELERS - LET YOUR HOSTS KNOW OF ANY CHANGES IN YOUR PLANS!

DIRECTORY USERS - PLEASE READ

HEALTH REQUIREMENT PLACEMENT

A single designation has been placed at the top of each page to remind you to always have all of your health and ownership papers with you. You, as users of this directory, should always assume that you will need a current Negative Coggins, Health Certificate, Proof of current immunizations, and Ownership papers. Some states also require brand inspection. It is your responsibility to find out what each state and what each individual overnight stabling facility require. Some might want a Negative Coggins test within 1 year, some within 6 months, some might even want one more current than that.

IT IS YOUR RESPONSIBILITY TO FIND OUT WHAT IS REQUIRED.

Any other requirements by individual stablers will be included in their listing in the Directory.

Notice to overnight stablers - some of our Directory users have told us that they were not asked to show their health papers and felt that host stablers should be concerned about seeing these papers. So, Hosts, please ask to see your overnight guests' equine health papers. This will make everyone feel better.

SPECIAL NOTE TO HOST STABLERS: We have had some complaints from customers who say they have called and made reservations but when they showed up (and this was evening, not late at night), no one was there to meet them and no written instructions were left for them. As frustrating as it is for hosts when travelers do not show up to honor reservations, it is also terribly frustrating for the traveler to show up and for the host to be missing. People - please be considerate of one another.

Janice J. Nelson
Executive Editor

James L. McDaniel
President of ETA

ADDITIONAL INFORMATION FOR DIRECTORY USERS:

Overnight hosts - if you would like to offer your overnight customers a chance to purchase their own directory, postage paid postcards are available for you to hand out to your customers. You might not want the Directory on hand to sell, but you might be interested in letting others know about the Directory. Just let us know if you are interested.

A word about maps used in the Directory. These maps are a guide only in locating the host towns and cities in an atlas. We want you to have some idea where the overnight spots are in relationship to the interstate system. So, please use them with your atlas.

This is a reminder that there have been literally hundreds of area code changes around the country the last several years. Lots of changes are still being made. If you have trouble with a telephone number listed in the Directory, the first thing you should check is the area code. Sometimes listers forget to let us know that their area codes has changed and sometimes the time of intercept messages is over.

Visit our new Web site: **www.overnightstabling.com**. The Directory content is not offered on the internet, but you will be able to read all about it and to order the Directory through the web site. You may also sigh up to be a host lister in the Directory, you can renew your listing and you can order Directories for retail re-sale.

ETA's e-mail address has changed to: **eta@hit.net** The old e-mail address still works, but we prefer you use the new one.

Please note our area code is now **620**.

CONTENTS

PUBLISHER
Equine Travelers of America, Inc.
P.O. Box 322
Arkansas City,
KS 67005-0322
Phone 620/442-8131
Fax 620/442-8215
Email: eta@hit.net
Web Site: www.overnightstabling.com

EDITOR IN CHIEF
James L. McDaniel

EXECUTIVE EDITOR
Janice J. Nelson

 Published annually, printed and mailed in USA, Media Mail Postage Pd., Arkansas City, KS 67005, in January/February, Return Postage Guaranteed.

All information contained in the directory is correct to the best knowledge of the publisher.

Listing deadline for the directory is Sept. 15.

Send all correspondence concerning editorial, advertising or circulation matters to ETA, P.O. Box 322, Arkansas City, KS 67005-0322

It is understood and agreed by members of Equine Travelers of America, Inc. and users of the Directory, that ETA is not responsible for injuries to persons or property occurring in or due to the accommodations provided by members or arranged for their use. Further, **it is agreed and understood that no portion of the directory will be reproduced and ETA's proprietary rights to the directory concept and the information therein is acknowledged.**

DIRECTORY & VACATION GUIDE USE

The Directory is organized for use as follows:

1. United States map with layover locations designated by red stars.

2. States are listed in alphabetical order and location of layover towns are shown on each state map with black stars or red stars for layover/vacation spots.

3. For each state, layovers are listed first by city/town and zip code, then alphabetically by last name or stable/farm name. Vacation spots are designated by red stars.

4. Each listing includes name, address, location, telephone number(s) and the facilities available.

Check the Directory for listings available in your area of travel or in your area of vacation interest. Correlate the actual time traveling with the type of terrain covered to estimate the number of miles logged in a day. Miles traveled should be adjusted according to the availability of layovers to meet your needs. BE SURE TO CALL IN ADVANCE to make stabling reservations for your horses or B&B reservations for yourself. Early morning or late evening may be the best time to reach hosts by telephone. You should always have ALL CURRENT HEALTH PAPERS with you.

The Directory is published yearly in January/February; listing deadline is September 15.

The latest issue of the Directory should always be used — layover information changes from day-to-day and old directories are soon out-of-date and unusable. (Also, tell your friends to buy their own copy of the Directory!)

There are two cards in the back of the Directory. A Change of Address Card to keep ETA advised of your current address and phone number, and an Order Form Card to share with others.

2003 Prices

Overnight Stabling Directory/Equestrian Vacation Guide -
$29.45 incl. hdlg.
Access to Information Service -
$19.95 per year.
ETA Membership - includes Directory & access to Service -
$42.45 incl. hdlg.
For those who wish to list facilities in the Directory/Guide,
the charge is $20 per year. (All listers are available through the Service.)
To list and receive the Directory - $39.45 incl. hdlg.
For new listers between printings of the Directory - your listing becomes available through the Service and you will be listed in the next available Directory.

TRAILER WISE

by

Genie Stewart-Spears

"The best thing I ever did was put hydraulic brakes on my truck. The second best thing was that I bought a gooseneck stock trailer," states Jan Worthington, who has hauled horses all over the U.S. and Canada and accompanied horses being shipped by air to Europe and the Middle East.

Worthington, who co-owns JG Ranch in Scales Mound, Illinois, has over 18,000 endurance miles, which means she has experienced a lot of road miles hauling horses to events. She finds a stock trailer, preferably a gooseneck, to be the best way to transport her horses.

"Gooseneck trailers are best because they pull more easily; there is less sway. I've pulled both, gooseneck and bumper pull. If a horse moves around, or there are high cross winds, the gooseneck will be steadier," explained Worthington who pulls a 26-foot trailer.

"And hydraulic brakes, rather than electric brakes, have saved our horses more than once. Hydraulic brakes don't throw the horses to the floor, and they always work. They are extremely reliable, expecially with the bigger trailers.

"Electric brakes will sometimes grab, causing the trailer to jerk. Sometimes electric brakes fail to work property," cautions Worthington

There are several reasons why Worthington prefers an open stock trailer over a closed trailer with dividers or partitions.

"It has always worried me about partitions. If you have a wreck, what do you take out first, the horse or the partitions? If you don't have partitions, you take out whatever horse is on top - you don't have to worry about untangling the horses from the partitions."

She says the ventilation is also reduced in a closed trailer. "I can't imagine what horses go through in an enclosed trailer. In the hot summer months, my horses get hot even in the open stock trailer. Enclosed trailers, with partitions that contribute to even less ventilation, are much much hotter."

What about too much ventilation in the cold climates? "If it is cold and/or rainy, they get a blanket," says Worthington. "I have a thermometer in my truck that measure the outside temperature. If it falls much below 65 degrees, I will blanket the horses.

"On a recent trip in the early fall, I started out with light blankets because the two horses were clipped. But by the time the temperature got up to 70 degrees, they were starting to sweat a little under those light blankets, so I took them off."

Worthington prefers a wooden trailer floor over metal. She had a wood floor specially installed in her aluminum trailer. "Wood has a more natural resilience; it has a certain amount of give, which I feel is less stressful on the horses' joints and legs."

But, whether wood or metal, trailer floors can be slippery. "I cover the floor with barn limestone - two or three shovel fulls - and a top layer of shavings," Worthington explained. "The limestone is granular and keeps them from slipping. And when I stop for the night or at my destination, I clean out the manure and any dampness. If you don't clean the manure and expecially the urine-soaked shavings, the strong ammonia odor isn't good for horses' respiratory systems.

Worthington feels that her horses travel more comfortably if they are not restricted by having their heads tied. Most always, they turn and face backwards, she pointed out.

What about feeding grain and hay while hauling? "The morning before leaving and throughout a trip, I give only half-rations of grain. I do this mostly to get their supplements into them. I will also add beet pulp, which is mixed with water, to their half ration. This helps to get moisture into their system.

"And, I always feed a grass hay," she added. "Timothy, orchard grass, brome, or any other of the grass hays."

If it is over a three-hour trip, Worthington places hay in nylon-rope nets, secured up where the horse can not get a foot tangled. And she offers the horses water when she stops for fuel or to rest.

Another important factor in monitoring a horse's health is checking the manure. "If it is dry, I increase their beet pulp which is soaked in water. It really pays off to get as much moisture into them as possible." said Worthington.

I don't electrolyte the horses as much as I should while traveling," she admitted. "But I highly recommend it in the hot summer months.

How many hours should one haul in a stretch? Some believe it is best to haul straight through - whether it is 6 hours or 24 hours. A lot depends on the situation and the horses being hauled. "I'll haul eight hours, but if the horses have had to perform strenuously, such as we do in endurance racing, I will stop on the return trip about halfway," she explained. "I like to stop over and let the horses stretch their legs and rest, and I can get some sleep, too."

The **Nationwide Overnight Stabling Directory** is extremely helpful in locating places to stopover. Calling ahead is more than just a courtesy, it also assures you that space is available and ready for you and your horse's arrival

While horses appear to be stout, tough creatures, their systems are actually quite fragile. Paying attention to details, and resting the horses at the fine facilities offered along your route in the **Nationwide Overnight Stabling Directory**, will contribute to your horse having a safe and healthly trip.

Author's Bio

The ***Nationwide Overnight Stabling Directory*** is a permanent fixture in Genie Stewart-Spear's truck. She frequently uses the directory when she travels with her horses, all over the U.S., photographing events and writing for such publications as ***Equus***, ***Western Horseman***, and ***Arabian Horse World***. When not traveling, she resides in Vienna, IL., with her husband and family, along with her horses and miniature donkeys on the 80-acre Runamuck Ranch.

GUIDE TO INTERSTATE HEALTH REQUIREMENTS – regulations effective as of January 2002

Each state establishes its own rules for animals entering its borders. These requirements are often amended. We advise that your check with the state veterinarian at your destination prior to shipment.

State	EIA Test Required	CVI*	Temp. Reading
Alabama	Yes (12 months) (L)	Yes	No
Alaska	**Yes (6 months) (B)**	**Yes (ii)**	**No**
Arizona	Yes (12 month) (B, L)	Yes (iv, †)	No
Arkansas	**Yes (12 months) (B, C, D)**	**Yes**	**Yes**
California	Yes (6 months) (B, C)	Yes	No
Colorado	**Yes (12 months) (C, G)†**	**Yes**	**No**
Connecticut	Yes (12 months) (B, J)†	Yes (iv, †)	Yes
Delaware	**Yes (12 months) (B, D)**	**Yes**	**Yes**
Florida	Yes (12 months) (B, C, L)†	Yes (iv)	Yes
Georgia	**Yes (12 months) (C)†**	**Yes (iv)**	**Yes**
Hawaii	Yes (3 months)	Yes (vi)	No
Idaho	**Yes (6 months) (B, C)**	**Yes**	**No**
Illinois	Yes (12 months) (A, B, C) †	Yes	No
Indiana	**Yes (12 months) (B, C, N) (iv)**	**Yes**	**No**
Iowa	Yes (12 months) (B, L)	Yes	No
Kansas	**Yes (12 months) (B, C)**	**Yes**	**No**
Kentucky	Yes (12 months) (B, C, D, G)	Yes	No **
Louisiana	**Yes (12 months) (D)**	**Yes**	**No**
Maine	Yes (6 months) (B)	Yes (v)	No **
Maryland	**Yes (12 months) (B, C) †**	**Yes (i, iv)**	**No** **
Massachusetts	Yes (12 months) (B, C, D, G)	Yes (iii, iv, †, *)	Yes
Michigan	**Yes (6 months) (M)**	**Yes**	**No**
Minnesota	Yes (12 months) (B, H)	Yes	No
Mississippi	**Yes (12 months) (A, C, G)†**	**Yes (iv, v, ix)**	**No**
Missouri	Yes (12 months) (B, C)	Yes (†)	No
Montana	**Yes (12 months) (C, L) (6 months) (vii) †**	**Yes (ii, vii, v)**	**No**
Nebraska	Yes (12 months) (A, C, E)	Yes	No
Nevada	**Yes (6 months) (B, C, G, I)**	**Yes**	**No**
New Hampshire	Yes (6 months) (C)†	Yes	No
New Jersey	**Yes (12 months) (L)**	**Yes**	**No**
New Mexico	Yes (12 months) (B)	Yes	No
New York	**Yes (12 months)**	**Yes (vi)**	**No**

North Carolina	Yes (12 months) (L, G)	Yes (iv, †)	No
North Dakota	**Yes (12 months) (B, E, C)**	**Yes**	**No**
Ohio	Yes (12 months) (A) †	Yes *	Yes
Oklahoma	**Yes (12 months) (C)**	**Yes †**	**No**
Oregon	Yes (6 months) (B, C, K, L) †	Yes (ii, vii)	No
Pennsylvania	**Yes (12 months) (B, C, G)**	**Yes**	**No**
Puerto Rico	Yes (6 months)	Yes (i, vi)	No
Rhode Island***	**Yes (12 months) (B, C)**	**Yes (iv)**	**Yes**
South Carolina	Yes (12 months) (B, C, G, L)	Yes (iii, iv, v, †, *)	No
South Dakota	**Yes (12 months) (B)**	**Yes**	**No**
Tennessee	Yes (12 months) (B, D, L)	Yes	No
Texas	**Yes (12 months) (C) †**	**Yes (ii, iv)**	**No**
Utah	Yes (12 months) (C)	Yes (iv)	No
Vermont	**Yes (12 months) (B)**	**Yes (viii)**	**No**
Virginia	Yes (12 months)	Yes	No
Washington	**Yes (6 months) (B, K)**	**Yes (vii)**	**No**
West Virginia	Yes (6 months) (F)	Yes (iv)	No
Wisconsin	**Yes (within calendar year) (C) †**	**Yes (iv)**	**No**
Wyoming	Yes (12 months) (B, C, G)	Yes (v)	No

†When EIA test is required, laboratory name and address, ascension number and test date with results must be included. *Certificate of Veterinary Inspection (CVI) filed with the State Veterinarian in state of origin are required. **Recommended. ***Import permit or all horses which will reside permanently in RI.

Footnotes - EIA Testing:

(A) EIA test required for equine over 12 months of age.
(B) EIA test required for equine less than 12 months of age. For age requirement, contact the state veterinarian's office. AZ, CA, CT, FL, ID, IL (no test is required for equine under 12 months in Illinois), IN, KY, MA, NC, ND, NV, OR, PA, SC, WA and WY: no pending EIA test allowed.
(C) Suckling foals accompanying EIA-negative dams are exempt. CA, FL, GA, ID, IL, IN, KY, NV, ND, OK, OR, PA, TX, WI and WY: no pending EIA test allowed.
(D) EIA test required within 6 months for sale or auction.
(E) EIA test required for equine from all states except SD. For specific states contact state veterinarian.
(F) 12 months if state of origin has a state EIA program.
(G) Test chart must accompany animal. Some states require original copy.
(H) Permit required if EIA test is pending when horse is shipped.
(I) Permit and EIA test required for National Rodeo Finals. Nevada: no permit required.
(J) EIA test within 60 days if going to public auction.
(K) Horses traveling between Oregon and Washington are exempt.
(L) EIA tests required for equines over 6 months of age.
(M) All equine must have neg. EIA within current calendar year or prev. 30 days
(N) Individually identified using a lip tattoo; individual brand, registration number if accompanied by registration papers; or a descriptive marking with name.

Footnotes - Certificate of Veterinary Inspection (CVI):

(i) Pre-approved CVI from state or origin required prior to shipment.
(ii) Permit from the state of destination is required prior to entry. Texas: slaughter horses only.
(iii) U.S. origin CVI, endorsed by a USDA approved veterinarian, valid 30 days from date of inspection.
(iv) Complete description of horse including brands or tattoos.
(v) Approved copy of CVI must be submitted to state veterinarian's office after entry.
(vi) State has requirements regarding vaccinations, testing or other.
(vii) 6 month CVI and permit available to reciprocal Western states of CA, ID, MT, NV, OR and WA.
(viii) Exhibition permit available for show season, contact state veterinarian office.
(ix) Official 6 month passport by reciprocal states of AR, TX, OK, LA, MS

OVERNIGHTING - FROM THE HOSTS' POINT OF VIEW

By

Lynda Layne

You're tired. You've been driving for hours and the lines on the road are getting blurry. You made advance reservations for overnight stabling and are just miles away from being able to unload your horse and get him settled into a stall. Then, you can head to a motel and settle yourself into a comfortable bed. No worries. Your horse will be in a safe stable with experienced caretakers.

This scenario shows how valuable the services of overnight hosts are to those of us who haul horses. That's why road weariness should never cause us to lose sight of the respect and courtesy we need to extend to the people who own and staff overnight stabling facilities. If they're happy with their business, they'll *stay* in business. That's what we all want to see. The best way to understand why they impose rules at their facilities is to put yourself in the host's position. Here are some of the problems they face, along with solutions that you, as a customer, can offer.

Make and Keep Reservations, Please

Some travelers have a "system" of making reservations at several overnight stabling facilities within a short distance, along their route of travel. When they get tired of driving, they stop at the closest facility, and just ignore the reservations at other stables. This is extremely difficult on the stable owners who have "no-shows." They have bedded stalls, turned down other travelers in need of a spot because they presume they were full, and often, they wait up through the night for their guests to arrive. Both labor and material expenses have been incurred.

As with motel reservations, some stable owners have had to begin asking for credit card numbers to reserve a spot. One stable owner interviewed said that she prefers to have reservations made three weeks in advance, then appreciates another call from the traveler a week or so in advance to reconfirm. If reservations must be canceled because of changes in the travel plan, stable owners really appreciate knowing as soon as possible.

Tell Them Ahead of Time About Your Horses

When you make your reservations, it's wise to tell the stable owner as much as possible about your horse(s). This helps in the stabling plans. For example, if you will be bringing a stallion, the stable owner might want to position this horse in a stall without horses next to it. There is a lot of planning involved to make your overnight stay successful. If your horse is a wall kicker or is aggressive to other horses, this is a factor the stable owner must know, in order to put the horse in the safest situation possible, given the personality issues.

Some travelers might be hauling two horses that they keep together at home. They'll ask if they can house them overnight in the same pen. There are stable owners who would rather not do this at their facility, since horses that are normally quiet at home can get rattled in a different place, especially if there are "new horses" all around them. Equine behavior is certainly subject to fast and radical change. It is safer to reserve separate stalls or pens for your horses.

Bringing Gear and Feed

While most stables have supplies of hay available, many hosts request that you bring your own feed. One stable owner said to think about the chances of colic, when your horse is having his feed altered several times on a long trip. When you make reservations, always ask if they prefer you bring your own feed. It will help in your pre-trip planning.

Also ask about water and feed buckets when you reserve an overnight place. One host commented that her barn has automatic waterers. While they are easy to sanitize before each horse arrives, not all horses will drink from them. Plastic buckets are not easily sanitized, and at an overnight stable, many horses will use them. This host suggested you bring your own buckets.

Another host said that she prefers use of buckets, because with the automatic bowls it is hard to gauge how much water a horse has actually consumed. On long trips, dehydration can become a factor and intake should be monitored. At this host's facility, she has good-tasting well water that horses never refuse, but there are places where horses balk at drinking because of a change in taste.

While you are packing your truck and trailer with feed and buckets, don't forget a flashlight. If you arrive at night, if your inside trailer lights don't work, or if there is not much lighting in the stall or pen area, a flashlight is invaluable.

Make A Call When You're Close

If you have a cell phone, or can stop and use a pay phone, one host suggests to her customers that they call when they're about 65 miles from the stable. This alerts the stable personnel of the arrival and they can watch for you. Or, if their place is hard to find, someone can wait for you in town and have you follow them in. Calling is especially helpful if you are arriving at night. If you drive in without being escorted, the stable owner will be on the lookout. One host said that she stands at the unloading area so she can signal the driver to park in the right spot.

Don't Unload Your Horses Until You Check In and Get the Go-Ahead

Even it it's a hot day, it's important *not* to unload your horses immediately. The stable owner needs to look at the Coggins and health certificates and make a visual check of your horses. With diseases such as Potomac Fever and West Nile virus on the spread, stable owners are even more concerned about checking paperwork and seeing the condition of the horses.

It won't take long, so just opening the trailer windows and (if safe) the back door, will cool the horse(s) off while this is being done. You should also check out the stalls or pens where you will be taking your horse, so you know the distance and route. You might want to move your trailer closer in, if you have a horse that doesn't lead well, such as a foal with its mother.

If you're planning on cleaning out your trailer after you unload, it's important to ask the stable personnel where the debris should be taken. Perhaps they have a wheelbarrow you can borrow. Hauling the manure to the designated area is much more polite than just kicking it out of the trailer.

Doggone Dogs

Many horse owners also have dogs in the truck when they travel. Some travelers just open the door and let the dogs jump out and run loose. This can result in the chasing of cats, kids and livestock, or "piles" left on manicured lawns. One host stressed that dogs be kept on a leash. If they're left in the truck until the check-in is completed, some stables have kennels where the dogs can stay, and the dog owner can be told when the coast is clear to take the dogs to that area.

Ask To Use Arenas and Other Facilities

Always ask permission to use the facility beyond your stalls or pens. One host said that horse owners are welcome to longe in her covered arena, but she doesn't want horses turned loose because of mirrors on the walls. Each stable will have its own rules and it's important that overnighters respect them.

Keep in mind that stable owners pay very high insurance rates. Horse safety is their first concern. They love horses or they wouldn't be in this business. But, in the back of their minds, the insurance issue is always there to haunt them.

Thank Them!

Always take the time to thank your hosts. They offer an invaluable service to all of us who travel with horses.

SideBar: The Directory publisher wishes to thank these overnight stabling providers who contributed greatly to the information for this article:

*Sally DeStafano, Carriage House Ranch, Big Timber, MT
*Carolyn Moe, Hobby Horse Overnight Stables, Mitchell SD
*Taydie Drummond, Drummond's Ranch Bed & Breakfast, Cheyenne WY

Author's Bio:
Lynda Bloom Layne has been writing for horse magazines since 1967. She recently co-authored two training/showing books which will come out in spring of 2003. She recently moved from the Midwest and was thrilled that the **Nationwide Overnight Stabling Directory** helped her hauler plan the trip with her horses. She currently lives in the Pacific Northwest and owns a Paint filly and a Thoroughbred mare. Having visited many stables since her move, she has seen the **Directory** on the desks of many trainers and breeders, not to mention the extra copy they usually have in their truck. They rely heavily on **ETA and the Directory** when they haul their horses.

DIRECTORY Yearly Advertising Rates

Full page ______________________________ $500.50

Second or Third Cover ________________ $555.00

4-3/8" x 7-1/2"

1/2 page ______________________________ $269.50

Second or Third Cover ________________ $295.00

Fourth Cover __________________________ $345.00

4-3/8" x 3-3/4"

1/4 Page ______ $148.50

2-1/8" x 3-3/4"

1/8 Page ______ $82.50

2-1/8" x 1-7/8"

or

For picture under listing apx. size of 4 3/8" x 1 1/2"

All rates are for black and white, camera ready ads. The color red is available for ads at no extra cost.

Artwork, layout, design, screens and bleeds are available at extra cost.

Ads appear for one year for the price stated.

Advertisers will receive a copy of the Directory.

Space, material and payment deadline: September 15.

Outline around listing in black or red - $15 above listing price.

Also, a listing can include your logo for $15 above listing price.

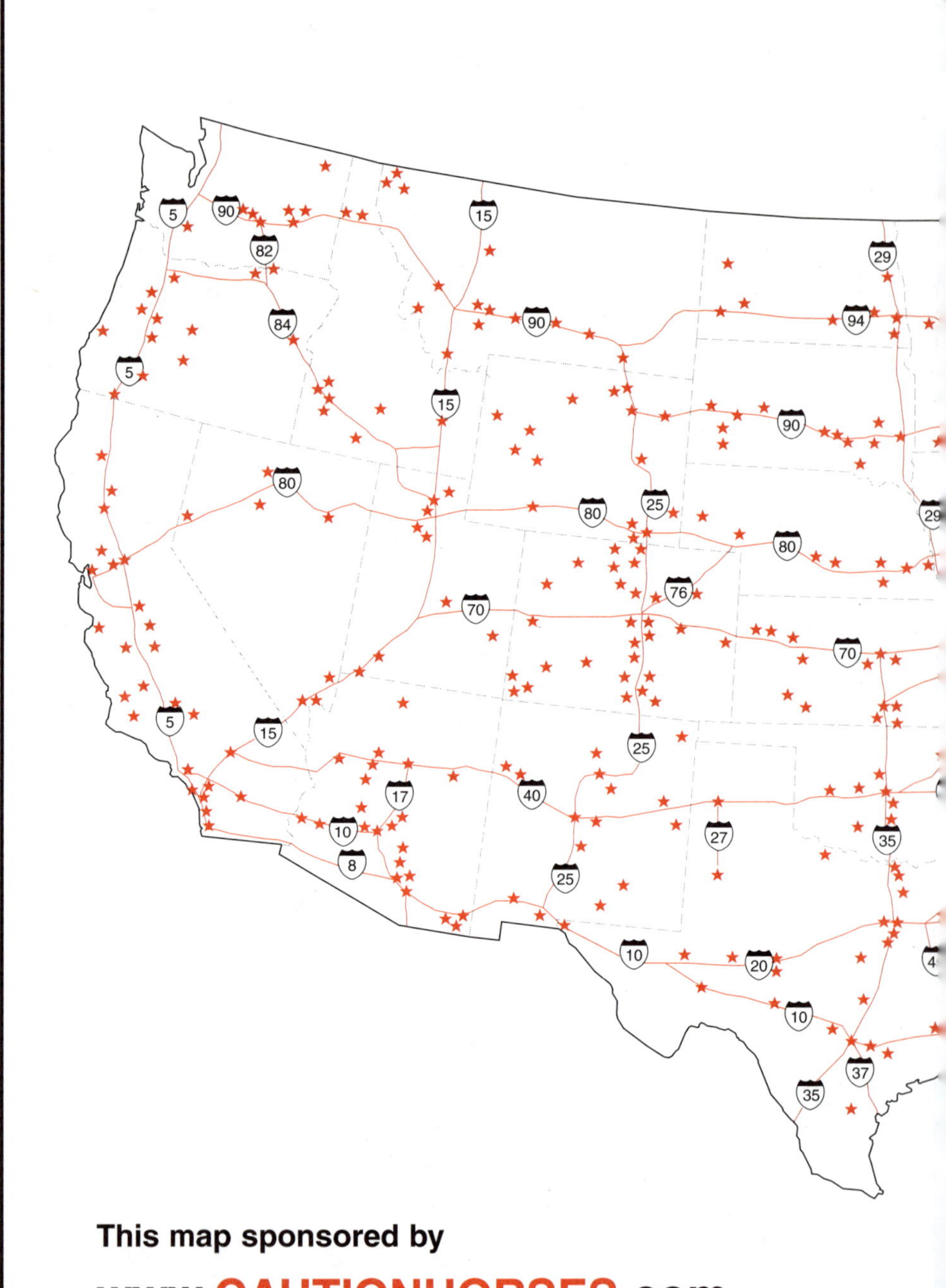
This map sponsored by
www.CAUTIONHORSES.com

United States Interstate System
★ Layover Locations

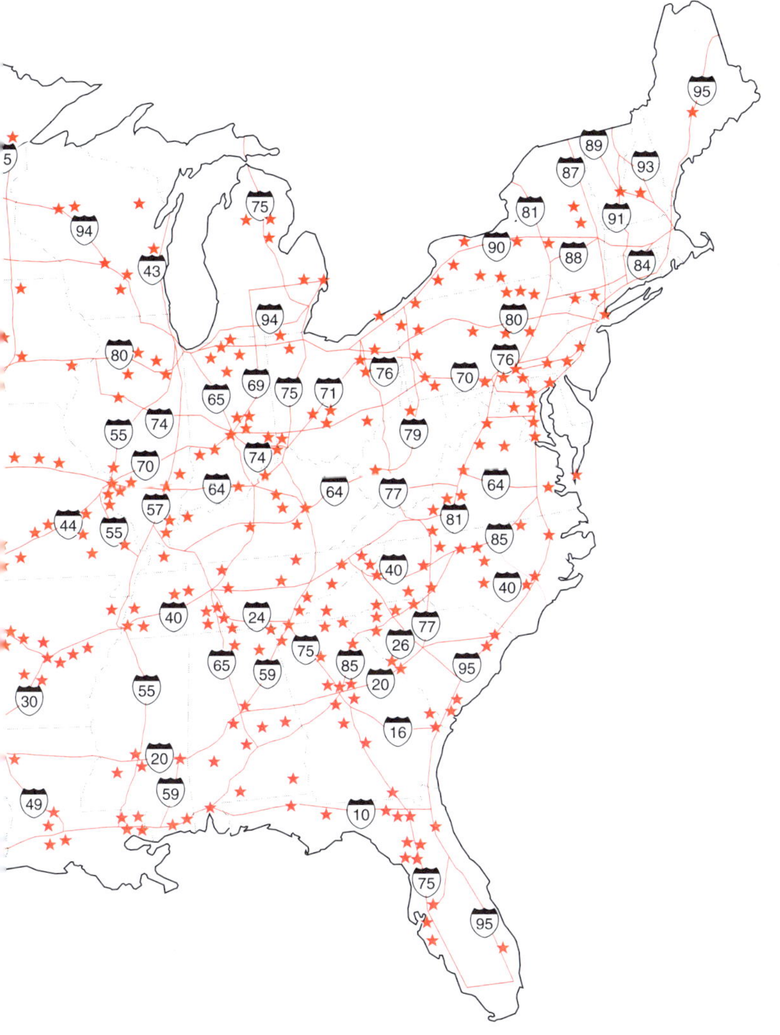

Safety Products for Horse, Rider & Trailer

COMMENTS FROM ETA CUSTOMERS

I'm purchasing a new Directory. I used your directory for a cross-country move with horses in 1989 and 1994. It was invaluable and the places at which we stayed were first class. Thank you! -- Euler WA

My friend from Georgia uses your Directory and thought we should offer facilities for overnighters. We have seen your publication and think highly of it's purpose. -- Kinz ID

A friend had the Directory and they traveled from WA to NC over ten days and every place they stayed was lovely. I'm purchasing my own Directory. -- Palmer AK

The Directory has really saved us several times this year. It also saved some friends who broke down on the road. We were able to give them information to use. They borrowed the Directory and we never got it back so are having to purchase a new one! -- Newport NY

Thanks for giving me the phone number out of the Directory when I called and for mailing me the Directory so promptly. The second night we planned to be in _____ CO, but had to stay in _____CO due to a snow & ice storm in the pass. The Directory had just arrived at our house that morning and my husband looked up _____ CO in the Directory and you had a listing there, so he passed it on to me on my cell phone, and we stayed there that night until the next day when the pass was melted enough to drive on. Thanks again. "Great Directory." "Both places we stayed at were absolutely great!" -- Sylvan Lake AB CAN

I used your Directory exclusively to trailer my horse from Ontario Canada to Phoenix AZ. Now I am married and live here full time and have two horses of my own. My husband and I own and operate an RV park. -- AZ

Host called because she was afraid she had missed nenewing her listing for 2003. They have had Shania Twain, the Budweiser horses, etc. and have enjoyed meeting all the people so much for the last 10 years. --WI

The Directory has been very useful in traveling. -- Marco Island FL

Have used the Directory for moves between NC and CO and are getting ready for another move, only using a different route this time. Every place they have ever stayed has been wonderful!!! - Norwood NC

No changes in listing. We always have good response. -- MO

I traveled cross country this spring with your directory, for the first time, with two horses. The people were very accommodating and the places were consistently nice. I know how wonderful it was to have several choices of quality places to stay, and decided I wanted to help fellow equestrienne travelers by listing my place as another option at the end o a long day. -- WA

Recommended by a friend. Found the Directory to be very informative -- KS

Comment after notifying customer that ETA had received their directory order from the web site: "Thank you, we look forward to seeing it. It comes highly recommended."

Well, another year has come & gone. Everything seemed to stop DEAD after 9-11, but come spring everything picked up and has gone steadily. I've had more commercial transporters this year and more private people. Busy is the word for it. We are so pleased. We even had a Fell pony in our barn this past week, one of only 45 here in the U.S. I took pictures of him. It was neat to see this rare breed. I do enjoy my people and their horses. -- IL

Purchaser of 2002 Directory - The Directory is very efficient, there is a lot in it.

I would like to be listed in your Directory. I have purchased and used your guide on a trip to FL. It was a huge help. We have purchased a piece of property and know it will be useful for traveling people as an overnight stop. -- MO

Someone gave us a 1995 Directory. It's been wonderful. We are now purchasing a 2002 Directory. -- Ft Collins CO

Thank you! You're a great resource for my business. -- AZ

Please take our name off your register and mailing list as we closed the business in March of this year. Thanks for the years of service you have provided the industry. We have met a lot of interesting people and made a lot of money offering overnight stabling. Should our circumstances change in the future, we will contact you. -- KS

Met a guy in a horsecamp in AR. He and his wife had a Directory. I copied the web address from the book and am now ordering one! -- Prairie Grove AR

New listers heard about ETA from horse transporter out of MT. When they asked about the demand for transports to stop along the way, since they are halfway between FL & TX, they were told that the transporters carry a copy of the Directory on all their trucks. -- MD

Last purchased Directory in 1998. Very grateful for service. Need a new Directry now. -- Sodus NY

We get a lot of boarders from your Directory. Thanks! - KS

(We appreciate all comments, especially good ones!)

Alabama

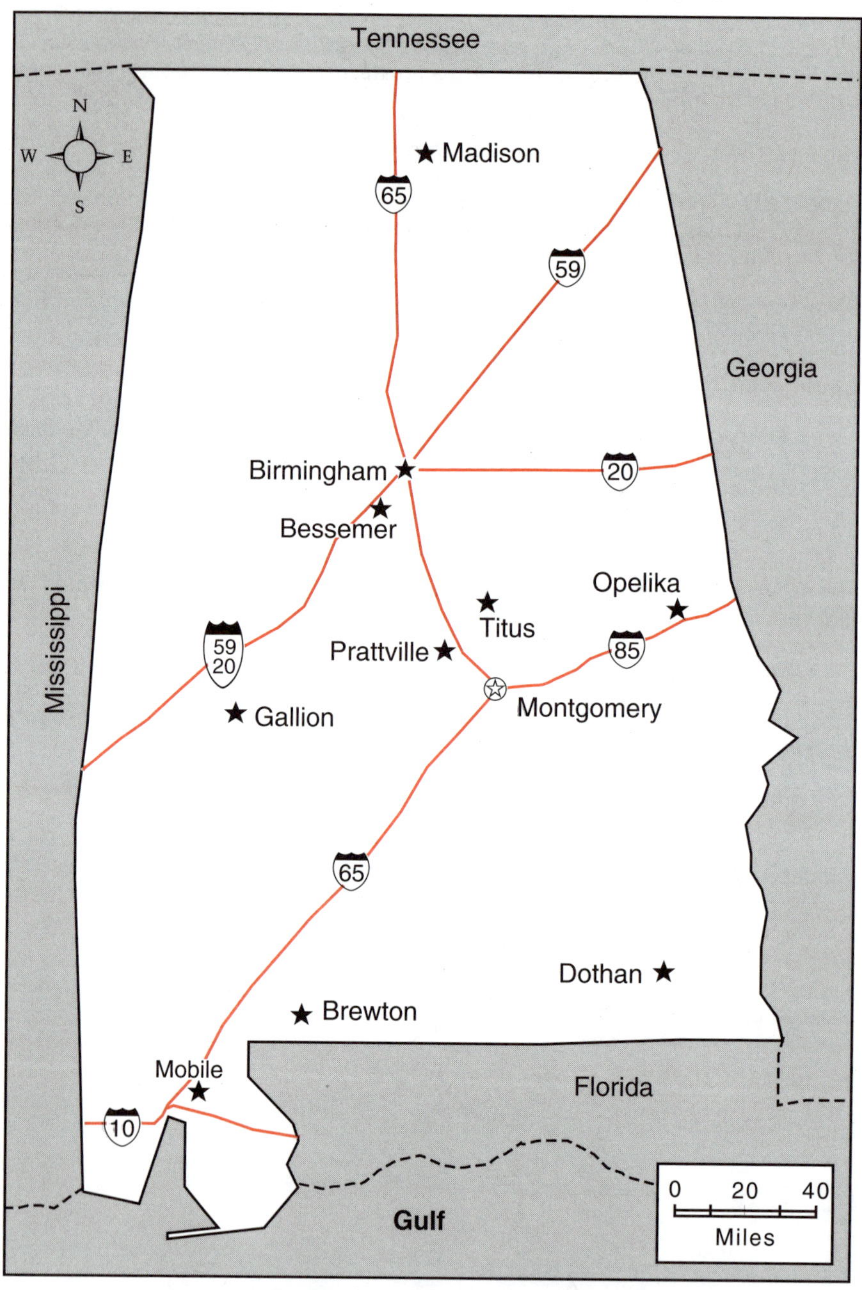

Vacation/Layover spots ★ Layovers only
State Capitol Hwy Junction cities

CURRENT NEGATIVE COGGINS, HEALTH CERTIFICATE & OWNERSHIP PAPERS REQUIRED - *see page 2 for details*

BESSEMER, 35022

Happy G Stables, Dale & Beth Gamble
7095 Dickey Springs Rd. (I-459, exit 6. Call for directions)
Ph. 205/477-5020 **Facilities:** 12 indoor stalls & parking w/elec.

BIRMINGHAM, 35244

Lonesome Dove Ranch, Ray McKinney
634 Cahaba River Estates (I-459, exit 10, Hwy 150 - 1-1/2 m. off interstate)
Ph./Cell 205/243-9770 Home 205/822-2705 Beeper 205/954-0358 **Facilities:** 8 indoor stalls, holding pens, pasture, bring your own feed & camper hookup.

BREWTON, 36426

"Just Passin' Through Stables", Lee & Wendy Merritt
1971 Shadow Hill Dr. (I-65, Flomaton exit #69)
Ph. 251/867-4166 **Facilities:** 10 clean & spacious indoor stalls, RV/camper-hookup with elec/water & overnight lodging. Call for reservations/rates. No smoking indoors.

DOTHAN, 36305

Corsage RV Rental Sites, W.T. Francis
3850 W. Main St. 806-37 (7 m. W. on US 84)
Ph. 334/692-4149 **Facilities:** Overnight paddock w/horse trailer parking. Full hookup, shaded RV facilities, located on a paved road off a four-lane hwy. Many nearby motels/restaurants. Call for reservations/rates.

GALLION, 36742

Bill Mackey Ranch
921 Hwy 80 W. Location: 205 Walters Rd. (4 m. N. of US 80, 3 m. E. of Demopolis AL)
Ph. 334/289-8470 Fax 334/289-8479 Email:bill@billmackey.com Barn ph. 334/289-3359 **Facilities:** 6 indoor/6 outdoor stalls, 4 paddocks, 3 pastures, round pen & wash rack. Call office to reserve: 334/289-8470 or 1-888/236-3994.

MADISON, 35757

Rainbow Riding Academy, Inc., Patricia Whitfield, owner
212 Capshaw Rd. (Apx. 15 m. E. of I-65)
Ph. 256/830-2911 837-7758 **Facilities:** 6-10 10x16 indoor stalls, 4 paddocks, 20 acres pasture/turnout, hay/feed avail, outdoor working pen, lighted outdoor arena, walker & wash stall. 10 min. to vets. Close to amenities. Close to US Space and Rocket Center.

MOBILE, 36608

Greenstone Stables, Jane Moore
830 Eliza Jordan Rd. N. (I-65, exit 3 W. Call for directions)
Ph. 251/649-7709 **Facilities:** 20 stalls, holding pens, pasture, feed, lighted arena, trails in area & parking avail.

CURRENT NEGATIVE COGGINS, HEALTH CERTIFICATE & OWNERSHIP PAPERS REQUIRED - *see page 2 for details*

OPELIKA, 36804

Bar 5 Ranch, Barry Brown
94 Lee Rd. 392 (I-85. 12 m. S. of Opelika; 60 m. E. of Montgomery; 25 m. W. of Columbus GA)
Ph.334/745-3816 Fax 334/745-6520 Email:bar5ranch@mindspring.com
Facilities: 9 stalls, round pen, lighted arena, hot walker, RV hookups, dump station, 2 shower rooms and men & women's restrooms. Buck bulls every Wed. night May-Oct: Sundays Nov-Apr.

PRATTVILLE, 36066

Tuff-e-Nuff Stables, Nell & C.H. Herrod
1033 Old Ridge Rd. E. (I-65, exit 179-181-186. 10 m. N. of Montgomery, 3.3 m. off I-65)
Ph. 334/365-5898 Email:nellch@bellsouth.net **Facilities:** 20 indoor stalls w/bedding & auto waterers, round pen, outdoor arena, wash rack, and space avail. for rigs while stabling. Vet on call. Facilities can be arranged for other animals. Motels & restaurants nearby.

TITUS, 36080-3428

Lucky 7 Ranch, Sherry Moore
180 Grass Farm Rd. (I-85, exit 6, 25 m. N.; I-65, exit 206, 22 m.)
Ph. 334/567-9752 Cell 334/315-9752 Fax 334-213/8702
Email:Sherry.Moore@jrsmith.com **Facilities:** 4 indoor stalls, round pen, 30 acres of pasture, bring your own feed, 150x120 arena and trails near property.

DON'T BE A "NO-SHOW"

For those providing overnight stabling, there's nothing worse. They work to prepare and clean stalls and wait up half the night waiting for those who never show up (they don't call to cancel or change plans either.)

Please plan ahead and be considerate of your stabling hosts in using this Directory. We have lost good listings because of too many "no-shows."

No-shows cause hosts much work and loss of income, especially if they turn down paying customers because they are holding the reservations for these "no-shows." This is very costly to those offering B&B.

Also, most hosts hold down other jobs, and it is very irritating waiting up half the night for late-comers or "no-shows."

PLEASE:

1. Always make reservations in advance - even if it's a repeat or return trip.
2. Cancel as soon as you know of changes in your plans. You could be charged.
3. Determine time of arrival with your hosts and let them know of any changes.
4. Don't just show up unexpectedly and assume your horses will be stabled at a moments notice. We know of people who have shown up a few days early or even a few days late and expected their reservations to be good.
5. Always have current health papers with you.

PLEASE TREAT YOUR HOSTS AS YOU WOULD LIKE TO BE TREATED. We realize that emergencies do arise and unforeseen delays do occur, but usually you would know well ahead of time if a reservation needs to be cancelled or changed. If you are unable to let your host know ahead of time, at least, call later and let them know what happened.

PLEASE READ. THIS INFORMATION IS VERY IMPORTANT!

Arizona

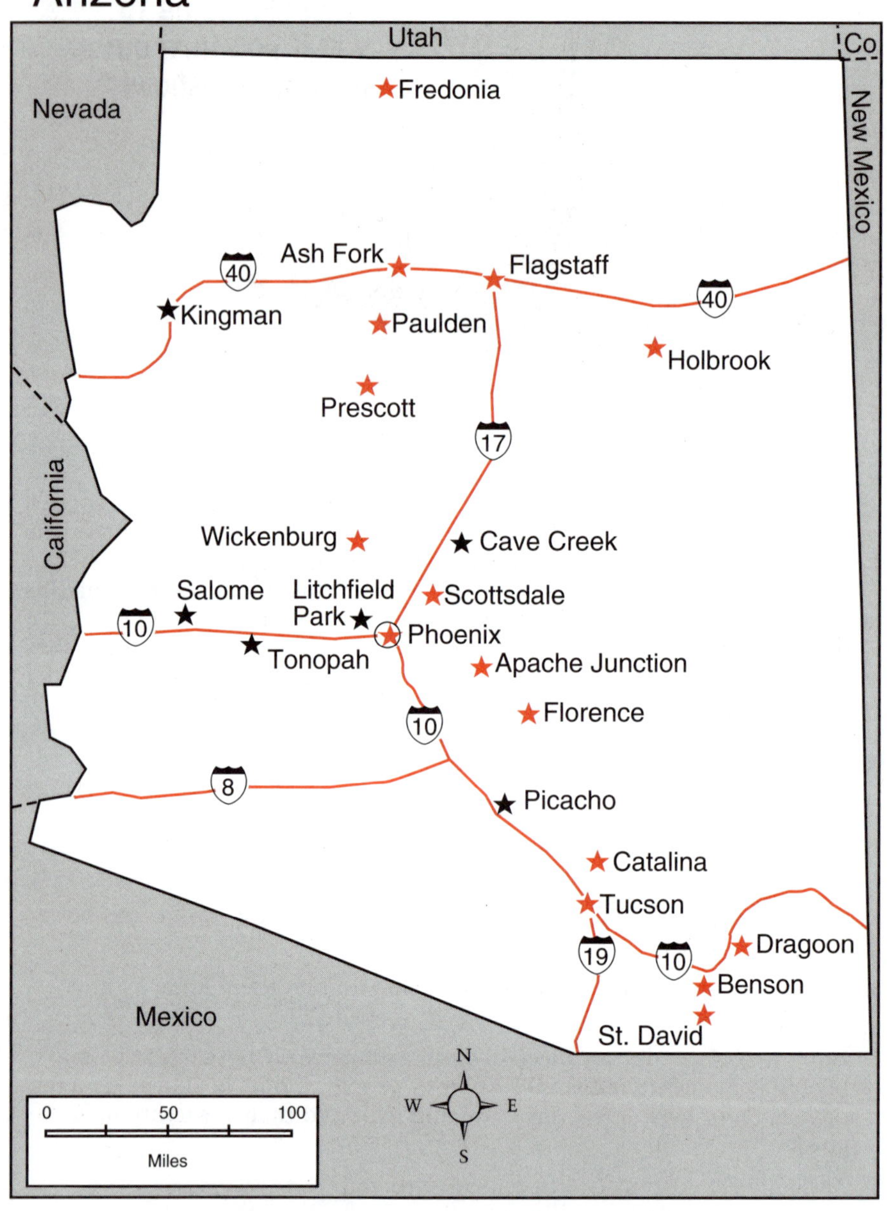

★ Vacation/Layover spots ★ Layovers only
✪ State Capitol ◉ Hwy Junction Cities

CURRENT NEGATIVE COGGINS, HEALTH CERTIFICATE & OWNERSHIP PAPERS REQUIRED - *see page 2 for details*

APACHE JUNCTION, 85217

★ **OK Corral Stables - at the foot of Superstition Mountain**
Mail: P.O. Box 528 Location: 2655 E. Whiteley (Hwy 60 - N. Tomahawk Rd. exit. N. 5 m.)
Ph. 480/982-4040 Web:www.okcorrals.com **Facilities:** 20-12x24 outdoor pipe corrals, alpha hay, 100x200 arena, miles of trails into Superstition Mt. Wilderness and 12 spaces for full camper hookup. Rental horses avail. Many motels within 3 m.

APACHE JUNCTION, 85219

D Horse Boarding, Wesley A. Diekman
1650 N. Vista (3 m. N. of Rt. 60 off Tomahawk exit)
Ph. 480/982-7778 **Facilities:** 40 stalls, hay incl., 3 turnouts & many trails. Various facilities 2 blocks to 3 m. radius.

ASH FORK, 86320

★ **Rocky Creek Ranch, Claudia Ladwig**
P.O. Box 355 (I-40, exit 146 onto Hwy 89 S. 1 m., easy access. 50 m. W. of Flagstaff: 50 m. N. of Prescott; 80 m. from Grand Canyon)
Ph. 928/637-2727 Emergency ph. no. 928/637-2289 **Facilities:** Barn w/6 indoor-outdoor pipe corrals, 6 portable stalls, 2-100x50 holding pens, feed avail., 100x300 arena, 60' round pen, trails in adj. Kaibab Nat'l Forest, elec & water for campers and limited camping. Daily - Weekly - Monthly rates. Open year round.

BENSON, 85602

★ **Circle R Ranch, Bobby Joe & Elly McFadden**
2856 W. Trails End Rd. (I-10, exit 299) The Hub of Southern Arizona's major attractions: 25 m. E. of Tucson, 29 m. from Tombstone, 8 m. from World Famous Karchner's Caverns.
Ph./Ranch 520/586-7377 Cell 520/249-2838 **Facilities:** 5 large pipe stalls w/shelter & auto waterers, feed by owners, arena avail., unlimited riding area, and parking space for vehicles & trailers. Reservations recommended. Motels within 4 m. $9.75 per horse.

CATALINA, 85737

★ **Spirit Dog Ranch, Kerry Dykes**
13750 N.Bowman Rd. Mail: P.O.Box 90404, Tucson AZ 85752 (Northern Tucson adjoining Catalina State Park & Coronado Nat'l Forest)
Ph. 520/237-4807 Fax 520/572-0075 Email:kerrydykes@yahoo.com **Facilities:** 4 pipe corrals w/shade covers, 2 holding pens, wash rack, RV hookups w/elec & water and primitive camping avail. Owners care for horses. On Catalina State Park w/unlimited trails for riding, biking & hiking. Motels/restaurants within several miles.

CURRENT NEGATIVE COGGINS, HEALTH CERTIFICATE & OWNERSHIP PAPERS REQUIRED - *see page 2 for details*

CAVE CREEK, 85331

Kukui Ranch, Joan M. Stearns
4150 E. Dynamite Blvd. (Between SR 51 & I-17, close to Carefree Hwy, off of Cave Creek Rd)
Ph. 480/585-0234 Email:jskukui@msn.com **Facilities:** Box stalls w/runs, 16x16 covered pens, 60' round pen, grass hay/alfalfa, arena, walker & trails. Hauling card. There are a lot of trails to ride and drive horses.

DRAGOON, 85609

★ **And The Horse You Rode In On**
P.O. Box 158 Location: 2400 W. Dragoon Rd. (7.3 m. off I-10 in the foothills of the Dragoon Mtns. in SE Arizona)
Ph. 520/826-5410 Fax 520-826-1078 Email:info@horseyourodeinon.com Web:horseyourodeinon.com **Facilities:** 10 shaded stalls, round pen, pellets/alfalfa/grain, ride in open country or in Cochise Stronghold or the Chiricaha Mtns., park your trailer in a large parking area & drive down the hill to the B&B w/4 guest rooms, guest kitchen and a spa. Full breakfast for guests.

FLAGSTAFF, 86001

★ **Hitchin' Post Stables, Inc.**
4848 Lake Mary Rd. (I-40, exit 195)
Ph. 928/774-1719 **Facilities:** 19 indoor stalls w/connected runs, grass/alfalfa mix & pellets, arena & many trails.

FLAGSTAFF, 86004

★ **Flying Heart Barn**
8400 N. Hwy 89 (I-40, exit 201 to Hwy 89 N. 3-1/2 m. N. of freeway next to Horseman Lodge Steak House)
Ph. 928/526-2788 **Facilities:** 18 indoor box stalls, bedded w/shavings, 6 stalls w/runs, feed avail., arena, walker, scenic mountain trails in Coconino Nat'l Forest, camper parking w/elec and Bed & Breakfast. Stallions accepted.

FLAGSTAFF, 86004

★ **The Roosevelt House**
2532 N. 4th St., #163 Location: 6655 Mariah Dr. (I-40 & 89A)
Ph. 928/526-6615 Email:Roosevelt_house@yahoo.com **Facilities:** 4 indoor stalls, 4 holding pens, 4 pastures, feed, incl., trails in Coconino Nat'l Forest, 2 camper hookups and Bed & Breakfast. Other meals avail.

FLORENCE, 85232

★ **Gotno Guest Ranch, Deb Johnson-Bailiff**
P.O. Box 2854 Location: 14152 N. Hexcel Rd. (65 m. NW of Tucson; 68 m. SE of Phoenix. US Hwy 79)
Ph. 520/868-2351 Email:gotno@cgmailbox.com
Web:www.gotnomorganranch.com **Facilities:** 12 stalls w/shade, 8 outdoor stalls, feed avail., roping arena w/lights, trails, RV hookups & parking space for trailers and guesthouse/ranch house rooms. Farrier on call. Call for reservations/rates. Motel/restaurants nearby.

CURRENT NEGATIVE COGGINS, HEALTH CERTIFICATE & OWNERSHIP PAPERS REQUIRED - see page 2 for details

FREDONIA, 86022

★ **Sand Creek Stables, Dennis & Cody Judd**
1855 N. Hwy 89A (near Kanab UT)
Ph. 928/643-7088 435/644-2452 **Facilities:** 25 indoor & outdoor stalls, training track, walker & trails. Facility is centered in the middle of 3 Nat'l Parks - Grand Canyon, Bryce Canyon, Zion Nat'l Park and Lake Powell recreation area.

HOLBROOK, 86025

★ **Belle Starr's "Silverado"**
9132 Washboard Rd. (I-40, exit 303/Adamana. Between Flagstaff & Gallup)
Ph. 928/524-9127 Email:silveradostarr1@juno.com Web:www.bellestarr.org
Facilities: Clean covered 20x24 stalls - water & elec., large area for exercising, RV hookups, hay avail. & unlimited trails. Pets welcome on leash. Truck stops, motels, restaurants nearby. Reservations required..

KINGMAN, 86401

Mohave County Fairgrounds, Errol Pherigo
2600 Fairgrounds Blvd. (Stockton Hill Rd. exit off I-40. Call for directions)
Ph. 920/753-2636 Office 920/753-1904 **Facilities:** 250-10x10 outdoor covered box stalls, water avail. year round, no hay/feed avail. & RV hookups. Open 24 hrs/night watch person. No boarding 2nd week in May or 2nd-3rd week in Sept. Stalls: $10/Hookups: $8. Motels within 1 m.

CURRENT NEGATIVE COGGINS, HEALTH CERTIFICATE & OWNERSHIP PAPERS REQUIRED - *see page 2 for details*

LITCHFIELD PARK, 85340

Dale Creek Equestrian Village
13424 W. Camelback Rd. (I-10, exit 129 - Dysart Rd. N. 3-1/2 m. to Camelback Rd., W. 1/4 m.)
Ph. 623/935-4513 623/935-2709
Facilities: 20 outdoor stalls, holding pens, feed, arenas & trails.

PAULDEN, 86334

★ **Little Thumb Butte Bed and Breakfast, Ann Nelson Harrington**
1252 Reata Trail (45 min. on Hwy 89 N. of Prescott & Yavapai Co. Fairgrounds and S. of I-40) Mail: P.O. Box 3947, Chino Valley AZ 86323
Ph. 928/636-4413 Fax 928/636-4452 Email:littlethumb@earthlink.com
Web:www.littlethumb.net **Facilities:** 10 stalls w/turnouts, hot walker, wash rack, round pen, roping arena, miles of trails & open spaces, parking and B&B sleeps 6. No hookups. At confluence of the Verde River & Grainite Creek. Ranch type breakfast. Common area w/2 porches; sun room has pool table. Rooms: $65-80.

CURRENT NEGATIVE COGGINS, HEALTH CERTIFICATE & OWNERSHIP PAPERS REQUIRED - see page 2 for details

PHOENIX, 85024

Lone Mountain Ranch
21152 N. 22nd St. (Loop 101 to Cave Creek Rd. N. 1 block to Rosegarden Ln., W. to 22nd St.)
Ph. 602/569-0078 **Facilities:** Large facilities with indoor stalls, turn-out areas, covered pens, round pen, 2-lighted arenas, walker, wash rack w/hot water, trail riding & camper parking. Also, covered patio area. Reservations req. Staffed 24 hrs.

PHOENIX, 85086

★ **Royal Ranch, Margaret Shearburn**
Mail: 515 E. Carefree Hwy #166, Phoenix, 85085 Location: 504 W. Galvin (2 m. E. of I-17 on Carefree Hwy)
Ph. 623/879-8054 Email:shearburn@earthlink.net **Facilities:** 12x12 indoor stalls with misting/fly system, 12x16 outdoor stalls, indoor wash racks, feed avail., trailer parking w/elec. and bathrooms w/shower.

PHOENIX, 85086

Stage Line Ranch, Michael & Sue Ewens
102 W. Desert Hills Dr. (I-17, exit 223, N. of Phoenix or Hwy 74 E. from Wickenberg)
Ph. **1-866/417-5539** 623/405-7492 Fax 623/465-5904 Email:slr@quixnet.net **Facilities:** 2 barn stalls, 7 open stalls, 16x16 & 65x70 holding pens, feed (market), 2 arenas, 7 m. to Nat'l Forest trails & 2 camper hookups. Farrier avail.

PICACHO, 85241

Picacho Campground
P.O. Box 368 (I-10, 40 m. from Tucson /exit 212 & 65 m. from Phoenix/exit 211A)
Ph. 520/466-7401 or **1-888/562-7453** Email:frnkiec@c2I2.com Web:www.picachocampground.com **Facilities:** 3 holding pens, 78 camper hookups & 1 cabin. Year round pool & spa; steakhouse, Dec 1- Mar. 31.

PRESCOTT, 86305

★ **The Davis Ranch**
1890 Pemberton Dr. (Hwy 89)
Ph. 928/778-0895 or **1-888/836-3211** Email:eileen@horse-books.com
Facilities: 5 indoor stalls, 3 outdoor pens, hay cubes, 100x200 arena, 4-horse hot-walker, many trails and Bed & Breakfast - call for rates & availability.

SALOME, 85348

Spirit Ranch, Dian Christensen
P.O. Box 87 Location: 64203 E. Hwy 60 (2 m. W. of Salome)
Ph.928/859-3373 **1-888/285-0270** Email:desertgem@tds.net **Facilities:** 3 stalls, small turnout paddock, 60' round pen, desert trails nearby & parking. Own RV Park w/full hookups 1 m. from ranch. 1 hr. from Wickenburg/Parker/Blythe CA; 115 m. from WestWorld in Scottsdale. Nice quiet place to make your stop before or after a show.

CURRENT NEGATIVE COGGINS, HEALTH CERTIFICATE & OWNERSHIP PAPERS REQUIRED - see page 2 for details

SCOTTSDALE, 85262

★ **Casa de Las Caballos LLC, Ethan S. Day**
31316 N. 152 St. (101 to Pima to Dynamite, E. to 152, go N.)
Ph. 480/471-7717 Email:ethan@houseofthehorses.com Web:www.houseofthe-horses.com **Facilities:** 96 stalls, 18 holding pens, 4 arenas & full cross country, pool, trails in Tonto Nat'l Forest, elec./water for campers and 1 bdrm apt. avail. Full Service Facility.

ST DAVID, 85630

★ **Lazy Horse Ranch, Charles Supplee**
1855 W. Patton St. (S. of I-10, S. of Benson on Hwy 80)
Ph. 520/720-9810 Email:charles@lazy-horseranch.com
Web:www.lazy-horseranch.com **Facilities:** Open pastures, round pen, lighted arena & sewer/water & elec. Guest Ranch w/3 meals per day provided, swimming pool, hot tub, washer/dryer & large front porch w/mtn. views. Perfect area for trail rides, beautiful views/sensation of the Old West. Guided rides upon request.

TONOPAH, 85354

Stewart & Betsy Runner Horse Motel, RV Park & Arena
35704 W. Indian School Rd. (I-10, exit 103. 2 m. N. of I-10, 10 m. W. of Phoenix)
Ph.623/386-5124 Cell 623/640-1524
Email:sbhorsemotelrv@mymailstation.com **Facilities:** 20-20x20 outdoor stalls, feed avail., arena & 8 full camper hookups.

TUCSON, 85719

★ **Morningstar, Susan L. Newman**
(Ride for miles in river or thru linear park along riverbed. Close to all services, but in quiet grandfathered, old Tucson pocket neighborhood where there are still more horses than people)
Ph. 520/321-0286 Email:snewsy@juno.com **Facilities:** Old racing stable on Rillito River across from track. 7-12x12 covered stalls w/24' runs, auto waterers, turn-out arena, 60' round pen, camper arrangements possible & trails in surrounding mtns. New guest house at one end of stable w/dble bd/bath/kitchenette/patio.

TUCSON, 85743-9699

★ **Rocking M Ranch, the place to stay with your horses in Tucson! Private Bed & Breakfast facility, hosts Pam & Lou Mindes**
6265 N. Camino Verde (3-1/2 m. from I-10 & Ina Rd.)
Ph. 520/744-2457 - residence **1-888/588-2457** Fax 520/744-0824
Cell 520/444-0306 or 520/444-0308 Email:lou@pamlou.com
Web:WWW.ROCKINGMRANCH.NET **Facilities:** 5 covered 13x12 pipe corrals, auto water, round pen, lighted arena, walker, trail access to Saguaro Nat'l Park. Horse facilities complimentary for B&B guests/includes breakfast - $75-$100. Guests responsible for feed/cleanup of horses. Reservations preferred.
Ph. 520/907-9208 or Stacey 520/398-2058 **Facilities:** 8 stalls, holding pen, pasture, feed, arena, walker, trails & guest house. B&B nearby.

CURRENT NEGATIVE COGGINS, HEALTH CERTIFICATE & OWNERSHIP PAPERS REQUIRED - *see page 2 for details*

WICKENBURG, 85390

★ **Horspitality RV Resort & Boarding Stable, Jan & Paul Sullivan**
51802 Hwy 60 (2 m. S. of Wickenburg on Hwy 60/93)
Ph. 928/684-2519 Fax 928/684-0148 Email:horspitality@hotmail.com
Facilities: 90 outdoor pens/20 covered, large arena & camper hookups, Full/WE/E. Monthly rates avail.

Arkansas

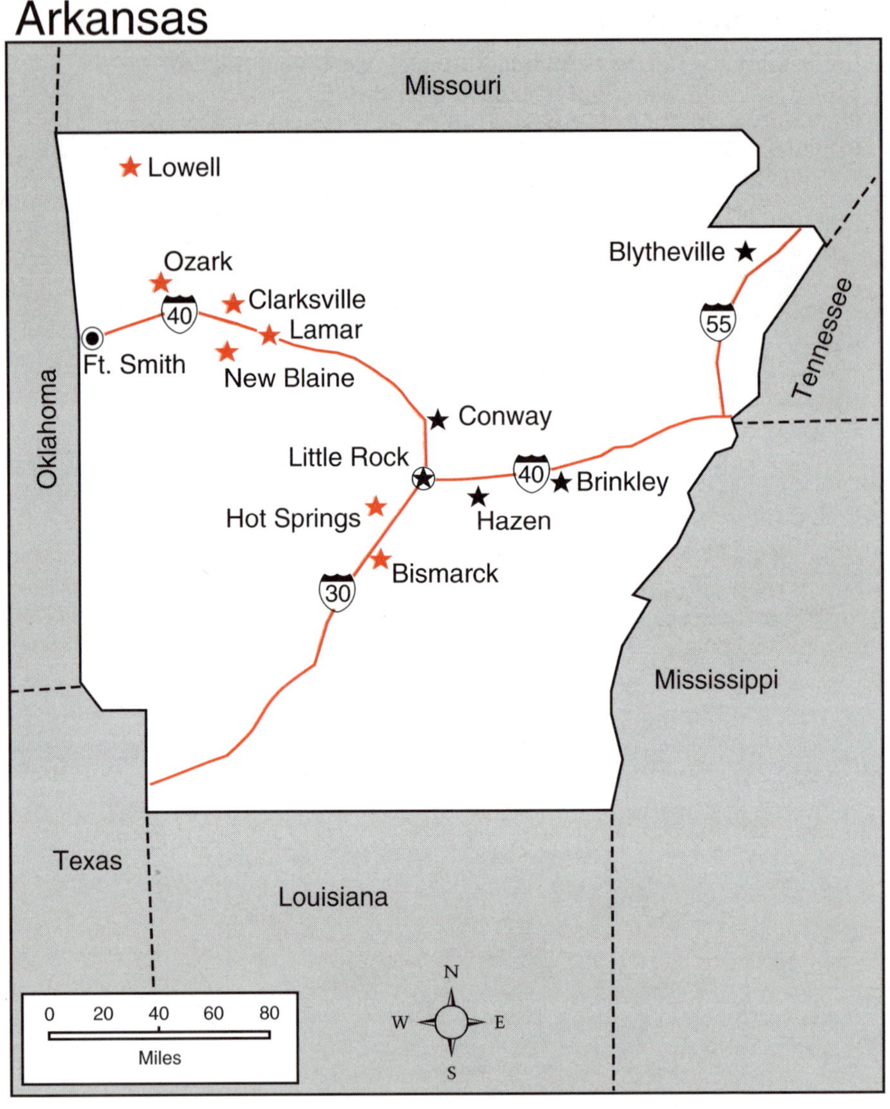

★ Vacation/Layover spots ★ Layovers only
State Capitol Hwy Junction Cities

CURRENT NEGATIVE COGGINS, HEALTH CERTIFICATE & OWNERSHIP PAPERS REQUIRED - see page 2 for details

BISMARCK (Hot Springs area), 71929

★ **Bar Fifty ® Ranch, Bette Clay & Julian McKinney, hosts**
18044 Hwy 84 (I-30, exit 91. 9 m. W. on Hwy 84. 20 min. to mineral baths/fishing/boating/racetrack.)
Ph. **1-888/829-9570** Fax 501/865-2633 Email:bclayb50@ipa.net **Facilities:** 360 acre ranch, 18 stalls w/cedar shavings, hay & feed avail., nice trail riding, trailer parking & full hook-ups. Lodge w/3-2rm suites. Full country breakfast incl. Pool/hot tub/sauna. Reservations req. MC/Visa accepted

BLYTHEVILLE, 72315

Circle S Horse Motel, Ronnie Self
3344 N. US Hwy 61 (I-55, exit 63. 1 m. S. on Hwy 61)
Ph. 870/763-9203 **Facilities:** 16 box stalls ($20 per head/per night) & camper hookup. Stud facilities avail. Tack shop. Reservations req. Cash only. Check-out by 11 a.m. No check-ins after 10 p.m. Motel 1 m.

BRINKLEY, 72021

Todd & Paige Mulloy
31326 Hwy 49 N. (I-40, exit 216. Take 490 6.3 m. on left. 1 hr. from Memphis & 1 hr. from Little Rock)
Ph. 870/734-0556 or 870/734-6436 **Facilities:** 8 indoor stalls, pasture, hay, elec. hookup avail., parking space for trailers, vet on call & other animals welcome. Easy in and out. Call for reservations/rates. Several hotels nearby.

CURRENT NEGATIVE COGGINS, HEALTH CERTIFICATE & OWNERSHIP PAPERS REQUIRED - see page 2 for details

CLARKSVILLE, 72830

★ **Standridge Circle S Ranch, Dennis Standridge**
(I-40, exit 64. 1/4 m. N., ranch on right. In Arkansas River Valley between the Ozarks & Ouachita Nat'l Forest. 4 hrs. W. of Memphis; 4 hrs. E. of Oklahoma City)
Ph. 479/754-8299 Fax 479/754-7082 Web:www.vulcancreative.com/standridge
Facilities: 19 indoor stalls, feed avail., round pen, arena, trails, guides optional, water & elec for campers & hot water wash bay. Washer/shower/dressing room in barn. Central to 3 mtn. trails. Use us as your base. Recommend BW Sherwood Motor Inn, exit 58, 479/754-7900.

Visit our Web site!
www.vulcancreative.com/standridge

CONWAY, 72032-4541

Miss Toby's Horseback Riding Academy and Dance Ranch, Toby Hart, owner/operator
255 E. German Ln. (N. of Little Rock off I-40)
Ph. 501/329-2233 Email:cjohnson@cyberback.com Web:www.MissTobys.com
Facilities: 10 stalls, 8 holding pens, 20 acres of pasture, grain/hay, outdoor arena, round pen, walker, wash rack, unlimited trails in area, water/elec for campers, parking for trailers/big rigs and overnight loft accommodations on premises. Cash or check. Reservation please.

CURRENT NEGATIVE COGGINS, HEALTH CERTIFICATE & OWNERSHIP PAPERS REQUIRED - see page 2 for details

HAZEN, 72064

Saddle Creek Stables, Patsy McMullen
P.O. Box 836 (Off I-40 between Memphis & Little Rock. Exit 193, head S. on Hwy 63 1 m. to Saddle Creek Rd., turn right)
Ph. 870/255-3037/call forwarding Email:stables@saddlecreekfarm.net
Web:www.saddlecreekfarm.net **Facilities:** 7 indoor 12x12 stalls, round pen & easy trailer access. No studs. Barn closes at 8 p.m. Reservations only.

HOT SPRINGS, 71913

★ **Step Ahead Farms & Training Center**
1301 Amity Rd. (25 min. from I-30 going N. & S.; 10 min. from Hwy 270 going E. & W. on I-40) Nearby restaurant has quality food at fast food prices.
Ph. 501/525-1667 **Facilities:** 25 box stalls w/mare & stud facilities, paddocks, feed, arena, walkers, 2 round pens, trails and 2 double rooms avail. for horse people w/continental breakfast. Large safe paddocks avail. for polo ponies. Vet. owner resides on premises. Reservations appreciated.

CURRENT NEGATIVE COGGINS, HEALTH CERTIFICATE & OWNERSHIP PAPERS REQUIRED - see page 2 for details

LAMAR, 72846

★ **Double W Ranch, Kevin & Jonna Webb**

(I-40, exit 64, to right/W 2 m. to Hwy 123, go right/N on 123 2-1/2 m. to Hwy 164, go left/W on 164 3/4 m. to Johnson Co. Rd. 157 [dirt rd/sign here], go right/N 1 m., ranch on left)

Ph. 501/754-4728 **Facilities:** 27-12x12 indoor concrete stalls, holding pens, pasture, feed, 300x100 outdoor lighted arena, trails and parking w/elec & water. Room for easy turn around. Arrive by 8 p.m. or call. At exits 55 & 58 are 9 motels within 5 m. of ranch. For directions from exit 58, call.

LITTLE ROCK, 72210

A M Ranch, Allen McKnight

13111 Col. Glenn Rd. (I-430, exit 4. 1 m. W. on left)

Ph. 501/312-2818 or 501/297-1953 Fax 501/227-5005 **Facilities:** 24 indoor stalls, 4 pastures, feed, arena, trails and overnight lodging w/continental breakfast.

LITTLE ROCK, 72210

Horsehead Arena and Stables, Tess Shell

13801 Lawson Rd. (2 miles off I-430 S. or 15 min. from I-40)

Ph. 501/224-0746 Fax 501/224-0730 **Facilities:** 5 stalls, holding pens, lighted indoor/outdoor arenas, wooded bridle trails, water & elec. hookup and trailer parking. Vet/farrier on call. Other animals welcome. Call for reservations/rates. Motels nearby.

LITTLE ROCK, 72210

Hungry Horse Stable, Sandy & Allison McMath

18100 Joanwood Ln. (Right off Col. Glenn from I-430)

Ph. 501/821-8777 **Facilities:** 7 indoor stalls, holding pen, pasture, arena, paddock, 10-20 m. of forest trails, may leave RV parked overnight and bunkhouse with 4 bunks, w/bath, when avail.

LOWELL, 72745

★ **Horse Haven, Judy Barnett**

1320 Bellview Rd. (In NW Arkansas, heart of the Ozarks. Less than 2 hrs. from Branson)

Ph. & Fax 479/621-0364 Email:jbarrett@ipa.net **Facilities:** Stalls, private turnout paddocks, indoor/outdoor arenas, wash rack & limited RV parking. Dog kennels. 10 motels within 4 m. Lots of fishing, golf, hiking, trail riding, state & Nat'l parks. Reservations required.

CURRENT NEGATIVE COGGINS, HEALTH CERTIFICATE & OWNERSHIP PAPERS REQUIRED - see page 2 for details

NEW BLAINE, 72851

★ **Lonesome "D" Horse Camp & RV Park, Dub Hamilton**
776 Cravens Ln. (S. of I-40. Hwy 22 & Cravens Ln)
Ph. 479/938-0149 Email:lonesomd@cswnet.com Web:www.lonesomed.com
Facilities: 57 outdoor holding pens, pastures, hay, round pen, 50x90 arena, 100 m. of trails, cabins for up to 4, 47 modern campsites w/corrals & primitive camping avail. Full facility bathhouse. Full time camp farrier on duty. Guides avail. Limited drive access.

OZARK, 72949

★ **Spirit Mountain Lodge and Cabins**
4117 Spirit Mountain Loop (18 m. N. of I-40, exit 35, Hwy 23)
Ph. 479/667-1919 Email:spiritmtnlodge@aol.com Web:www.spiritmountainlodge.com **Facilities:** 8 indoor/8 outdoor stalls, 3 holding pens, pasture, arena, trails and cabins. No stallions.

California

Oregon
Idaho
N
W
E
S
Redding
Red Bluff
Orland
5
80
Vacaville
Woodland
Sacramento
Nevada
Point Reyes Station
San Francisco
580
Westley
Carmel Valley
Santa Nella
Winton
5
Fresno
Lost Hills
Templeton
Bakersfield
SanLuis Obispo
Tehachapi
15
Agua Dulce
Barstow
40
Pacific Ocean
Los Angeles
Chino
San Bernardino
Huntington Beach
Chino Hills
Cherry Valley
10
0 50 100
Miles
San Diego
8
Arizona
Mexico
Vacation/Layover spots
Layovers only
State Capitol
Hwy Junction cities

CURRENT NEGATIVE COGGINS, HEALTH CERTIFICATE & OWNERSHIP PAPERS REQUIRED - see page 2 for details

AGUA DULCE, 91390

★ **Casa Dulce Riding & Guest Ranch, Joyce Guenther**
8035 Clayvale Rd. (40 m. N. of Los Angeles. 405 N. to 5 N. to 14 N. exit at Sierra Hwy. Then right, 14 m. to Johnnie Rd., then left to Clayvale, turn right)
Ph. 661/268-8946 Fax 661/268-8947 Email:HorseRanch@aol.com Web:www.TheGuestRanch.com **Facilities:** Large covered pipe corrals, round pen, arena & 1000's m. of open trails. Pacific Crest Trail within 15 min. 5 acre Bed & Breakfast Guest Ranch w/3 country syle rooms + bunkhouse/sleeps 11. Rental horses avail. Children & pets, campers & trailers welcome.

BAKERSFIELD, 93307

Galbraith's End of the Road Ranch
9010 Hermosa Rd. (Hwy 58. exit on Weedpatch Hwy S. to Hermosa, 1/2 m. to trailer sales)
Ph. 661/845-3013 After 6-8 rings, leave message. Will return call. **Facilities:** 8-13x48 stalls undercover, 2 holding pens, feed, arena & camper parking w/elec & water.

BAKERSFIELD, 93307

Triple C Ranch, Cathy P. Splonick
5818 S. Fairfax Rd. (3-1/2 m. S. of Hwy 58 on Fairfax; 5-1/2 E. of 99 on Panama Ln.)
Ph. 661/845-6937 Fax 661/846-5820 Web:www.crittercleaners.com **Facilities:** 40 indoor stalls, alfalfa avail., indoor arena, 2 outdoor arenas w/lights, camper hookups & parking for trailers/big rigs. $25 w/o feed. Economy Inn-5 m., Comfort Inn-8 m. & Motel 6-5 m.

BARSTOW, 92312

★ **Pan McCue Ranch**
P.O. Box 541 (1/2 m. N. of I-15 & the KOA at Yermo, CA. Take Ghost Town Rd. toward Calico)
Ph.760/254-2184 Email:pmcskl@msn.com
Facilities: 10 indoor/10 outdoor stalls, 2 holding pens, 96x96 exercise ring, feed & trails. KOA & Calico Ghost Town Camp areas. Motels nearby. Vet/farrier on call. Call for reservations/rates.

CARMEL VALLEY, 93924

Jon & Mary Sutherland
550 W. Carmel Valley Rd. (Off Hwy 1.E. 9.2 m. on right)
Ph. 831/659-2553 Email:jon@worrall.com **Facilities:** 1 indoor stall, paddock, feed & trails. Accommodations nearby.

CURRENT NEGATIVE COGGINS, HEALTH CERTIFICATE & OWNERSHIP PAPERS REQUIRED - see page 2 for details

CHERRY VALLEY, 92223

Gee Jay Ranch, Judi Brey
38660 Vineland St. (I-10, exit Beaumont. N. apx. 3 m., left on Vineland, 1/2 m. on right)
Ph. 909/845-5859 Cell 909/318-3449 **Facilities:** 8 indoor stalls, 15 holding pens, feed avail., 80x120 arena & camper hookup. Please call ahead. Will find overnight stabling if full. Clean, modern & safe.

CHINO, 91710

Burroughs Stock Farm & Transportation
4043 Francis Ave. (Ramona Ave. exit off US 60)
Ph. 909/465-6965 Email:elitestitch@aol.com **Facilities:** 30 box stalls, 10-12x24 holding pens w/covers, alfalfa or bermuda, 150x250 arena w/lights & 4-horse walker.

CHINO HILLS, 91709

Western Horse Co., Bud Grice
14536 Peyton Dr. (1 m. S. of 60 Freeway off the 71 Freeway in Chino Hills)
Ph. 909/597-1876 **Facilities:** 6 stalls w/runs, call for holding pens, hay/water, 2 turnout arenas, walker & camper/trailer parking.

FRESNO, 93706

Westfork Stables, Tricia Selsor, owner/mgr.
3201 W. Whitesbridge (Hwy 99, exit Belmont Ave. W to stop sign, left to Whitesbridge. 2 min. from Hwy 99)
Ph. 559/233-0982 **Facilities:** 25 indoor stalls, 10 holding pens, pasture, alfalfa/oats avail., round corral, 4 arenas, wash rack, walker, lots of trails, camper parking & tack shop. All in grass and trees. Very clean facilities.

HUNTINGTON BEACH, 92648

★ **Huntington Central Park Equestrian Center**
18381 Goldenwest Blvd. (405 Freeway & Goldenwest Blvd.)
Ph. 714/848-6565 Fax 714/842-9229 Email:hcpec@aol.com
Web:www.hcpec.com **Facilities:** 159 box stalls/228 pipe corrals, half-covered, turnouts, hay & cubes, arena, walker & trails.

LOST HILLS, 93249

★ **Lost Hills K.O.A.**
P.O. Box 276 (I-5 & Hwy 46)
Ph. 805/797-2719 Reservations only: **1-800/562-2793** **Facilities:** 4 holding pens, trails & camper hookup. Motels/restaurants/service station within walking distance.

CURRENT NEGATIVE COGGINS, HEALTH CERTIFICATE & OWNERSHIP PAPERS REQUIRED - see page 2 for details

ORLAND, 95963

Fox Hunter Farm, Judy & Bob Holzapfel
5960 County Rd. 200 (3 m. W. of I-5)
Ph. 530/865-5599 Email:jholz@glenncounty.net **Facilities:** Indoor stalls, holding pens w/runs, pasture & feed avail., large arena w/jumps, dressage arena & parking space for horse trailers or self-contained campers. Motels, campgrounds and B&B nearby. Close to Black Butte Lake. Please call ahead for reservations.

POINT REYES STATION, 94956

★ **Bar-or Ranch, Gal Bar-or**
P.O. Box 778 Location: 11925 Hwy 1 (Located along the Point Reyes seashore, less than an hour N. of San Francisco & W. of the Napa-Sonoma wine country)
Ph. 415/663-9596 Fax 415/480-1317 Email:gal@bar-or.com Web:www.bar-or.com **Facilities:** Premier B&B, private cottages, world-class equestrian center. 25 fully-bedded stalls, feed 3xdaily, h&c wash racks & ample horse trailer parking. Ride to town, hitch up & have a drink at the Western Saloon or ride the 24,000 acres of the Pt. Reyes Nat'l Recreation Area.

RED BLUFF, 96080

Bar $\overline{\text{M}}$ Ranch, Barbara Secor
20105 Callahan Rd. (5 m. W. of I-5. 2-1/2 hrs. N. of Sacramento; 30 m. S. of Redding)
Ph. 530/527-2107 Email:barmrch@tco.net **Facilities:** 5 large indoor stalls, 2 large holding pens w/shelters, pasture, feed, round pen, arena, parking and/or hookup & pull through access for large rigs. Motels & restaurants nearby.

REDDING, 96003

3-D Ranch, Vicki Donovan
20567 Conestoga Trail (I-5 to 299E E. Stillwater Way)
Ph. 530/549-4999 **Facilities:** 10 indoor stalls, holding pens, pasture, feed, arena, walker, trails & elec. for self-contained campers.

SACRAMENTO, 95827

Cracker Jack Ranch, Jeanee & Lew Conner
10004 Jackson Rd. (7/10 m. E. of Bradshaw Rd.)
Ph. 916/363-4309 916/441-8179 - voice mail **Facilities:** 8 stalls, 2 w/corrals, paddocks avail., arena & parking for self-contained campers w/water & elec.

SAN DIEGO, 92154

Jeraldine Hickman 'Donkey Lady'
1666 Sunset Ave. (15 m. S. of the city of San Diego. South Bay near all attractions)
Ph. 619/575-4509 **Facilities:** 6-24x24 covered stalls, 2 wash racks, overnight parking w/elec & water, and beach trails 1-1/4 m., ride on beach.

CURRENT NEGATIVE COGGINS, HEALTH CERTIFICATE & OWNERSHIP PAPERS REQUIRED - see page 2 for details

SAN LUIS OBISPO

★ **Barbi Breen-Gurley's Sea Horse Ranch**
2566 Sea Horse Ln., Los Osos CA 93402 (11 m. W. of US 101/San Luis Obispo, on the central CA coast)
Ph. 805/528-0222 **Facilities:** 30 paddocks, oats/alfalfa, 4 arenas, access to beach & Montana de Oro State Park trails and B&B 3 m. Motels/campgrounds nearby.

SANTA NELLA, 95322

★ **San Luis RV Resort, Jo Martindale**
28485 Gonzaga Rd. (2-1/2 m. W. of I-5; Hwy 152 & 33, left on Gonzaga Rd)
Ph. 209/826-5542 Fax 209/826-4875 Email:john@cell2000.net Web:www.san-luisrv.com **Facilities:** This is an RV resort w/4 stalls & a round pen. Full hook-ups for RV's and all pull thru sites; tent areas are also avail.

TEHACHAPI, 93561

Horse Apple Ranch, Ray & Beverly Billingsley
21832 Ferncuko (Hwy 58, Sand Canyon exit)
Ph. 661/822-6416 823-VET-1 **Facilities:** 10 indoor/12 outdoor stalls, alfalfa, 2 arenas, walker, near Pacific Crest Trail and parking w/elec & water. DVM on premises.

TEMPLETON, 93465

★ **Carriage Vineyards, Bed - Barn & Breakfast**
4337 S. El Pomar (Hwy 101, near Paso Robles & San Luis Obispo)
Ph. 805/227-6807 Fax 805/226-9969 Web:www.carriagevineyards.com
Facilities: 4 indoor/20 outdoor, covered stalls, corral, hay, arena, trails and Bed & Breakfast. 100 acres w/gardens, sitting areas, creek, mtn. bikes avail, hiking & 2400 sq. ft. carriage house w/12 antique carriages. Central Coast: ocean 30 min/near Hearst Castle/wine country.

VACAVILLE, 95696

Ranchotel Horse Center, Delbert Berg, owner
P.O. Box 6 (I-80, 1 m. W. of Vacaville/Pena Adobe exit)
Ph. 707/451-8225 **Facilities:** 12x12 stalls w/wood shavings & 80x120 indoor lighted arena/2 outdoor arenas w/grandstands. Advance reservations req. Complete Tack Store on premises, 10 am to 6 pm (closed Mondays), 448-TACK. Restaurants/factory stores nearby. Motel on grounds.

WESTLEY, 95387

Henderson's Walkers, Daymond & Sue Henderson
P.O. Box 316 Location: 3565 Howard Rd. (1 m. E. of I-5, 7 m. N. of Patterson & 19 m. S. of Tracy)
Ph. 209/894-3360 - evening only Email:hendersn@evansinet.com **Facilities:** 8 indoor stalls, holding pens, pasture, walker, feed, trails & camper hookup. Motels nearby.

CURRENT NEGATIVE COGGINS, HEALTH CERTIFICATE & OWNERSHIP PAPERS REQUIRED - *see page 2 for details*

WINTON, 95388

The Do Daaw Ranch, Hannah Miller
8175 Almond Ave. (Hwy 99 N. or S., exit Central 1 m., right on Almond)
Ph. Office 209/357-7947 Cell 209/761-0203 Email:thedodaawranch@aol.com
Facilities: 10 outdoor stalls, 4 holding pens, feed avail., arena use extra w/stay, wash rack, saddle mounting rack & trailer parking. No business conducted Friday night or Saturday daytime - Torah observant.

WOODLAND, 95695

Woodland Stallion Station
34270 County Rd. 20 (Exit Hwy 16 W. off I-5, N. of Woodland)
Ph. 530/661-1358 530/662-1354 **Facilities:** 54 indoor stalls, 12x24 covered pens, feed incl., indoor/outdoor arenas, walker, 1200 acres of trails & camper parking, $25 per night.

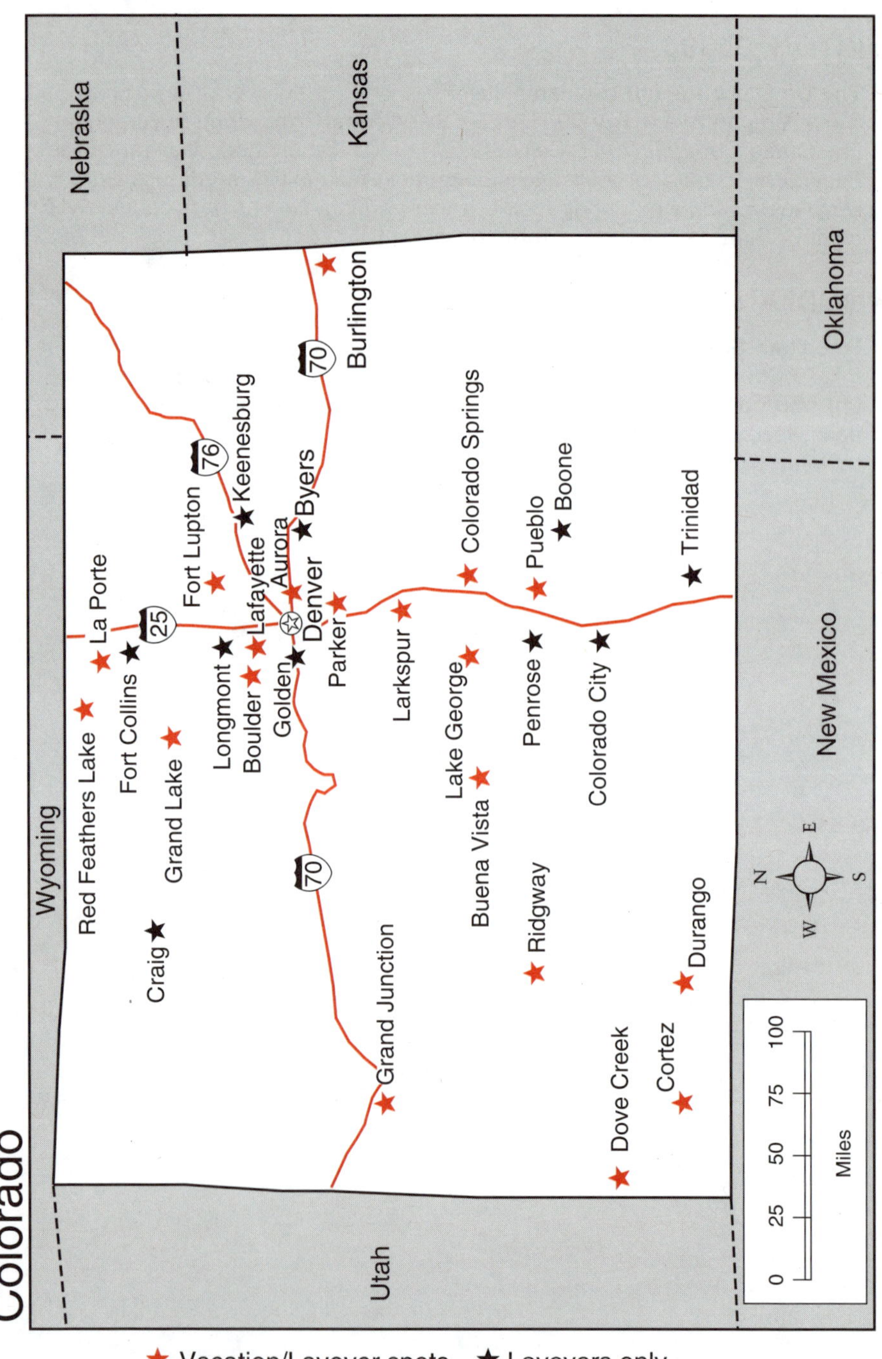

★ Vacation/Layover spots ★ Layovers only

✪ State Capitol ◉ Hwy Junction Cities

CURRENT NEGATIVE COGGINS, HEALTH CERTIFICATE & OWNERSHIP PAPERS REQUIRED - see page 2 for details

AURORA, 80011

★ **Kenlyn Stables, Ken & Linda Fisher**
1000 Salida St. (E. off I-225, exit 6th Ave., 2 m. to Airport Blvd., N 1/4 m. to 10th; or S. off I-70, exit Airport Blvd., 2 m. to 10th Ave. E.)
Ph. 303/364-9556 Cell 303/807-0062 **Facilities:** Show barn box stalls, holding pens & turnouts, grass & alfalfa hay avail., indoor/outdoor arenas, river bottom trails & camper parking. .

BOONE, 81025

4 A's Boarding Stable, Brian & Rose Ancona
Mail: P.O. Box 114 Location: 58520 E. U.S. Hwy 50 (Between mile markers 337 & 338 on S. side of US 50)
Ph. 719/947-3698 **Facilities**: 3 indoor stalls, 3 holding pens, 900 acres of pasture, feed incl., arena coming soon, trail riding permitted and RV's & large trailers welcome. Vet/farrier on call. 25 m. E. of Colorado State Fair Grounds.

BOULDER, 80026

★ **Mary Bradley**
5610 Baseline
Ph. 303/665-9247 **Facilities**: Stables and boarding. See Lafayette listing.

BUENA VISTA, 81211

★ **Wapiti Run Trakehners, Judith L. Moore**
17900 Vista Dr. (Hwy 24, between US 50 & I-70)
Ph. 719/395-8543 Email:dialogue@amigo.net Web:www.helpyourdog.com **Facilities**: 4 indoor stalls, paddock & pens w/shelters, indoor/outdoor arenas, cross-country course, dressage/jumping instruction, feed, wilderness trails & camper hookup. Two studio apts. avail. w/wo breakfast - advance reservations only.

BURLINGTON, 80807

★ **JB's Horse Motel - Joan B. Chandler, Owner & Mgr.**
19790 Hwy 385 N. (I-70, exit 438/Rose Ave. 1-1/2 blks. W. on Rose, right on 385 N. 2 m. on right)
Ph. & Fax 719/346-8217 **Facilities**: 7 indoor stalls w/pipe runs, outdoor pens, pastures, feed avail. at extra charge, outdoor arena , camper hookup/overnight parking & B&B when avail.. 20 m. from Bonny St. Park (25,000 acres) w/trails, fishing, boating, water skiing, camping. Advance reservations appreciated.

BYERS, 80103

Hennesy's Country Acres
P.O. Box 325 Location: 71777 County Rd. 10 (Close to I-70 & Hwy 36)
Ph. 303/822-8446 **Facilities**: Indoor stalls, pasture & pens avail. Close to motels & restaurnats. Nightly, weekly & monthly rates.

CURRENT NEGATIVE COGGINS, HEALTH CERTIFICATE & OWNERSHIP PAPERS REQUIRED - see page 2 for details

COLORADO CITY, 81019

Stewart Thoroughbreds, Shirley Pigg, Facilities Mgr.
P.O. Box 19107 Location: 6888 Hwy 165 West (1-1/2 m. W. of I-25, exit 74. 20 m. S. of Pueblo)
Ph.719/676-3323 **Facilities**: 50 stalls, $12 + bedding, pasture w/shelter, $12, round corrals, outdoor arena, trail riding area avail., lots of parking room/semis okay. Stallions welcome. Security lights/elec. in barn for late arrivals. KOA, motel, convenience store within a mile.

COLORADO SPRINGS, 80908

★ **H2 Ranch, Edwin Housley**
6665 Walker Rd. (I-25, exit 161, Hwy 105 E. to Hwy 83, then 3 m. on Walker Rd.)
Ph. & Fax 719/495-2338 Email:h2stables@mindspring.com Web:h2stables.com
Facilities: 8 indoor stalls, 3 holding pens, pasture, hay, round pen, indoor/outdoor arenas, trails within 5 m. and B&B on premises - 2 bdrms w/bath. Reservations necessary. No smoking. Evening meals by reservations only. Pikes Peak/Garden of the Gods/AF Academy within 10 m.

CORTEZ, 81321

★ **Jones Livery, Jerry & Carol Jones**
P.O. Box 1378 Location: 20225 County Rd. G (Rd. G is S. of Cortez next to the DOT off Rt. 666/160. W. on Rd. G 2-1/2 m. past airport)
Ph. 970/565-9639 **Facilities**: New barn w/12x32 stall areas, arenas, trails, wash rack, large parking area. Private & secure. Owners live on property. Four Corners area: Mesa Verde Nat'l Park, ski resorts, Ute Mountain Casino. Motels in city.

CRAIG, 81625

TWO SHUE'S HORSE RANCH, Bill & Dona Shue
696 County Rd. 22 (4 m. N. on Hwy 13, 1 m. W. on CR 22)
Ph. 970/824-0105 Cell 970/629-5760 **1-877/259-2315** Email:wfs1019@hotmail.com Web:www.twoshueshr.8k.com **Facilities**: Indoor/outdoor stalls, pasture, feed avail., round pen, camper hookup w/elec & water, Bed & Breakfast, tent camping spots, picnic area & parking space for horse trailers. No smoking. Call for reservations/rates. Motels/restaurants nearby. Checks or cash.

CURRENT NEGATIVE COGGINS, HEALTH CERTIFICATE & OWNERSHIP PAPERS REQUIRED - see page 2 for details

DOVE CREEK, 81324-0860

★ **Sun Canyon Ranch, Mac McMahon**
P.O. Box 860 Location: 02082 Co. Rd. 8 (6-1/2 m. N. of Dove Creek on CR 8, off US 666. Located in the spectacular 4 corners area of SW Colorado between Durango, Telluride & Moah UT. Mesa Verde nearby)
Ph. **1-866/737-3377** Email:mail@suncanyonranch.com
Web:www.suncanyonranch.com **Facilities**: 7 indoor stalls, 10 paddocks, round pen, outdoor arena, heated wash stall, 12 RV sites w/50 amps & a B&B room in barn. Brand new: Sun Canyon Lodge sleeps up to 20+, solar powered, w/a spectacular view. Trailhead access to Dolores River Canyon Rim. Ride or tour area.

DURANGO, 81301

★ **ALMOSTARANCH, Terry & Rhonda Hunt**
4618 C.R. 203 (4.6 m. N. of town - Big Red Barn with metal roof)
Ph. 727/647-8060 Fax 727/945-1647 Email:TL1955@aol.com
Web:www.almostaranch.com **Facilities**: 4 stalls, 2 holding pens, parking space for trailers, beautifully decorated 3-bdrm farm house w/historic Red Barn, located in the heart of the San Juan Mtns. 2 night minimum. Call for reservations/rates/info. Durango has rodeos, abundance of trails, etc.

FT. COLLINS, 80524

Brown Quarter Horses, Ted or Lynn K. Brown
325 E. County Rd. 56 (4 m. off I-25; 3 m. off 287)
Ph. 970/493-0953 - best time to call is before 7 a.m. or after dark. Leave a phone or cell number; they will call back. **Facilities**: 5 indoor stalls, 4 holding pens, 2 pastures, alfalfa/grain, arena, elec/water for campers.

FT. LUPTON, 80621

★ **Renegade Ranch, Maryann & Ken Abeles**
8711 WCR 23 (Easy access from I-25 or CO Hwy 85, 30 min. N. of Denver & Nat'l Western Complex. Easy commute during Stock Show)
Ph. 303/857-2189 Email:arenegade01@aol.com **Facilities**: 7 stall barn w/outside runs, attached to indoor arena, outdoor pens w/shelter, outdoor arena, round pen, turnout areas, feed avail. & trailer parking/hookups. Motels & restaurants close or stay in fully equipped RV. Great place to rest up & enjoy area sites.

GOLDEN, 80401

Jefferson County Fairgrounds
15200 W. 6th Ave. (I-70, exit 262 W.; I-70, exit 261 E.; 6th Ave & Indiana)
Ph. 303/271-6600 Fax 303/271-6606 Email:sburgene@jeffco.us Web:fairgrounds.jeffco.us **Facilities**: 90 indoor/10 outdoor stalls, 26 holding pens, 3 outdoor/1 indoor arenas and 23 camper spaces w/elec. only.

GRAND JUNCTION

★ **Alamar Stables, Kimberly Shipard**
3363 C Rd., Palisade Co 81526 (10 min. from I-70, exit 37)
Ph. 970/523-1445 **Facilities**: 30 indoor/20 outdoor stalls, full exercise training facility & trailer/RV parking.

CURRENT NEGATIVE COGGINS, HEALTH CERTIFICATE & OWNERSHIP PAPERS REQUIRED - see page 2 for details

GRAND LAKE, 80447

★ **Winding River Resort, Wes House**
P.O. Box 629 Location: 1447 Co. Rd. 491 (W. entrance to Rocky Mtn. Nat'l Park & Arapaho Nat'l Forest. 3 m. from Grand Lake & 100 m. NW of Denver on paved roads)
Ph. 970/627-3215 Fax 970/627-5003 Email:trailboss@rkymtnhi.com
Web:www.windingriverresort.com **Facilities**: Housekeeping cabins, lodge rooms, campsites w/horse pens at the site or the barn, trail rides, hay rides, animal farm and chuckwagon breakfasts & dinners. Ride directly to the trails from your campsite or cabin. Open May 15-Oct. 1.

KEENESBURG, 80643

Pam Booghier
29391 Weld County Rd. 8 (7-1/2 m. E. of I-76 & 52. 30 min. to Denver Intn'l Airport; 40 min. to downtown Denver)
Ph. 303/478-8695 303/732-4919 **Facilities**: 3 indoor stalls, pasture, grass hay & country dirt roads for riding. Certified hay avail. KOA at I-76 & 52. Motels 3 m.

LAFAYETTE, 80026

★ **Mary Bradley**
1375 N. 111th St. and 4277 N. 109th
Ph. 303/665-9247 **Facilities**: Indoor/ outdoor stalls, holding pens, pasture, arena, feed, trails and Bed & Breakfast.

LAKE GEORGE, 80827

★ **Mule Creek Outfitters/M Lazy C Ranch**
P.O. Box 461 (40 m. W. of Colorado Springs on Hwy 24. Nestled in high mountain valley, about 8200' elevation)
Ph. 719/748-3398 **1-800/289-4868**
Web:www.mlazyc.com **Facilities**: 2 indoor/10 outdoor stalls, 2 holding pens, grass hay/3 way grain at market price, 7 RV hookups w/elec. and 5 cabins for Bed & Breakfast. An actual working cattle ranch, homesteaded in the early 1900's and surrounded by 25,000 acres of National Forest.

CURRENT NEGATIVE COGGINS, HEALTH CERTIFICATE & OWNERSHIP PAPERS REQUIRED - see page 2 for details

LaPORTE, 80535

★ **Copper Top Acres, Lee & LoraLee Carter**
4625 Kiva Dr. (Intersection of CR 54G & Hwy 287 which is 6 m. NW of Ft. Collins on Hwy 287. Located within 2 m. of Lory State Park, Rist Canyon & Poudre Canyon)
Ph. 970/221-4382 Email:LLJTC4x4@cs.com **Facilities**: New 3 stall Morton barn w/runs & 120x90 working arena, wash rack, hay avail. & limited trailer hookups. Well mannered horses. Overnight accommodations avail. in owner's home, air-conditioned room w/dbl bd & 2-twin trundle bds, private bath.

LARKSPUR (35 m. S. of Denver), 80118

★ **Spring Canyon Ranch, Camping & B&B, Bobbi Richine**
6203 Valley High Rd. (I-25, exit 172 or 173; 4-1/2 m. W.)
Ph. 303/681-3237 Barn 303/681-2942 Cell 303/808-9730 Fax 303/681-2844 Email:bobbi@rmtc.net Web:www.rmtc.net **Facilities**: A beautiful mountain valley with hundreds of miles of America's most scenic riding trails. Camper hookups/showers avail. Indoor stalls, pens, pasture & covered arena. Horses: $15/day. Condition your horse for edurance/racing.

LARKSPUR, 80118

★ **That Special Place, Steve & Wendy Hickox**
6145 S. Perry Park Rd. (Just off I-25, 20 m. S. of Denver. Convenient to Castlerock, Parker, Colo. Sprgs. & entire Denver Metro area_)
Ph. 303/681-0187 Fax 303/715-1012 Email:hickox@1031x.com **Facilities**: 14 stalls, 3 holding pens, 6 pastures, round pen, lighted outdoor arena and 5 nicely appointed guest rooms & cabins. Situated in the West Plum Creek Valley. We only accept people w/horses and horses w/people. Satisfaction guaranteed with our facilities & care.

LARKSPUR, 80118

Leslie Terry
6510 E. Lorraine Rd. (Intersection of Hwy 83 & Lorraine Rd./Co. Rd. 82)
Ph. 303/688-4147 Fax 303/688-0266 Email:PSEC6510@aol.com **Facilities**: 12 indoor stalls, large holding pens, feed avail., large outdoor/indoor arena 2 m. away, small outdoor arena on property, trails 4 m., and parking w/elec & water. Call in advance for B&B/apt/room. Reservations required.

LONGMONT, 80504

CR Livestock & Animal Care, Inc., Rick & Chris Foster
757 Weld County Rd. 18 (20 m. N. of Denver off I-25)
Ph. 303/651-7193 **Facilities**: Stalls & runs, holding pens, feed, indoor/outdoor arenas, round pen & walker. 48 hrs. reservations req.

CURRENT NEGATIVE COGGINS, HEALTH CERTIFICATE & OWNERSHIP PAPERS REQUIRED - see page 2 for detail

PARKER, 80138-4909

★ **Wine Glass Ranch, LLC, Victoria Long**
1765 Michael Gates Dr. (Located between I-70 & I-25, just E. of I-470. A map can be found on our website)
Ph. 303/840-7772 Fax 303/840-7773 Email:thewineglassranch@hotmail.com
Web:www.thewineglassranch.com **Facilities**: 6 indoor (5-12x12 w/runs/1-15x16) stalls w/bedding, round pen, 4 pastures 125x250 outdoor arena, trails located nearby and a beautiful European styled apartment.

PENROSE, 81240

Caballo Casa, Jim & Nancy McEnulty
60921 Hwy 50 E (I-25 at Pueblo, take Canon City/Royal Gorge exit. 28 m. W. of Pueblo on Hwy 50)
Ph. 719/372-6182 **Facilities**: 4 indoor stalls w/runs, large pipe pen, round pen, feed avail. upon request, 15 m. to Beaver Creek Trails, elec. only for campers & plenty of room for parking. Trailer repair nearby.

PUEBLO, 81004

★ **Greenhorn Horse Hotel, Gay Powell Christie**
8055 S. I-25 (Apx. 20 m. S. of Pueblo on I-25, exit 77/Cedarwood. W. side of interstate, entrance is on service rd)
Ph. 719/676-2528 Email:info@greenhornhorsehotel.com
Web:www.greenhornhorsehotel.com **Facilities**: 4-12x12 stalls w/30' runs, 2-12x42 pens, round pen, well lit & secure. Opern 24/7. Ride from stalls into adjoining countryside or leave horse with us and enjoy attractions of southern Colorado. Hook up trailer or RV next to horses. Discount for multiple horses.

PUEBLO, 81008

★ **Five Star Ranch & Equestrian Center, LLC**
18550 Midway Ranch Rd. (Halfway between Pueblo & Colorado Springs on I-25. From S. exit 119, from N. exit 122)
Ph. 719/382-5601 Fax 719/392-7561 Email:fivestarreq@aol.com
Web:www.fivestarranch.com **Facilities**: 45 stalls, 20 paddocks, wash racks, 3 outdoor/2 indoor arenas, elecrical RV hookups and 2 guest houses w/9 rooms, sleep approx. 19.

PUEBLO, 81008

Lena Fox, Fountain Valley Stable
2580 Overton Rd.
Ph. 719/545-8350 **Facilities**: Indoor/outdoor stalls, holding pens & arena.

CURRENT NEGATIVE COGGINS, HEALTH CERTIFICATE & OWNERSHIP PAPERS REQUIRED - see page 2 for details

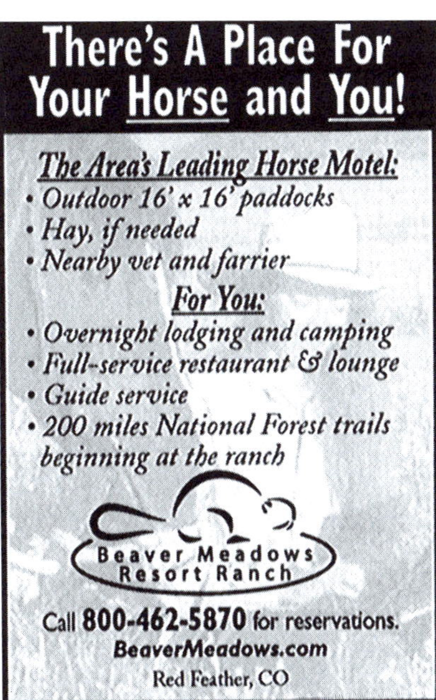

RED FEATHER LAKES, 80545

★ **Beaver Meadows Resort Ranch**
100 Marmot Dr., Unit 1 (Northern CO)
Ph. **1-800/462-5870** Fax 970/881-2643 Email:info@beavermeadows.com Web:www.BeaverMeadows.com **Facilities**: 16x16 paddocks, pasture & 200 m. of riding trails through Roosevelt Nat'l Forest adjacent to resort. Open year round. On-site campgrounds, condominiums, family cabins, log cottages & lodge rooms. Full-service restaurant & lounge. Call for reservations/rates.

RED FEATHER LAKES, 80545

★ **Red Feather Ranch B&B and Horse Hotel, Steve Horsmon**
3613 CR 68C (1 hr. NW of Ft. Collins and 2 hrs. from Denver_
Ph. 970/881-3715 Fax 435/514-1151 Email:rfranch@earthlink.net Web:www.red-featherranch.com **Facilities**: Up to 5 paddocks & barn w/20 ac. fenced pasture, grass hay upon request, arena, round pen, trailer parking w/easy access, B&B w/5 bdrms & private baths and 40 ac. backing Roosevelt Nat'l Forest riding trails. Clinics w/John Lyons certified trainer. Campfires & guitars!

RIDGWAY , 81432

★ **Angel Ridge Ranch, Denise Fisher**
177 County Rd. 10 (25 m. S. of Montrose off Hwy 550)
Ph. 970/626-4287 Email:angelridge@frontier.net Web:www.angelridgeranch.com **Facilities**: 14 indoor/4 outdoor stalls, 4 holding pens, 80' round pen, loafing sheds, 52 acres of pasture, completely fenced, supply your own feed, 80x120 outdoor arena, hot-walker, trails, camper hookup and 4 rooms for Bed & Breakfast.

RIDGWAY (Ouray County), 81432

★ **Ouray County Fairgrounds, Louie Schlosser**
P.O. Box 188 (Corner of Hwy 550 & Hwy 62 in Ridgway. In the spectacular San Juan Mtns.)
Ph. 970/626-9775 Fax 970/626-4439 or after hours/weekends 970/626-5796 Web:www.co.ouray.co.us **Facilities**: 20 new 12x12 stalls, 10 holding pens, water, feed avail. upon request, outdoor arena, trails nearby & parking. Vet/farrier on call. Other pets welcome. Reservations required.

CURRENT NEGATIVE COGGINS, HEALTH CERTIFICATE & OWNERSHIP PAPERS REQUIRED - *see page 2 for details*

TRINIDAD, 81082

LP Boarding & Overnight Stables, Ken & Denise Pfalmer
101 W. Indiana (I-25, exit 15, W.)
Ph. 719/846-7094 Email:d_pfalmer@hotmail.com **Facilities**: 10 covered stalls w/paddocks, 2 holding pens, arena nearby, riding area & parking space. Reservations required.

TRINIDAD, 81082

Rogers Quarter Horses, John & Mary Rogers
17615 CR 75.1 (I-25, exit 18, 4 m. E.)
Ph. 719/846-4634 or 719/846-6030 Email:rogersqh@amigo.net **Facilities**: 4 box stalls w/runs, holding pens, pasture, feed, arena, trails, camper parking w/elec. & water and one room. Horses in good health only.

NOTES

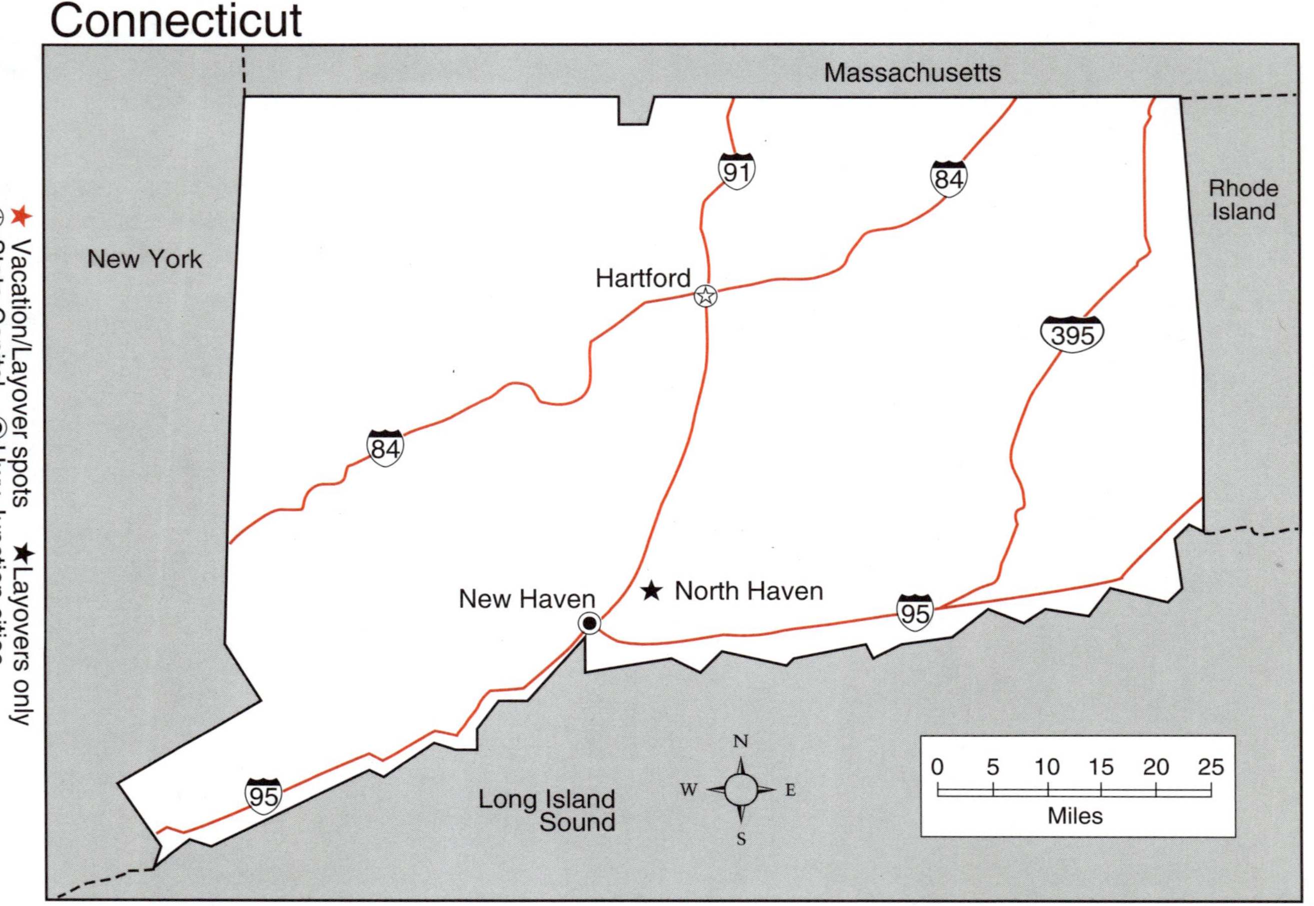
Connecticut
Massachusetts
New York
Rhode Island
Hartford
New Haven
North Haven
Long Island Sound
91
84
395
84
95
95
N
W
E
S
0 5 10 15 20 25
Miles
Vacation/Layover spots
Layovers only
State Capitol
Hwy Junction cities

CURRENT NEGATIVE COGGINS, HEALTH CERTIFICATE & OWNERSHIP PAPERS REQUIRED - see page 2 for details

NEW HAVEN, 06473

Sugarloaf Farm, Debbie or Rick Rallo
420 Barberry Rd. (I-91 N. or S., exit 9, Call for directions)
Ph. 203/234-7884 Email: sugarloafdjr@aol.com **Facilities:** 25-12x14 indoor box stalls, 5 large grass turnouts, feed, indoor/outdoor lighted arenas, round pen & trails. 6 p.m. arrival. Call ahead.

Delaware

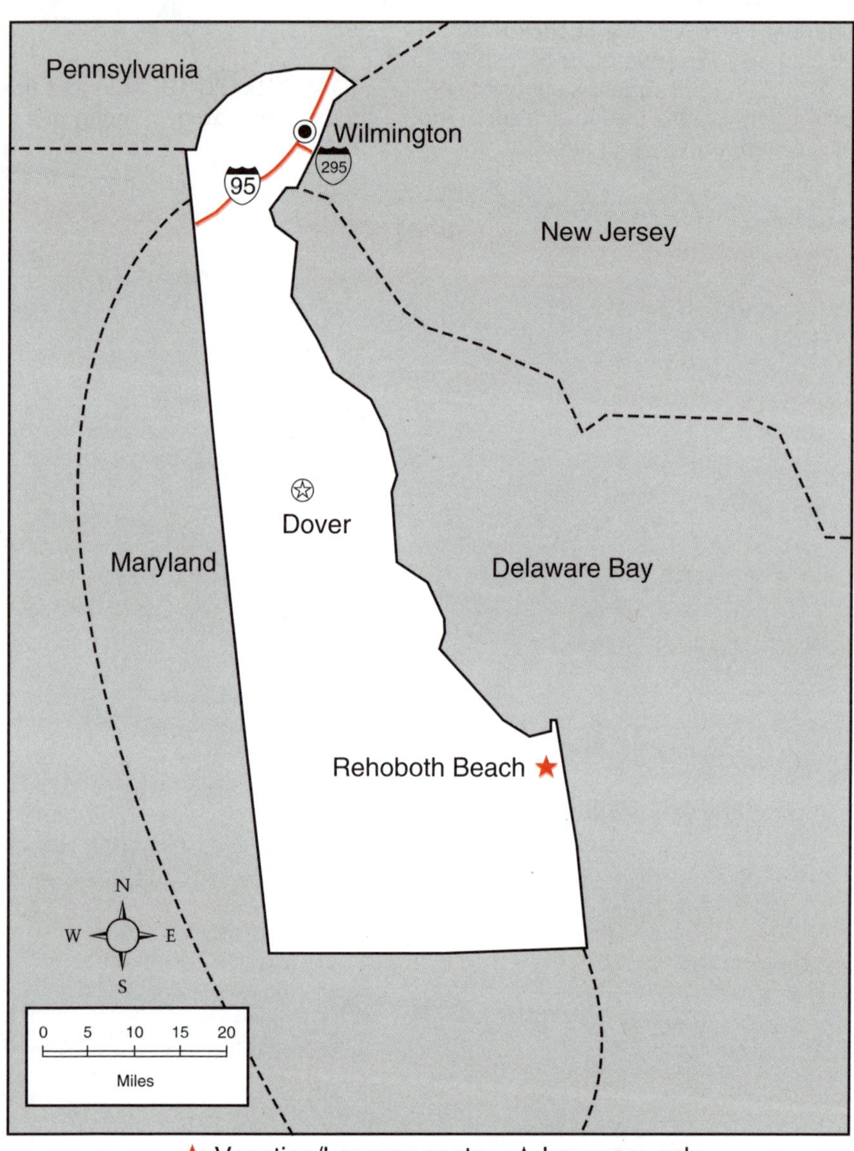

★ Vacation/Layover spots ★ Layovers only
✪ State Capitol ◉ Hwy Junction cities

CURRENT NEGATIVE COGGINS, HEALTH CERTIFICATE & OWNERSHIP PAPERS REQUIRED - see page 2 for details

REHOBOTH BEACH

★ **1776 Farm, Ken & Linda Butler**

Mail & location: 27189 Martins Farm Rd., Milton DE 19968 (Apx. 5 m. W. of SR 1 Tnpk off US 9W & SR 5S. Delaware & Maryland State Parks within minutes)
Ph. 302/684-3416 - barn Business 302/645-9355 Fax 302/645-0854 Email:LJae1776@aol.com Web:www.1776ofRehoboth.com
Facilities: 11 indoor/2 outdoor stalls, 5 paddocks, hay/feed, outdoor arena, round pen, water/elec for RV/Campers, parking & guest suite on property. B&B within 1 m. Vet/farrier on call. No stallions. Beach rides our specialty. 24 hr. reservations req. Credit cards accepted.

(Riding on the beach of Delaware Seashore State Park) Rehoboth Beach Delaware

Florida

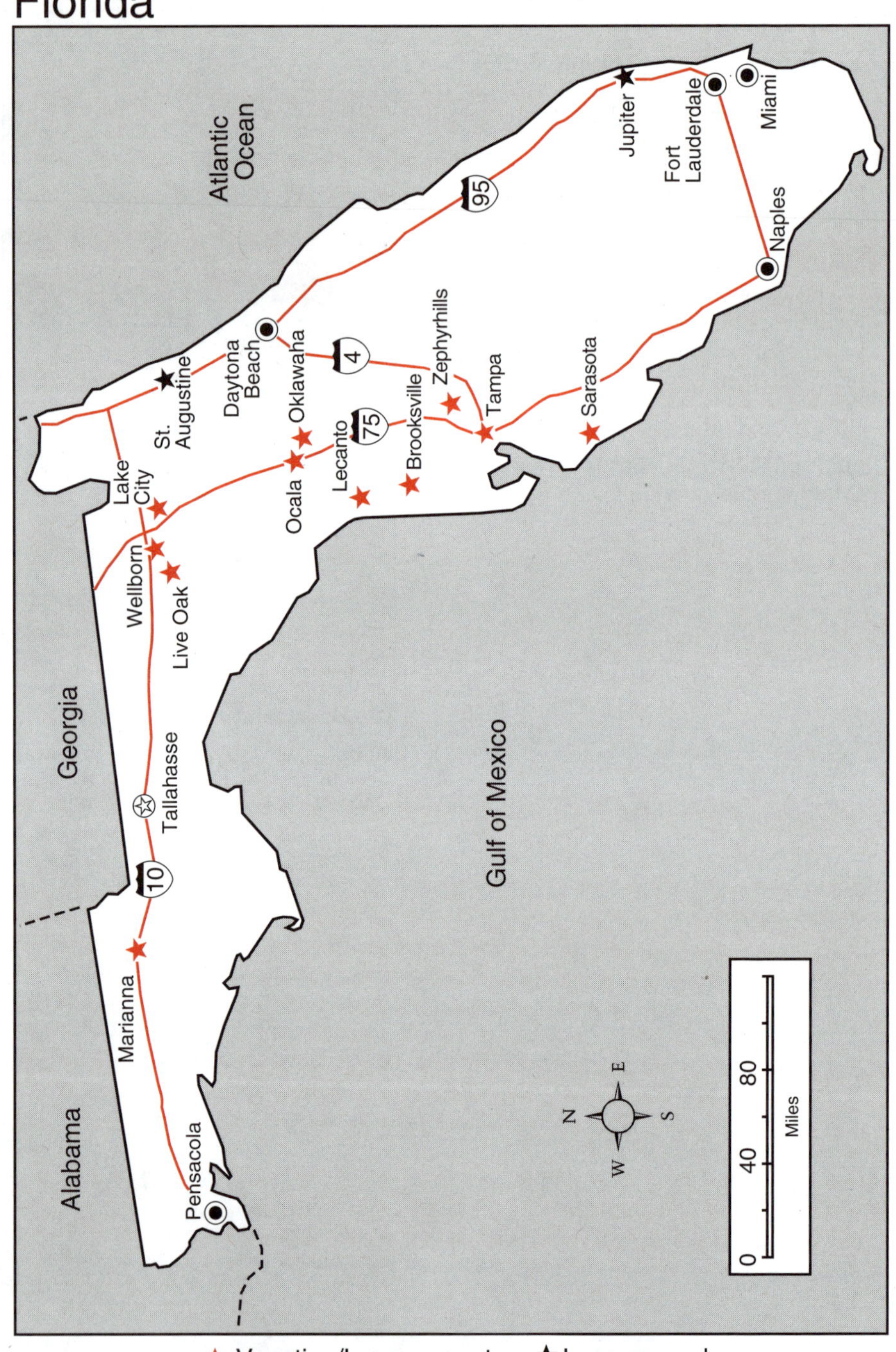

★ Vacation/Layover spots ★ Layovers only
State Capitol ◉ Hwy Junction cities

CURRENT NEGATIVE COGGINS, HEALTH CERTIFICATE & OWNERSHIP PAPERS REQUIRED - see page 2 for details

BROOKSVILLE, 34601

★ **H & L Ranch and Blueberry Farm, Bill & Karen Hartley**
24537 Evaline St. (I-75, exit 61, Hwy 50 W. to US 41)
Ph. 352/797-0822 Fax 352/797-0994 Cell 727/460-1706 or 727/480-7201 Email:Ranchhl@aol.com **Facilities:** Stalls, pasture, feed, trails, camper hookup and Bed & Breakfast. Bring your horses or use ours. Ride for hours in the Withlacoochee State Forest on the rustic & relazing Croom Horse Trails. The Forest offers miles of scenic horse/hiking/biking trails..

JUPITER, 33478

Lady Jean Ranch, Inc.
10333 Randolph Siding Rd. (4 m. from I-95, exit 59 & exit 116 off Florida Turnpike)
Ph. 561/745-1300 **Facilities:** Stalls, holding pens, pasture, feed, arena, walker, trails & camper hookup. Prices vary by season.

LAKE CITY, 32024

★ **Hala Arabians, Helmy W. Ehrler, owner/manager**
Rt. 11, Box 111-C (Off I-75, exit 427, 1/8 m. W. on Hwy 90; 3-1/2 m. W. on Hwy 252-C, Pinemont Rd. Turn right on Duckett Rd., 1st entry on right)
Ph. 386/752-4276 **Facilities:** Training Facility. 8 indoor stalls, pasture, feed, exercise ring, tack room, restroom, shower & space for camper. Motels within 3.5 m. Offering disaster emergency shelter for horses through the Red Cross. Stable avail. for winter lease.

LECANTO, 34461

★ **Renab Ranch, Lillian Baner**
5338 S. Lecanto Hwy, Rt. 491 (W. of I-75, 10 m. from Gulf of Mexico, Homosassa/Crystal River area)
Ph. Day 352/628-2716 Evenings & Sundays 352/628-9816 Email:renab@digitalusa.net **Facilities:** Access to premium State Forest trails. Stalls, pasture, feed (own feed store - free delivery to campsite),.lighted exercise ring, hot walker, camper hookup, shower, campfire, pool, laundry. Owner lives on premises. "Horse Heaven!" Rolling hills & shady trails.

LIVE OAK, 32060

Crystal Stables, David Fields
7321 E. Co. Rd. 136 (Easy access from I-10 & I-75. 5.8 m. from I-75)
Ph. 386/364-7745 **Facilities:** All paved roads up to the ranch. Can accommodae semi's for parking. Provisions for overnight stabling & camping. UNDER DEVELOPMENT. Call for info on availability of facilities

CURRENT NEGATIVE COGGINS, HEALTH CERTIFICATE & OWNERSHIP PAPERS REQUIRED - see page 2 for details

LIVE OAK, 32060

★ **Spirit of the Suwanee Music Park, James Cornett**
3076 95th Dr. (US Hwy 129. 4 m. off I-75 & 4 m. off I-10. 80 m. from Jacksonville; 80 m. from Tallahassee; 20 m. from Lake City; 30 m. S. of GA stae ine; 40 m. from Valdosta GA)
Ph. Main Park/Reservations 386/364-1683 Doris O'Brien/barn 386/963-4927 Fax 386/364-2998 Email:spirit@musicliveshere.com
Web:www.musicliveshere.com **Facilities:** 50 barn stalls, portable stalls avail., camping area w/portable bath house, hookups w/water & elec. avail. in horse area, sewer in other areas that do not allow horses. Laundry facilities, restaurant, 700 seat music hall, cabin rentals, trails guides, etc.

MARIANNA, 32446

CIRCLE D RANCH
AND
WESTERN SHOP

★ 3121 DRYDEN DRIVE
5 MILES WEST ON HIGHWAY 90
MARIANNA, FLORIDA 32446

Ph. 850/352-4882 352-4324
Call for reservations.

Facilities: Indoor stalls & camper parking.

Store hours:
Mon. thru Sat., 9 a.m. to 6 p.m.

Largest and Most Complete Western Shop East of the Mississippi

OCALA, 34476

★**The Haas-ienda, M-M Haas**
(I-75, Exit 68...apx. 5-1/2 m. to residence)
Ph. 352/873-9331
Email:hasienda@mac.com **Facilities:** 5 separate board fenced paddock turnouts, stalls & kennel. RV hookup avail. Coachhouse bdrm suite for non-smoking couple - min. two-night stay. Trails in immediate area. Reservations/pet deposit req. Payment upon arrival - cash only.

OCALA, 34482

★ **Dancing Horses Farm. Bob Walla**
8711 W. Hwy 40 (I-75, exit 252W. Straight on 40W. After intersection with 225A, 6/10th m. on right)
Ph. 352/873-7084 **Facilities:** 12x12 block barn, auto waterers, pest control, pasture. turn-out, dressage ring & overnight RV hookup. Apt. avail. at times - call. Attendant on grounds.

OCALA, 34482

★ **Rose-Creek Farm, Annie Martin**
6235 NW Hwy 27 (2 m.W. off I-75, exit 70)
Ph. 352/840-0448 Fax 352/840-5932 Email:AnnieOPro@aol.com **Facilities:** Stalls, paddocks, pastures, wash racks, round pen, 6-horse walker, 5/8 m. training track, 620 ac. of trails, 2-bdrm guest quarters/sleeps 5, fully furnished w/washer-drying, full kitchen, satellite & trailer parking. Adults only.

CURRENT NEGATIVE COGGINS, HEALTH CERTIFICATE & OWNERSHIP PAPERS REQUIRED - see page 2 for details

OKLAWAHA, 32183

★ **Wit's End Farm**
P.O. Box 964 (I-75, exit 67. 20 m. E. on 484; 11 m. S. of Ocala)
Ph. 352/288-4924 Caretaker352/288-8157 **Facilities:** 7 indoor box stalls, 2 holding pens, pasture, feed, walker, trails, limited RV parking and lodging avail. No smoking except in designated areas. Call for reservations/rates. Fish/swim/canoe/hike/golf.

SARASOTA, 34240

★ **Willoughby Farms Bed & Breakfast, Larry & Shirley Friedman**
1201 Sinclair Dr. (4 m. E. of I-75, exit 210. 8 m. from downtown Sarasota)
Ph. 941/379-5220 Fax 941/377-4845 Email:bigkidstoy@aol.com
Web:www.willoughbyfarms.com **Facilities:** 10x12 & 12x12 stalls, pastures, round pens, arenas, wash racks, trails and new/modern 3-rm apt. w/TV, washer & dryer and full kitchen. Come for a night, weekend or short stay. Breeders/trainers of Haflinger horses; home of Grand Champion stallion Amadeus.

ST. AUGUSTINE, 32086-9325

The Irish Acre, Margie & Francis O'Loughlin
1925 St. Rd. 207 (State Rd. 207, 1 m. E. of I-95 exchange)
Ph. 904/829-3771 or Stable 904/823-1952 **Facilities:** 12 indoor stalls, 4 holding pens, pasture & trails available. $20 per horse per day.

TAMPA, 33625

★ **In The Breeze Horseback Riding Ranch & Childrens Camp**
7514 Gardner Rd. (5 m. N. of Tampa International Airport off exit 7, Expway 589. 10 min. to beaches, Busch Gardens, racetrack, fairgrounds)
Ph. 813/264-1919 Fax 813/986-2655 Web:inthebreeze.net **Facilities:** 30 indoor/5 outdoor stalls, 3 holding pens, Seminole Premium Feed, arena/daily rental, round pen, trails (must sign insurance release) & camper hookup

WELLBORN, 32094

★ **Wellborn Quarter Horses, Andrea & Joe Schomburg**
8660 CR 137 (1/2 m. N. of I-10, exit 292)
Ph. 386/963-1555 Fax 386/963-1557 Email:ahfind@aol.com **Facilities:** 4 indoor/2 outdoor stalls, round pen, pasture, feed, outdoor arena, trails & parking w/water & elec. Dogs on leash. Also, fishing pond & new swimming pool. McLeran House B&B 5 m. S. Motels at I-75, exit 439. Many area attractions.

ZEPHYRHILLS, 33541

★ **Take A Break Ranch, Barbara Wolf**
8720 Fort King Rd. (I-75, exit 285 at SR 52. Close to Zephyrhills, Dade City & Tampa. Call for further directions)
Ph. 813/715-1767 813/714-6053 Fax 813/715-4618
Email:Takeabreakranch@cs.com **Facilities:** 4 stalls, pasture, arena, wash rack & camper hookup. Several motels, B&B's & restaurants nearby. Vet/farrier close by.

Georgia

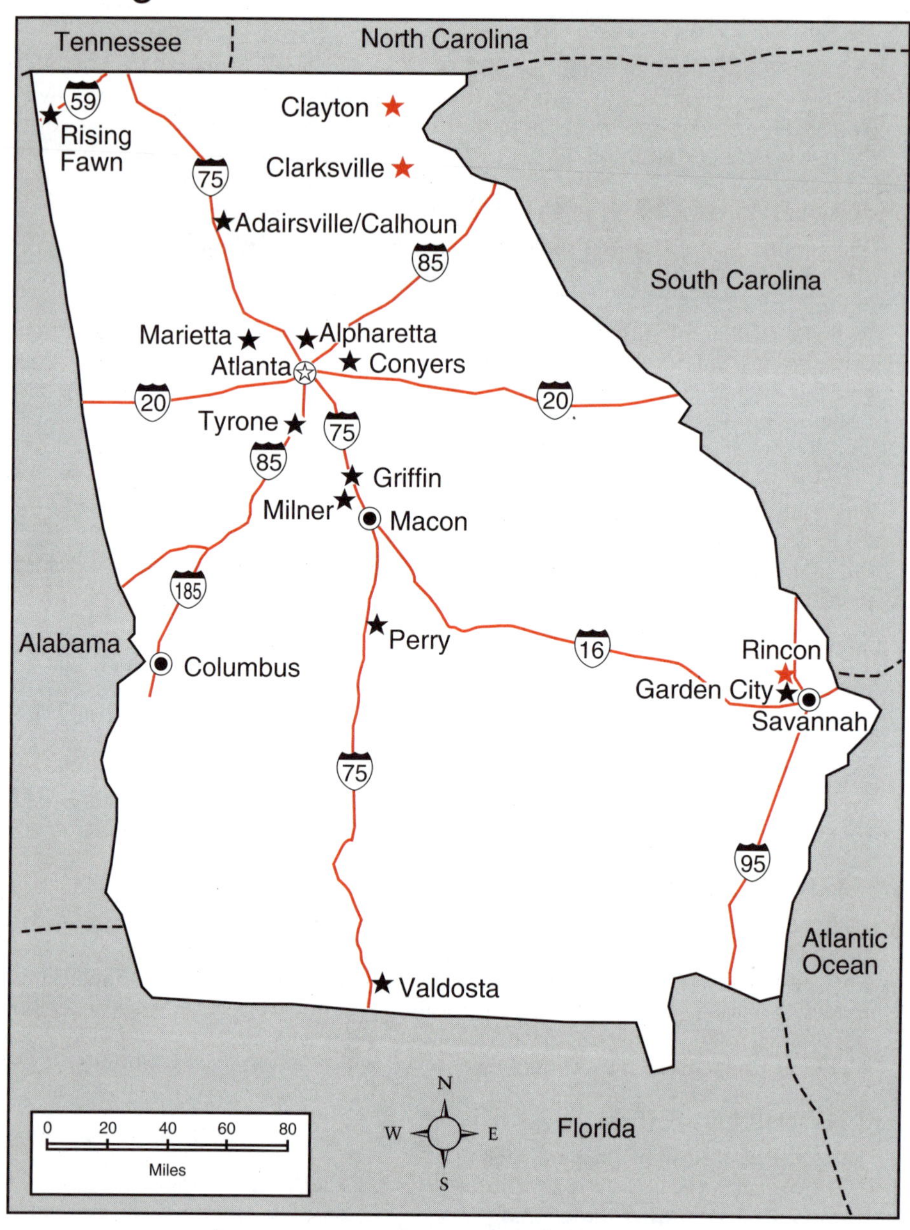

Vacation/Layover spots ★ Layovers only

State Capitol ◉ Hwy Junction Cities

CURRENT NEGATIVE COGGINS, HEALTH CERTIFICATE & OWNERSHIP PAPERS REQUIRED - see page 2 for details

ADAIRSVILLE/CALHOUN

CJE Erwin Farm, Jon & Billie Erwin
1750 Union Grove Church Rd. S.E., Adairsville GA 30103 (I-75, exit 312 at Calhoun. 60 m. N. of Atlanta)
Ph. Home/Barn 706/629-4882 Office 706/629-2877 Cell 706/271-6352
Facilities: 9 stalls, 2-15 acre pastures, as avail., feed, 80x128 arena, 28' round pen, B&B w/continental breakfast avail. Stable license with state of Georgia.

ALPHARETTA, 30004

Carolyn McCall/Chevaun Gillson
15570 Birmingham Hwy (GA 400, exit 11, 6 m. W., 3 m. left on 372)
Ph. 770/777-2143 **Facilities:** 9-18 indoor stalls, 2 broodmare stalls, 4 pastures, quality orchard grass hay, round pen, 1 jumping/grass footing arena, hot/cold water washrack & 1 double w/private bath avail.

CLARKESVILLE, 30523

★ **Double K Farm, Aubrey & Mary Kay**
1111 John Wood Rd. (Apx. 1 m. from intersection of Hwy 441 & Alt. 17. Hwy 441 N. is the main Hwy from Atlanta to Cherokee NC)
Ph. 706/754-3323 Email:awkay@hemc.net **Facilities:** 12 indoor box stalls, 3-80x100 paddocks, 3-ac. pasture, outdoor lighted riding arena and within easy driving distance of trails in Chattahoochie Nat'l Forest, Willis Knob horse camp on the Chatooga River & the Southern Nantahala Wilderness

CLAYTON, 30525

★ **Powerhouse Properties, Julia Mather**
52 Trillium Ln. (Rabun County)
Ph. 706/782-3318 Fax 706/782-6625 Email:power.house@mindspring.com Web:www.mindspring.com/~power.house **Facilities:** 30 ac. pasture or 2 ac. paddocks, 6 stall DIY barn, hosing facilities, 28 m. of Nat'l Forest managed trails, mtn. views, trailer parking and large luxury house w/all ammenities/can sleep from 2 up to 21. Other pets welcome. Vet/farrier services by appointment.

CONYERS, 30094

Linda Greene Ridley, Linda's Riding School, Inc.
3475 Daniels Bridge Rd. (7 m. from I-20. E. of Atlanta)
Ph. 770/922-0184 **Facilities:** 20 indoor/8 outdoor stalls, shavings for sale, arena, walker & trails.

GARDEN CITY, 31418

Triple B Ranch, Rayford W. Barnwell
P.O. Box 7362 Location: 60 Triple B Trail (2 m. W. of I-95, exit 106)
Ph. 912/964-6698 **Facilities:** 40 indoor stalls, round pen, 50 acres of pasture, feed, arena, trails & parking/elec. for 2 campers. Motels nearby.

CURRENT NEGATIVE COGGINS, HEALTH CERTIFICATE & OWNERSHIP PAPERS REQUIRED - *see page 2 for details*

GRIFFIN, 30223

Silver Horseshoes Stables
3010 High Falls Rd. (I-75, exit 205, 40 m. S. of Atlanta. 45 m. N. of Macon)
Ph. 770/227-7681 770/227-7717 **Facilities:** 40 indoor stalls, pasture avail., hay & grain, 2 arenas, 100 acres of trails & camper hookup.

MARIETTA, 30064

Hymnbrook Farm, Barbara & Bill Dawson
150 Mt. Calvary Rd. (I-75, exit 269. 20 m. N. of Atlanta)
Ph. 770/428-1065 Email:hymnbrook2@yahoo.com **Facilities:** 12 indoor stalls, ring, & trailer parking w/elec. 6 motels within 5 m.

MILNER, 30257

Pegasus Riding School, Inc., Linda & Warren Abrams
392 Philip Weldon Rd. (Off I-75, exit 201 Southbound or exit 198 Northbound)
Ph. 770/228-3865 **Facilities:** 7 indoor/10 covered stalls, holding pens, pasture, feed dealer nearby, 3 arenas, trails, camper hookup & apt/ room w/kitchenette & bath. Most major motels, stores, etc. 10 min. away in Griffin.

PERRY, 31069

Sandy Hill Stables, Charles & Tricia Nelson
P.O. Box 332 Location: 2315 Marshallville Hwy. (I-75, exit 135. 1 m. W. on Hwy 127 to stables)
Ph. Farm 478/987-7187 Home 478/987-2156 **Facilities:** 30 indoor stalls, outdoor arena, 4-horse walker, 1 m. training track w/gate & parking w/elec & water. No bath house/restroom only. Reservations preferred.

RINCON, 31326

★ **Hi Ho Hills Farm, Robin Hughes, owner**
939 Goshen Rd. (I-95, exit 109. Hwy 21 N. 4 m. to Goshen Rd., turn left, 1-1/2 m. on left)
Ph. 912/826-5808 **Facilities:** 12 indoor stalls w/auto waterers & fans, 3 holding pens, round pen, 3 large fields of pasture, 12% sweet feed, 2 show rings, 20 m. of trails & 2 camper spaces. 5 new major motels nearby.

RISING FAWN, 30738

Harvest Home Bed & Breakfast, Cheri Miller
P.O. Box 272 Location: 1330 Holder Loop Rd. (3 m. from I-59, exit 1 at Rising Fawn)
Ph. 706/462-2146 **Facilities:** 2 outdoor paddocks w/shelter, feed/hay avail., miles of scenic mtn trails adajacent to property within short driving distance and room w/bath & kitchenette with private entrance. Vet/farrier on call. KOA within 10 m. Trail maps avail.

CURRENT NEGATIVE COGGINS, HEALTH CERTIFICATE & OWNERSHIP PAPERS REQUIRED - see page 2 for details

TYRONE, 30290

Trickum Creek Ranch, Debbie Lowe
213 Lincoln Rd. (2.2 m. E. of I-85 at exit 56. 15 min. S. of Hartsfield Airport. Also, easy access to I-75)
Ph. 770/487-2146 Fax 770/486-1075 Email: horsehotel@juno.com Web: www.debbielowe.com **Facilities:** 2 stud stalls w/acre runs, 8 indoor stalls, 3 separate pastures, hay avail., round pen, 1 m. wooded trails, parking & elec. for campers & large rigs welcome. Vet/farrier on call. Motels nearby. Call for reservations/rates.

VALDOSTA, 31601

Windy Willow Stables, Nanci Kendall
5203 Phillips Rd. (8 m. W. of I-75, exit 16)
Ph. 229/247-4399 Email:nanci_kendall@hotmail.com **Facilities:** 14-12x12 stalls, turnout, feed/hay, wash rack, jumps, parking/RV space, boarding & riding lessons. Owners on premises.

Idaho

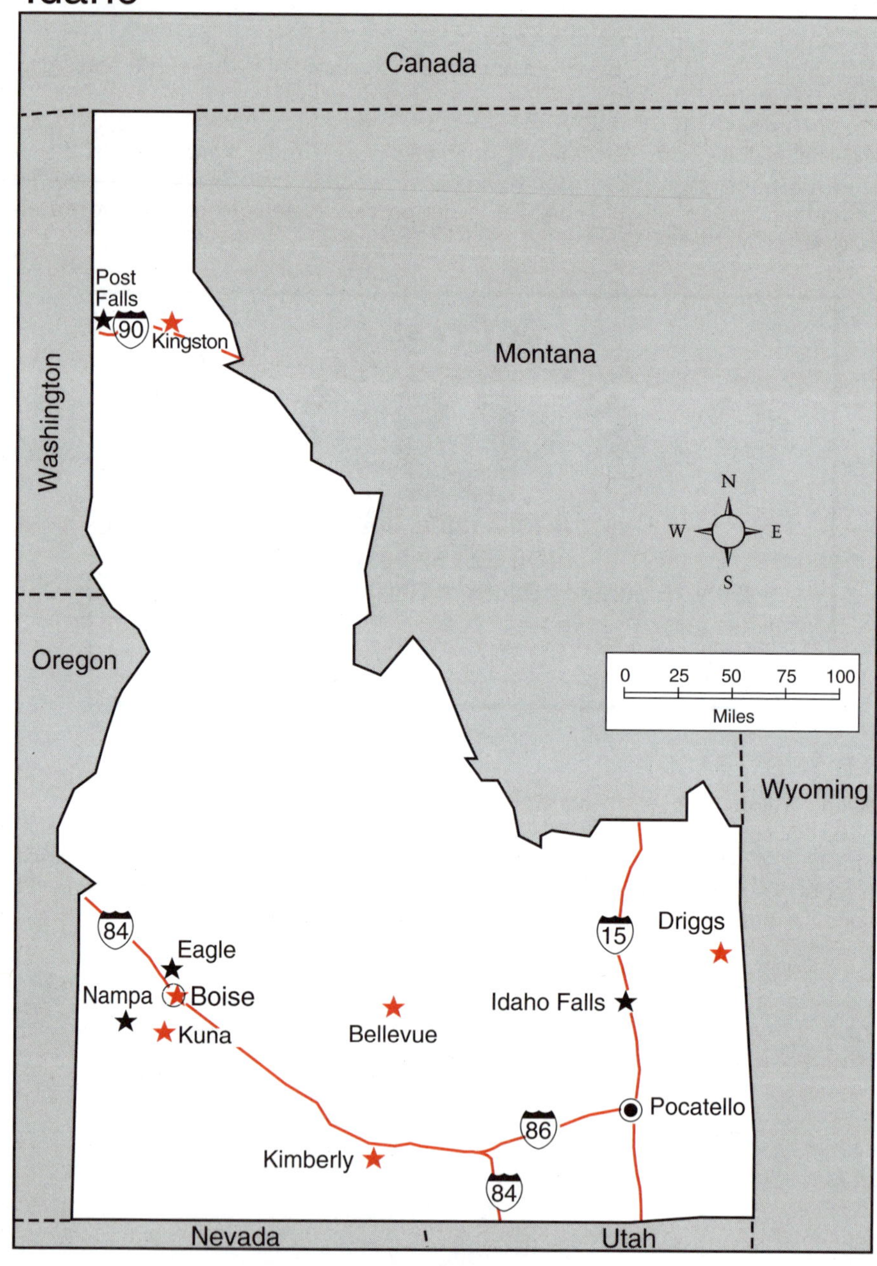

★ Vacation/Layover spots ★ Layovers only
State Capitol ◉ Hwy Junction cities

CURRENT NEGATIVE COGGINS, HEALTH CERTIFICATE & OWNERSHIP PAPERS REQUIRED - see page 2 for details

BELLEVUE, 83313

★ **Fullmoon Farm, Justin & Heather Jones**
Mail: P.O. Box 487, Hailey ID 83333 Location: 20 Prairie Sun East (Off Hwy 75. Call for directions)
Ph. 208/788-1388 Email:fullmoonfarm@juno.com **Facilities:** 21 stalls, 7 in barn/14 covered 12x24 pens, 100x200 indoor & 100x200 outdoor arenas. No hookups.

BOISE, 83709

★ **Hidden Valley Ranch, Sabrina Leonard**
8699 S. Gantz Ave. (5 m. from I-84, Eagle Rd. exit #46)
Ph. 208/362-4345 Fax 208/362-4242 Email:brina@rmci.net
Web:hiddenvalleypaints.com **Facilities:** 4 barn stalls w/runs, 3 holding pens w/run-in shed, 3 corrals, pasture, alfalfa hay, 120x200 arena, wash bay, trails, camper hookup and Bed & Breakfast. Great, friendly care.

DRIGGS, 83422

★ **Marilyn Monroe Farmhouse, Chuck & Janet Kunz**
364 N. 150 E. (Hwy 33; 2 m. E. toward Grand Tetons. 1 m. from WY border, 22 m. from Jackson Hole WY)
Ph. 208/354/2403 Cell 208/313-4728 Email:mmfarmhouse@aol.com **Facilities:** 4 outdoor covered stalls, holding pen, some pasture by creek, feed, if necessary, arena, many trails near area, camper/RV hookup/no dump station & apt./sleeps 4. Free guide service avail. All local facilities 10 min. from Farmhouse.

EAGLE, 83616

Lonesome Dove Ranch, Chuck Nichol & Carmen Graham
P.O. Box 1387 Location: 8 m. N. of I-84 - 1505 Riverside (I-84, exit 46, 8 m. N. to St. Hwy 44, E. 1 m. to Riverside/traffic light, turn S.)
Ph. 208/939-2183 Email:ccdove@juno.com **Facilities:** Indoor stalls, paddocks, pasture, alfalfa or grass hay, arenas & round pen. $15 per head/night.

IDAHO FALLS, 83401

C & D Stables, Donna Garriott
3909 N. 15 E., St. Leon Rd. (I-15, exit 119, Hwy 20 2-1/2 m. E., exit 15th E., 1/4 m. S. Easy access)
Ph. 208/522-1439 **Facilities:** 24 indoor bedded stalls w/water, alfalfa pellets, indoor arena, washrack, 20 acres for riding & plenty of parking. Reservations req.

IDAHO FALLS, 83402

Ellis Supreme Arabians
1438 W. 97th S. (Exit 133 off of I-15)
Ph. 208/524-7247 Email:tmellis@f.rmci.net **Facilities:** 27 indoor stalls & electrical hookups.

CURRENT NEGATIVE COGGINS, HEALTH CERTIFICATE & OWNERSHIP PAPERS REQUIRED - see page 2 for details

KIMBERLY, 83341-0176

★ **Carol L. Sherman**
P.O. Box 176 (I-84, Kimberly/Twin Falls exit 182)
Ph. 208/423-6340 Email:csherman@onewest.net **Facilities:** 8-12x12 box stalls, 6-24x24 pipe corrals, 100x100 arena, camper hookup and Bed & Breakfast. Close to Twin Falls/Shoshone Falls/ Magic Mt. Ski area.

KINGSTON, 83839

★ **Kingston 5 Ranch Bed & Breakfast, Walt & Pat Gentry**
Mail: P.O. Box 130 Location: 42,297 Silver Valley Rd. (I-90, exit 43. Easy access. 1 hr. E. of Spokane WA & 2-1/2 hrs. W. of Missoula MT)
Ph. 208/682-4862 **1-800/254-1852** Fax 208/682-9445
Web:www.k5ranch.com **Facilities:** 2 paddocks off round pen, 2 indoor/outdoor stalls, open pasture, round pen, exercise track, full arena, 1000 m. of trails, and B&B. No smoking or pets indoors. Overnight stabling w/B&B stay only. Featured: KHQTV's "Wkend Getaways"/H&R mag. & "Guide to Food & Romance."

KUNA, 83634

★ **Aspenbreak Stables, John & Karen Vehlow**
330 N. Eagle Rd. (8 m. S. of I-84 at Meridian/Kuna exit/#44)
Ph. 208/922-4563 **Facilities:** 10 indoor stalls/2 turnouts, feed avail., indoor/outdoor arenas, trails & parking avail. $15 per night. Vet/farrier on call. Call for reservations. Motels nearby.

NAMPA, 83653

Idaho Horse Park, Terry Calnon
P.O. Box 279 Location: 16200 Can-Ada Rd. (Near Boise. Easy access from I-84, exit 38/Garrity)
Ph. 208/442-3232, Mon-Fri. 10-4 or after hrs. 208/484-2071 Fax 208/442-3312
Email:info@idahocenter.com Web:www.idahocenter.com **Facilities:** Covered stalls, outdoor pens, outdoor arena & wash rack.

CURRENT NEGATIVE COGGINS, HEALTH CERTIFICATE & OWNERSHIP PAPERS REQUIRED - see page 2 for details

POST FALLS, 83854

PrairieStables LLC, Alice Jordan
11875 W. Manitoba Ct. (I-90. From Spokane WA, take exit Hwy 41/Rathdrum)
Ph. **1-877/977-7958** Fax 208/773-5379 Email:prairiestables@aol.com
Facilities: 52 stalls, holding pens, feed, indoor/outdoor arenas & walker.

Illinois

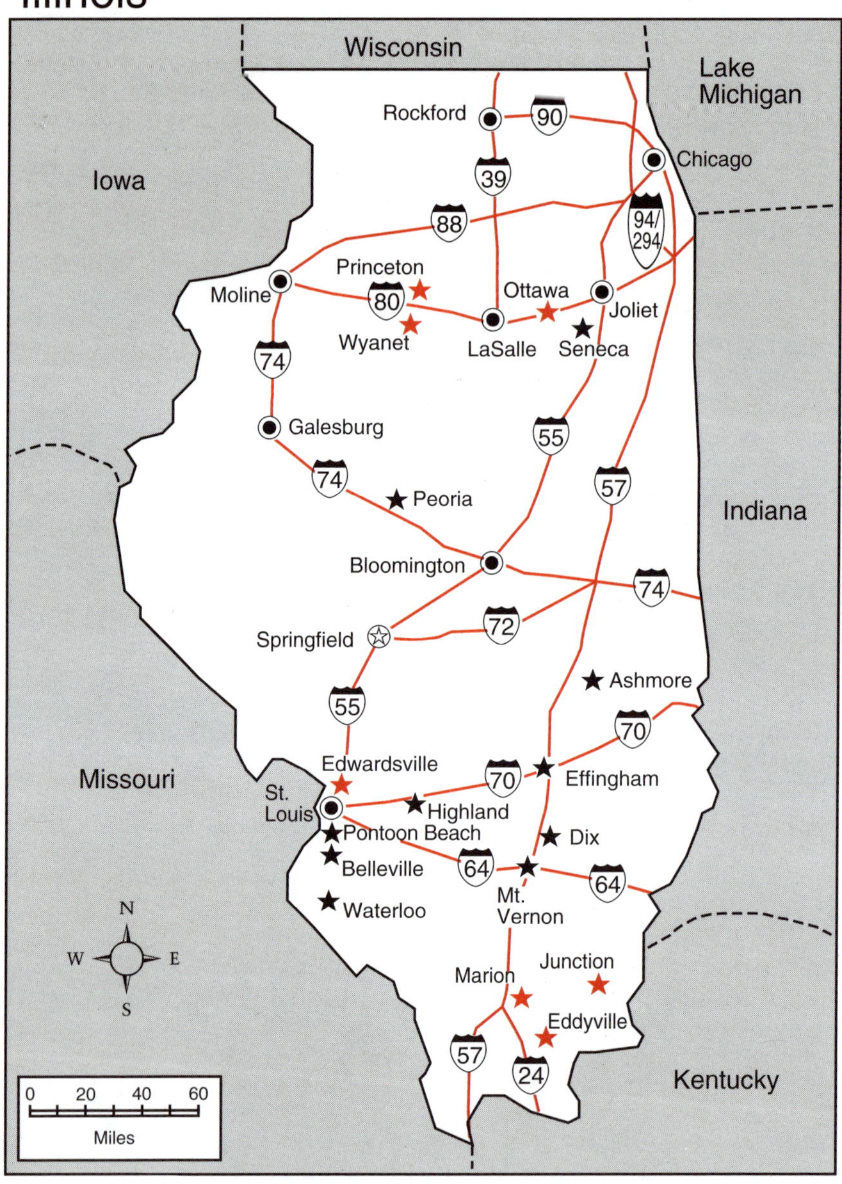

★ Vacation/Layover spots ★ Layovers only
State Capitol Hwy Junction cities

CURRENT NEGATIVE COGGINS, HEALTH CERTIFICATE & OWNERSHIP PAPERS REQUIRED - see page 2 for details

ASHMORE, 61912

Dream On Farm, Dale & Dee Greathouse
9739 NCR 2250 E. (14 m. E. off of I-57/Mattoon-Charleston exit)
Ph. 217/349-8430 Fax 217/348-0057 Email:dalendee@advant.net **Facilities**: 6 stalls w/individual runs, auto waterers, fans, grain/hay avail., small outdoor arena, pasture for longer stays, large barn & tack room.

BELLEVILLE, 62223

Arch View Stables, Dolores Williams
9000 Old St. Louis Rd. (From I-255, exit 17A/Hwy 15E to 157 S. to 13 E./3 m. from I-255/15 m. from St. Louis)
Ph. 618/538-7866 Fax 618/538-5628 Email:archviewminis@aol.com **Facilities**: 30-10x12 indoor stalls, 100x200 indoor arena & plenty of trailer parking space. No camper hookups. Other animals (cats & dogs) okay. Reservations required. Motels nearby.

DIX, 62830

Huff Farms, Brian & Mist Huff
23484 N. IL Hwy 37 (I-57, Dix exit. 1-1/2 m. E. to 37N, 2 m. N. on E. side)
Ph. 618/266-7041 **Facilities**: 6 indoor/2 outdoor stalls, 60' round pen, pasture for turnout, feed avail. & trailer parking. Farrier on premises. Motel nearby.

EDDYVILLE, 62928

★ **Bear Branch Horse Resort**
P.O. Box 40, Hwy 145 (15 m. S. of Harrisburg IL, on Hwy 145, 1-57, exit Hwy 13 E. or 35 m. off I-24, Paducah KY exit Hwy 45 on Hwy 145 N. Centrally located in 280,000 acre Shawnee Nat'l Forest)
Ph. 618/672-4249 Fax 618/672-4739 Email:manders@shawneelink.com Web:www.bearbranch.com **Facilities**: 40 box stalls, 12 holding pens, 2 pastures, feed avail. in tack shop, 300 miles of trails, 80 sites for campers & cabins/lodge. Log cabin restaurant & tack shop on grounds. 2 ac. lake for fishing or swimming. Playground for children. Vet/farrier on call.

CURRENT NEGATIVE COGGINS, HEALTH CERTIFICATE & OWNERSHIP PAPERS REQUIRED - see page 2 for details

EDWARDSVILLE, 62025

★ **The Sleepy P - John & Victoria Piel**
6309 Miller Dr. (I-270 N. 25 m. from downtown St. Louis)
Ph. 618/659-1051 **Facilities:** 20 stalls, pasture/turnout, trails, wash area, B&B, camper/RV hookup, primitive camping, parking, feed/hay & vet/farrier on call. Scenic area, tourist attractions, museums, antique shops, horse racing park & golf course. Drafts & other animals welcome.

EFFINGHAM, 62401

Pine Tree Stables, Becky & Ron Althoff
11091 E. 1550th Ave. (I-70, exit 160, W. on Rt. 32-33. 2 m. left on Nazarene Rd., 1 m. left on 1550th Ave., first place on right)
Ph. 217/868-5182 Email:armymom1116@yahoo.com **Facilities**: 5 indoor box stalls, large corral & camper parking w/elec & water.

HIGHLAND, 62249

Highland Horse Boarding Stables, Kevin Gleason
12118 Ellis Rd. (12 min. off I-55/70, exit 17A/Troy, Highland/St. Jacob)
Ph. 618/654-3401 Cell 618/792-5570 Email:kgleasonhotdj@hotmail.com **Facilities**: 75 indoor box stalls, holding pens & paddocks, some pasture, indoor arena w/round pen, walker, indoor exercise track and trailer parking w/water & elec. B&B avail. within 3 m. along with major motels. Call for reservations.

JUNCTION, 62954

★ **Double M Campground, Heath A. Mann**
5320 Thacker Hollow Rd. (Off I-57. Rt. 1 S.)
Ph. 618/275-4440 Web:www.doublemcampground.com **Facilities**: Panel stalls, 100 campsites w/full hookups, showerhouse, dumpstation, cabins, playground, laundry facilities, restaurant open weekends & holidays Mar-Nov, miles of horse trails in Shawnee Nat'l Forest & cabins w/full bath, full bed & 2 sets of bunks..

CURRENT NEGATIVE COGGINS, HEALTH CERTIFICATE & OWNERSHIP PAPERS REQUIRED - see page 2 for details

MARION, 62959

★ **WildHorse Stables, Rich & Brenda Rybak**
5094 S. Market Rd. (Near I-57 & I-24)
Ph. 618/964-1165 Email:wildhors@midwest.net **Facilities**: 9-10x20 stalls w/rubber mats, turnout pens, outdoor arena, round pen, trails in nearby Shawnee Nat'l Forest, camper hookup & continental breakfast. Overnight room for rider w/bathroom & laundry. Motels at exits 53 & 54 off I-57.

MT. VERNON

Richardson Stables, Judy & C. Wayne Richardson
Mail: 9208 N. Log Cabin Ln., Opdyke IL 62872, Woodland Drive (easy access from I-57 & I-64)
Ph. 618/242-6566 - home, after 7 p.m. Barn 618/242-1232 or 242-0972 **Facilities**: 12 stalls, feed, outdoor arena, 1 camper hookup & parking space. Reservations preferred.

OTTAWA, 61350

★ **Marcia's Bed & Breakfast and Horse Facility**
3003 N. Rt. 71 (I-80 & IL 71, exit 93. 2nd house on right going S)
Ph. 815/434-5217 Web:www.go-illinois.com - Scroll to Ottawa **Facilities**: 3 stalls, 3 lots, camper space, Bed & Breakfast for 9, and private cottage w/kitchenette. Grill, bonfires, trails by Fox River. Reservations/deposit req. Vet 1 m. Near Starved Rock, Catlin Park, Matthiessen Park Trails, canoe rentals, area trail rides every Sunday.

OTTAWA, 61350

Tree Farm Stable Bed & Breakfast, Barbara Hendrix
2734 E. 1809 Rd. (I-80)
Ph. 815/434-0593 **Facilities**: Horse facility w/overnite Bed & Breakfast for travelers. 4 stalls, 3 holding pens, pasture and space for campers & hookups. B&B is self-contained 3-rm suite. Safe, quiet, casual. Close to Starved Rock, Matheison State Park & Catlin Park for trail riding.

CURRENT NEGATIVE COGGINS, HEALTH CERTIFICATE & OWNERSHIP PAPERS REQUIRED - see page 2 for details

PEORIA, 61615

Heart of Illinois Arena
9201 N. Galena Rd. (Rt. 29 N. 14 m. from I-74/Murray Baker Bridge - downtown. Rt. 29 & Galena Rd. are same. 1-1/2 m. S. of Rt. 6 bypass on Rt. 29)
Ph. 309/693-1805-barn Home 309/693-9680 **Facilities**: 160+ indoor/outdoor stalls, holding pens, feed avail., indoor/outdoor arenas & camper hookup. Studs welcome.

PONTOON BEACH, 62040

Gateway Stables, Kellly Arnold
3514 Lake Dr. (Convenient to all St. Louis area interstates hwys - call for directions. Within sight of Gateway Arch in St. Louis)
Ph.618/931-3527 **Facilities**: 25 indoor stalls, feed avail., indoor/outdoor arenas, trails in Horseshoe Lake State Park & trailer parking w/elec. (bring extension cord) Call day of reservation to confirm arrival - will not wait late hours if you don't call. Motels nearby. Clean.

PRINCETON, 61356

Bureau County Fairgrounds
P.O. Box 238 Location: 611 W. Peru St., IL Rt. 6 (I-80, exit 56 S)
Ph. 815/875-1003 815/659-3160 **Facilities**: 80 stalls - semi open barn, outdoor arena & 50 RV spaces avail. close to barn. Call ahead for barn reservations as mgr. does not live on premises.

PRINCETON, 61356

★ **The Prairie Hill - Barn, Bed & Breakfast**
25457 1275 N Ave. (12 m. off I-80)
Ph. 815/447-2487 Cell 773/251-7044 **Facilities**: 15 indoor stalls, 5 pastures, paddocks, feed incl., sand arena, 35-fence cross-country course, 90+ m. of scenic trails & accommodations in historic farm house w/continental breakfast - homemade breads, pastries, etc.

SENECA, 61360

The Pony Place, Elaine Owens
2945 N. 37th (Adjacent to I-80. I-55 & I-39. Rt. 71 & Rt. 52)
Ph. 815/695-5913 **Facilities**: 12x12 box stalls, turnouts, feed avail., riding area & elec/water for campers. Cash please. Welsh Cobs and Morgans.

CURRENT NEGATIVE COGGINS, HEALTH CERTIFICATE & OWNERSHIP PAPERS REQUIRED - see page 2 for details

WATERLOO (St. Louis area), 62298

Elite Equine Center (formerly Chance Stables), Karl Probst/Pat Costin
5545 G Rd. (S. of I-255 on IL Rt. 3, 20 min. from St. Louis)
Ph. **1-888/517-4533** 618/939-1536 Cell 618/604-7663 **Facilities**: New boarding facility. Several indoor stalls, outdoor runs, pasture, feed & hay avail., wash rack and adequate parking for semis & trailers; motels, restaurants & shopping nearby..

WYANET, 61379

★ **Huskey's Horse Motel, Richard & Karen Huskey**
13051 1200 N. Ave. (3 m. S. of I-80, exit 45/Hwy 40)
Ph. 309/895-3181 If no answer try Cell 815/866-9598 **Facilities**: 6 large box stalls, arena & camper hookup. Motels within 11 m. Call for reservations & directions. Same day usually okay. $15 per horse per night. 3 m. from historic Hennepin Canal - 70 m. of trails.

Indiana
Lake Michigan
Michigan
Ohio
Illiniois
Kentucky
94
80
90
65
69
74
70
70
74
64
164
Gary
Middlebury
LaPorte
Valparaiso
Winamac
Noblesville
Pendleton
Fortville
Indianapolis
Terre Haute
Cloverdale
Brookville
Greensburg
New Albany
Branchville
0
20
40
60
Miles
N
W
E
S
Vacation/Layover spots
Layovers only
State Capitol
Hwy Junction cities

CURRENT NEGATIVE COGGINS, HEALTH CERTIFICATE & OWNERSHIP PAPERS REQUIRED - see page 2 for details

BRANCHVILLE, 47514

★ **Jubin Creek Lodging & Livery, Christine & Wayne Trumbo**
23250 Oxen Rd. (8 m. SE of I-64, exit 79. Surrounded by Hoosier Nat'l Forest. 50 m. W. of Louisville KY)
Ph.812/843-5485 - leave message Email:jubin@psci.net **Facilities:** 12x12/12x18 stalls, feed & room/sleeps up to 4 w/bathroom & kitchen. Offering solitude, peace & quiet-no phones/TV. Nature sanctuary/Nat'l Forest fishing & recreation lakes/designated horse trails. No pets in rooms. No smoking in bldgs/no drugs/alcohol.

BROOKVILLE, 47012-8805

G & AK Horse Farm c/o Gary & Alta Kimble
7159 Shop Rd. (14 m. from I-74; 60 m. E. of Indianapolis; 50 m. W. of Cincinnati)
Ph. 765/647-2722 Email:gandakhorse@cnz.com **Facilities:** 5 indoor stalls, small & large turnout pens, 3 fenced pastures & sweet feed. B&B in Brookville. Motels in Batesville & Brookville. Numerous campgrounds & RV parks around Brookville Lake.

CLOVERDALE, 46120

Shaky Hill Ranch Horse Motel, Darrell & Kathy Jordan
7837 S. US Hwy 231 (I-70, exit 41. N. 231 1 m.)
Ph. 765/795-6344 or Cell 765/721-3378 Email:ranch@ccrtc.com **Facilities:** 6 indoor stalls, round pen, turn-out area avail. & feed. 4 motels within 1 m. & campground 1/2 m.

FORTVILLE, 46040

Jubilee Stables, Debbie Massey
8794 W. 1000 St. S. (4 m. off I-69, exit 13. 30 m. from Indianapolis & 18 m. from Anderson)
Ph. 317/485-5259 **Facilities:** 30 indoor stalls, holding pens, pasture, feed, indoor arena, trails & 3 camper hookups.

GREENSBURG, 47240

Flatrock River Valley Ranch
6290 N. Co. Rd. 350 W. (I-74, Rushville State Rd. 3 North)
Ph. 812/663-2496 Email:ggebele@alltel.net **Facilities:** 20 indoor stalls, holding pens, pasture, feed, arena and elec & water for campers.

INDIANAPOLIS, 46205

Indiana State Fairgrounds, Dave White, Mgr.
1202 E. 38th St. (I-70, Keystone exit)
Ph. 317/925-5457 - a.m. calls Cell 317/698-3870 **Facilities:** 220 indoor stalls, holding pens, feed, indoor arena & 120 full camper hookups. Motel nearby. Open 24 hr. w/security.

CURRENT NEGATIVE COGGINS, HEALTH CERTIFICATE & OWNERSHIP PAPERS REQUIRED - see page 2 for details

LaPORTE, 46350

Gillerlain Quarterhorse Farm
0102 E. 200 N. (Severs Rd.) (4 m. from I-80/90, exit LaPorte Rd.; 8 m. from I-94, exit 40A) Call for directions.
Ph. 219/362-1122 **Facilities:** 8-10x10 indoor stalls, turn-out w/shed, feed incl. & 60x80 indoor arena. Call for reservations. Motels & RV hookup within 1 m.

MIDDLEBURY, 46540

★ **Mary D. Hankins at Coneygar Bed & Breakfast**
54835 County Rd. 33 (5 m. S. of IN Toll Rd. [I-80-90], Bristol or Middlebury exits)
Ph. 574/825-5707 **Facilities:** 10-12x12 stalls, pasture, feed, excellent riding trails, space for campers/trailers and Bed & Breakfast - sleep 10/full breakfast. Campgrounds, indoor/outdoor arenas nearby. Good place to relax self & horses.

PENDLETON, 46064

Windara Farms, Wanda & Mark Dodd
7979 W. Fall Creek Dr. (2 m. off I-69, exit 14, NE of Indianapolis. Call for directions)
Ph. 317/485-4604 Fax 317/485-4228 Web:windarafarms.com **Facilities:** 12-12x12 stalls, 2-12x16 stalls, holding pens, feed/hay avail., pasture/turnout, round pen, indoor/outdoor arenas, heated washrack, auto waterers, parking & elec. for vehicles. Lounge/shower & restroom, washer/dryer. 24 hr. on-site supervision. Safe/Private.

NOBLESVILLE, 46060

Janet Keesling Stables
11930 E. 211th St. (1/2 m. E. of St. Rd. 37 on E. 211th)
Ph. 317/773-5482 Fax 317/776-7019 **Facilities:** 30-12x12/+16-10x10 indoor stalls, 60x120 indoor arena, 63' round pen and camper parking w/elec & water. Stallions accepted. Accommodations: Super 8 in Noblesville.

TERRE HAUTE, 47802

Persimmom Hollow Farm, Bill & Donna Isaacs
2966 E. Harlan Dr. (S. of I-70 on Rt. 41; to Stuckey's, 1 m. E)
Ph. 812/299-4754 **Facilities:** 5 indoor stalls & 3 holding pens. Camping/motels nearby.

VALPARAISO, 46385

Victoria's Hope Equine Rescue/and B&B
131 W. 850 N. (3 m. S. of both I-94 and I-80, off Hwy 6. Call for directions)
Ph. 219/331-1261 Fax 219/926-4008 **Facilities:** Indoor stalls, small paddock w/large pasture attached, 2 RV hookups w/water & elec and 2 private rooms & bath, very homey. Heated pool & hot tub. Meals avail. upon request. 15 min. from Lake Michigan and Nat'l Lakeshore beaches & horse trails.

CURRENT NEGATIVE COGGINS, HEALTH CERTIFICATE & OWNERSHIP PAPERS REQUIRED - *see page 2 for details*

WINAMAC, 46996

★ **Riparian Farms Equestrian Centre' & Tortuga Inn B&B, Gordon & Lee Heinsen-Ligocki**
2142 N. 125 East (1-1/4 m. off US 35 N. of Winamac)
Ph. 574/946-6969 Fax 574/946-3500 Email:riparian@pwrtc.com **Facilities:** 90 indoor/outdoor stalls, turnout paddocks, 72x200 indoor arena, wash racks, heated tack rooms, heat avail. for stalls, trails along Tippecanoe River, camper hookups, and Bed & Breakfast w/gourmet breakfast. Dorm/bunks avail. Large driveway for semis.

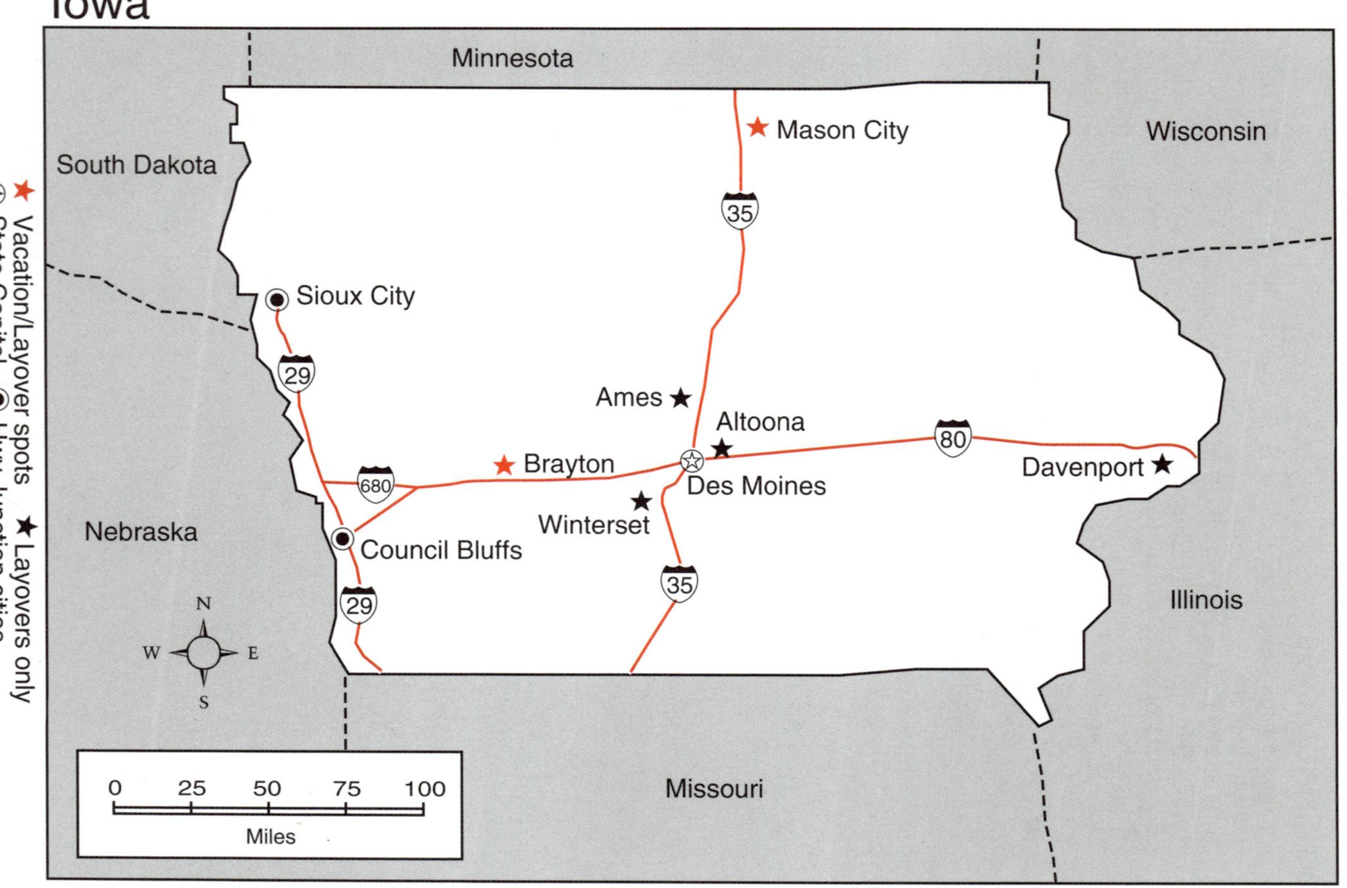
Iowa
Minnesota
South Dakota
Wisconsin
Nebraska
Illinois
Missouri
Mason City
Sioux City
Ames
Altoona
Brayton
Des Moines
Winterset
Davenport
Council Bluffs
35
29
680
80
35
29
N
W
E
S
0 25 50 75 100
Miles
Vacation/Layover spots
Layovers only
State Capitol
Hwy Junction cities

CURRENT NEGATIVE COGGINS, HEALTH CERTIFICATE & OWNERSHIP PAPERS REQUIRED - see page 2 for details

ALTOONA, 50009-9527

Georgia's Arabian Stables, Georgia Campbell
5055 NE 96th St. (4-1/2 m. off I-80, exit 143. 5 min. from I-35)
Ph. 515/967-5553 **Facilities:** 38 box stalls, 3 tie stalls, 8 sheds, 6 holding pens, pasture, feed, 4 round pens, 120x96 indoor arena, walker, 3 camper hookups & tackroom. Motels nearby. Vet/farrier nearby.

AMES, 50010-1652

Stage Coach Stables, Mary Jo Schmitt
P.O. Box 1652 (1 m. off I-35)
Ph. 515/232-0999 Fax 515/233-6229 **Facilities:** 32 indoor/7 outdoor stalls, holding pens, pasture, feed, 120x80 indoor/125x275 outdoor arenas & trails.

BRAYTON, 50042

★ **Hallock House Bed & Breakfast, Guy & Ruth Barton**
P.O. Box 19 (I-80, exit 60. 3 m. N. on Hwy 71; 1 m. E. of Brayton)
Ph. **1-800/945-0663** 712/549-2449 Email:halhsebb@metc.net **Facilities:** 4 box stalls, 5 holding pens & pasture. Add'l 8 indoor stalls & arena across road. Country roads for riding. Full Bed & Breakfast, 2 air-conditioned rooms. Gas grill & deck. Call for reservations. Visa/MC accepted.

DAVENPORT, 52806

Cedar Ridge Ranch, Larry or Deb Hansch
4750 W. 60th St. (I-280, exit 1)
Ph. 563/391-0624 **Facilities:** 10 indoor stalls, 8 holding pens, indoor/outdoor arenas and parking for 3 w/elec. hookup, but no water hookup.

MASON CITY, 50401-1590

★ **North Iowa Fair Complex**
3700 4th St. S.W. (Hwy 122/Bus. 18 & Eisenhower. 6 m. E. of I-35, exit 194 or 3 m. N. of Eisenhower, exit 183 from Hwy 18/Ave. of the Saints)
Ph. 641/423-3811 or 641/424-6515 Email: office@northiowafair.org **Facilities:** Indoor stalls, holding pens, outdoor arena & camper hookups. Call ahead. Not available some weekends. Can send Visitor's Guide and NIFG Events brochure.

WINTERSET, 50273

B/K Stable & Training Facility, Don Shiverick
2853 220th St. (7 m. W. of I-35; 12 m. S. of I-80)
Ph. 515/462-1269 Email:dshiverick@hotmail.com **Facilities:** 13 stalls, 4 large paddocks w/run-in sheds & pasture, 60' round pen, 100x235 outdoor arena, parking w/elec & water and Bed & Breakfast avail. Circle driveway. See the "Bridges of Madison County" & John Wayne's old stomping grounds in area.

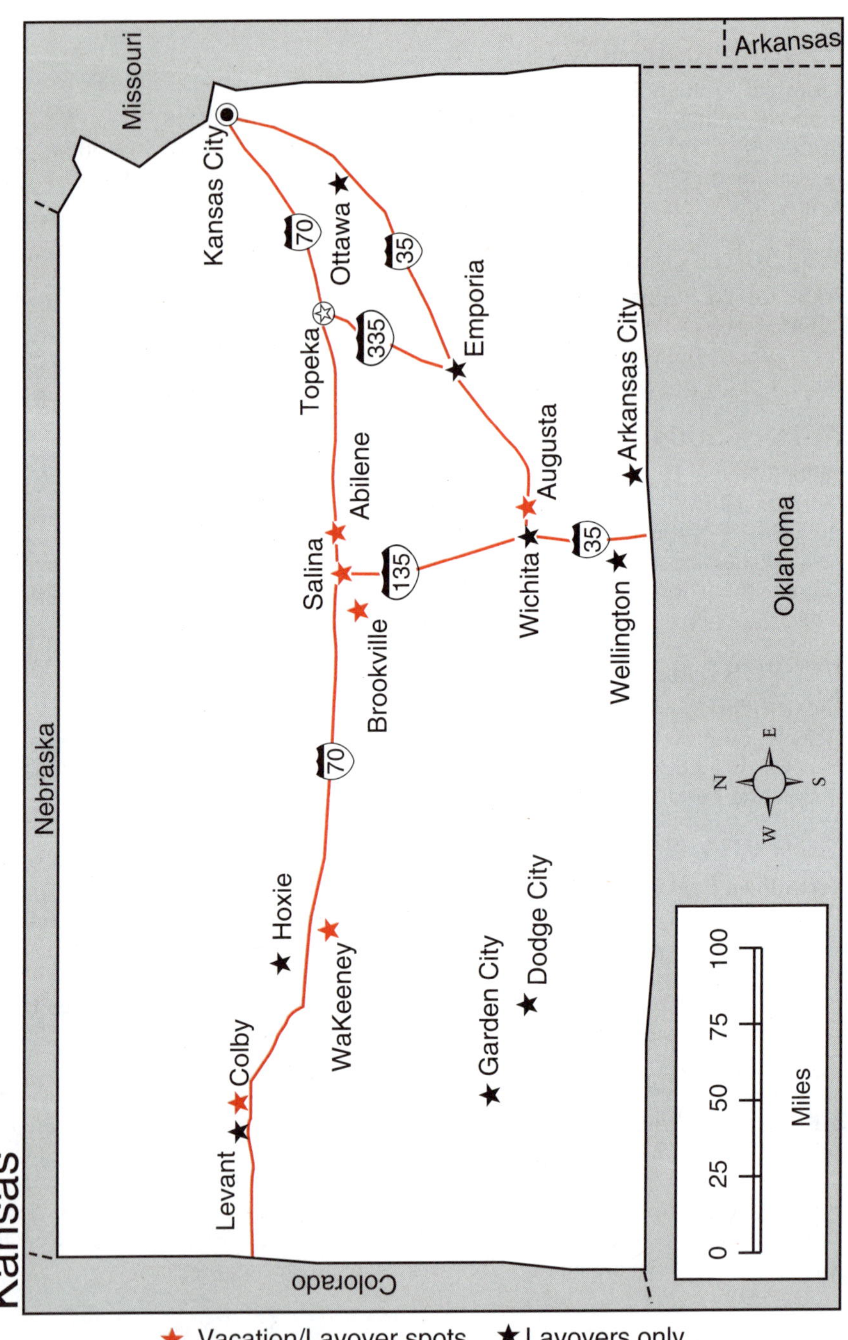

★ Vacation/Layover spots ★ Layovers only
☆ State Capitol ◉ Hwy Junction cities

CURRENT NEGATIVE COGGINS, HEALTH CERTIFICATE & OWNERSHIP PAPERS REQUIRED - see page 2 for details

ABILENE, 67410

★ **Covered Wagon R.V. Park, Richard & Cathy Osborn**
803 S. Buckeye (I-70, Abilene exit 275. S. on Buckeye 2-1/2 m. Within 3 blocks of Eisenhower Center & Old Abilene Town)
Ph. **1-800/864-4053** Email:cwoodosborn@access-one.com Web:access-one.com/asvra/ **Facilities:** 4 outdoor stalls and 6 full camper hookups. Must call ahead. Open year-round. Full hookups, pull-thrus, laundry, clean restrooms & shower, pool, ice, playground, dump station, instant phone service & cable TV. Pets welcome on leash. Check out by noon.

ARKANSAS CITY, 67005

George Blatchford
1012 Running Horse Ln. (2 m. E. of town on Madison Ave.)
Ph. 620/442-4687 Cell 580/761-2397 **Facilities:** Indoor/outdoor stalls, holding pens, pasture, walker, feed, exercise track and a 3-horse training gate.

ARKANSAS CITY, 67005

Erickson Quarter Horses, Ed & Alice Erickson
12357 US 166 (5 m. E. of Ark City on US Hwy 16, S. side)
Ph. 620/442-1853 Cell 620/441-8590 **Facilities:** 12 stalls, holding pens, pasture, feed, round pen, trails, hookup w/elec & water, large vehicle parking and 2 bdrm apt/sleeps 8 people. 6 p.m. arrival or call for late arrival.

AUGUSTA, 67010

★ **Briar Fox Farm**
9718 SW Hwy 54 (E. US Hwy 54, Mile Marker 233)
Ph. 316/775-7577 or 316/775-5512 **Facilities:** 20 covered stalls in summer barn + limited # in main barn, paddocks, if avail., feed avail. upon request, trails & camper hookup. Vet/farrier on call. Kennels avail. Reservations req. Prepay by check or Visa/MC. Motels within 2 m.

BROOKVILLE, 67425

★ **Castle Rock Ranch Bed & Breakfast**
1086 29th Rd. (20 m. W. of I-135, exit 92; 8 m. S. of I-70, exit 238)
Ph. **1-888/225-6865** toll free or 785/225-6865 **Facilities:** 5 stalls w/exits inside & out, holding pen, 2 ac. pasture surrounding barn, exercise area & Kanopolis Lake trails 5 m., guided rides by apt. and 8 dbl rms for B&B w/private baths. Retreats can be arranged.

COLBY, 67701

★ **Tin Acres Quarter Horses, Theron & Jane Johnson**
2626 N. Kansas Hwy 25 (9 m. N. of I-70, exit 53, right on Hwy 25)
Ph. 785/462-7525 or 785/462-3600 Email:jjohnson@colby.ixks.com **Facilities:** 14 indoor stalls, 6 outdoor stalls w/runs, 2 holding pens, pasture, feed daily, indoor arena, 2 camper hookups and Bed & Breakfast in new passive home w/country breakfast/4 rooms. Designed for semi turnaround.

CURRENT NEGATIVE COGGINS, HEALTH CERTIFICATE & OWNERSHIP PAPERS REQUIRED - see page 2 for details

DODGE CITY, 67801-6528

Slash L Farm, Jean Lantis
10782 US Hwy 50 (1 m. W. of city limits on Hwy 50)
Ph. 620/227-6364 **Facilities:** Indoor/outdoor stalls. Motels 1 m. & campground 1/2 m.

EMPORIA, 66801

Shamrock Bed & Board, Tim & Carol McLaughlin
1323 S. Hwy 99 (2-1/2 m. S. of Emporia. 5 m. from I-35)
Ph. 620/342-5941 Email:shamrock@osprey.net Web:www.shamrockranch.com
Facilities: 12x12 barn stalls, small lot w/pole barn, turnout corrals, large lighted arena, round pen, parking space w/elec. and bunkhouse for up to 4, limited cooking facilities, w/continental breakfast. Reservations preferred. Prefer no smoking. No credit cards accepted.

GARDEN CITY, 67846

Steve Burgess
P.O. Box 686 Location: 5185 E. Hwy 50
Ph.620/275-0114 620/275-2324 **Facilities:** Stalls, holding pens, pasture, feed & arena. Will accept other livestock.

HOXIE, 67740

Pat & Bill Weeks, Overnight Stable
RR 2, Box 52 (I-70, Grainfield exit 95. N. 12 m. just past mile marker 174, right)
Ph. 785/675-3770 **Facilities:** 2 indoor/2 outdoor stalls, 1 large holding pen (accommodate polo ponies or rodeo horses) & electricity for campers.. Cash payment.

LEVANT, 67743

West Kansas Horse Motel, Janette M. McDowell
2145 County Rd. 12 (I-70, exit 45. 3-1/2 m. N. on Hwy 407)
Ph. **1-888/478-6272** Email:JANKS97@hotmail.com Web:www.westkansashorsemotel.com Fax 785/586-2287 **Facilities:** 24 indoor stalls, $5 unbedded, $10 bedded, holding pens, hay/grain, 150 acres of pasture to ride on & indoor arena. Vet/farrier avail. Colby 8 m. E. w/9 hotels, 25 restaurants, camping facility w/all services.

OTTAWA, 66067

68 Ranch LLC, Kevin & Sheri Pietro
3732 K-68 Hwy. (I-35 to 68 Hwy/exit 187. Just 3 m. off I-35. Call for directions)
Ph. Reservations only:785/242-9955 Cell 913/238-0918
Email:kspietro@grapevine.net **Facilities:** 12 indoor stalls, turnout lots & arenas, brome/grain, trails and parking lot w/water & outlet. Multiple horse discount. Motels nearby.

CURRENT NEGATIVE COGGINS, HEALTH CERTIFICATE & OWNERSHIP PAPERS REQUIRED - see page 2 for details

SALINA, 67401

E Bar Z Stables, Dexter Eggers & Ann Zimmerman
3904 N. Ohio (1.8 m. N. of I-70 at exit 253/Ohio St.)
Ph.785/825-7135 Email:overnight@ebarz.com Web:www.ebarz.com
Facilities: 7 indoor/10 outdoor stalls, pasture & feed avail., indoor/outdoor arenas, trails & easy trailer parking. Call or email for reservations/rates. Motels & campground nearby. EASY access from I-70 or I-135.

SALINA, 67401

★ **Hunters Leigh Bed & Breakfast, Lee & Wynona Mason, owners**
4109 E. North St. (Crossroads of America, I-70 & I-35)
Ph. 785/823-6750 **1-800/889-6750** Web:www.huntersleigh.com **Facilities:** Safe, clean, well lit indoor stalls w/bedding furnished, feed avail., parking w/elec./water for RV's. Bed & Breakfast has 3 luxurious rooms w/private baths. Full breakfast served. $20 per stall/$20 for RV's/$80 per rm. Hunters Leigh is for sale.

SALINA, 67401

Saline County Livestock & Expo Center
900 Greeley (I-70, Ohio exit S; I-135, Crawford St. exit)
Ph. 785/826-6531 or 785/826-6532; after 5 p.m. & weekends call 785/825-0840
Email:bobbiewallace@saline.org **Facilities:** 50+ indoor/50+ outdoor stalls & elec. for camper hookup. Bedding required and is avail. for $2 per bale.

CURRENT NEGATIVE COGGINS, HEALTH CERTIFICATE & OWNERSHIP PAPERS REQUIRED - see page 2 for details

WaKEENEY, 67672

★ **Saline River Hunting Lodge & Guide Service, Inc., Roger & Kelli Flax**
Rt. 1, Box 47 (I-70, exit 128, 7 m. N. on Hwy 283, 2 m. W. on CR 422)
Ph. 785/743-6676 Cell 785/769-6095 Work 785/743-6603
Email:rogflax@ruraltel.net Web:www.salinelodge.com **Facilities:** Indoor facilities for up to 3 horses, 2 large/2 small holding pens, camper/trailer parking & lodge for up to 6. Overnight stablng avail. Reservations req. Full home cooked breakfast incl. w/lodging. Stable & pens nearby lodge. Dog kennels also avail.

WaKEENEY, 67672

★ **Thistle Hill Bed & Breakfast, Dave & Mary Hendricks**
Rt. 1, Box 93 (I-70, exit 120, 1-1/2 m. from exit - will give exact directions when reservations are made)
Ph. 785/743-2644 Email:wildflowermary@yahoo.com Web:www.thistlehillonline.com **Facilities:** 1 indoor stall, 4 holding pens and 3 rooms for Bed & Breakfast. Overnight stabling avail. for B&B guests only. Reservations req. Full country breakfast incl. w/lodging. Stay near your horse.

WELLINGTON, 67152

Willow Brook Acres, Christie
786 E. 35th St. S. (I-35, exit 19/Wellington)
Ph. Mobile 316/708-1660 Home 620/326-5550 **Facilities:** 6 stalls, 6 holding pens, pasture w/excellent fencing, feed avail., indoor riding arena & parking w/elec & water. Breakfast by reservation. Private shower avail. - handicap accessible. In by 7 p.m. or call and out by 12 p.m.

WICHITA, 67207

Shadow Ridge Stable, Donna & Don O'Gorman
7303 E. Harry (Apx. 2 m. S. of US 54/400 on Rock Rd., then W./right on Harry St. W. apx. 1/3 m. to entrance on S./left)
Ph. 316/686-7303 or 316/688-0865 Email:dnogo1790@aol.com **Facilities:** 24 stall barn w/wash stall & grooming stalls, turnout avail., 2 outdoor arenas (1 w/ights), round pens, 56 acres to ride with some trails & 2 ponds and limited elec. hookups & water for camping.

CURRENT NEGATIVE COGGINS, HEALTH CERTIFICATE & OWNERSHIP PAPERS REQUIRED - *see page 2 for details*

ELIZABETHTOWN, 42701

★ **Heartland Quarter/Thoroughbred Horses, Charlie & Rhonda Hogan**
600 Upper Colesburg Rd. (I-65, exit 94. US Hwy 62 E. Call ahead. Secure location w/security gates)
Ph. 270/737-1821 Email:RQuarters2@aol.com **Facilities**: 20 indoor stalls, 9 turnout fields, 3 aluminum round pens, 110x120 indoor/250x300 outdoor riding arenas, vinyl fencing around farm & trailer drop spaces. Dogs on leash & w/owner. All children must be well behaved. Up-to-date shots requied. $20 per horse per day.

FRANKFORT, 40383

Lakeside Arena, Bruce & Connie Brown
1385 Duncan Rd. (I-64, exit 58. 1.2 m. off interstate on St. Rt. 1681)
Ph. 859/873-9155 859/489-4885 **Facilities**: 120 indoor stalls, feed avail., 130x227 indoor arena, shavings & camper hookups w/elec & water. Vet on call.

HARRODSBURG, 40330

A Peaceful Place Farm
642 Keenon Rd. (SW of Lexington. Use Blue Grass Pkwy)
Ph. 859/734-7054 Email:kataaffe@ax.net **Facilities**: Barn has 7 new oak stalls, 2 pen-sized paddocks, 3-acre paddock w/large run-in shed, 2 large fields/1 with run-in access, 20-25 acres of riding area, wash rack & room for trailer. Beautiful campsite on KY River 7-8 m. & hotel/motel accommodations 5 m.

HARRODSBURG, 40330

★ **Shaker Village of Pleasant Hill**
3501 Lexington Rd. (US 68 at intersection of KY 33)
Ph. **1-800/734-5611** or 859/734-5411 Email:diana@shakervillageky.org Web:www.shakervillageky.org **Facilities**: 20 indoor stalls, 2 paddocks, 25 m. of riding trails, trailer parking & 81 lodging rooms in Nat'l Historic Landmark. No pets. Dining room on premises-res. req. Other services: 19th century restored Shaker Village, crafts, carriage rides, riverboat excursions.

IDLEWILD, 41080

★ **First Farm Inn, J.S. Warner**
2510 Stevens Rd. (I-275, belt around Cincinnati, to exit 11. 1/2 hr. from downtown Cincinnati)
Ph. 859/586-0199 **1-800/277-9527** Email:firstfarm@goodnews.net Web:www.bbonline.com/ky/firstfarm **Facilities**: 5 indoor stalls, 20 acres of pasture, grass arena and 2 rooms for Bed & Breakfast in historic 1870's farm home. Many attractions in area

CURRENT NEGATIVE COGGINS, HEALTH CERTIFICATE & OWNERSHIP PAPERS REQUIRED - see page 2 for details

KEVIL, 42053

Willoway Stables, Jerry & Sherrye Dublin, owners
3740 Magruder Rd. (I-24, exit 4. Hwy 60 W. 10 m. to Magruder Rd. Right 1/2 m.)
Ph. 270/488-3444 - barn House 270/488-3646 **Facilities**: 6 indoor stalls, 2 holding pens, pasture, feed, indoor/outdoor arenas, & trails within 1 m. Campers using water & elec. for the night will be charged $10. 24 hr. notice req.

LEXINGTON, 40511

Meoldie's Farm, Glenda & Mike Meadows
4222 Iron Works Pike (I-75, exit 120, across from KY Horse Park)
Ph. & Fax 859/252-9908 Mobile 859/321-0568 **Facilities**: 5 stalls, 6 paddocks & feed incl.

SHELBYVILLE, 40065

★ **Sanorosa Farm, Laura Sanor**
850 McMakin-McMullen Rd. (Shelbyville exit 35 off I-64. 1/2 way between Lexington & Louisville)
Ph. 502/647-3324 **Facilities:** 5 stalls, 60' holding pens, pasture, feed, 80x150 arena, camper hookup and 3 rooms for Bed & Breakfast w/fireplace, whirlpool tub. Farrier on premises. Vet on call. Animals welcome.

SULPHUR, 40070

Crystal Pines Ltd.
9591 Sulphur Rd. (I-71, exit 28. Hwy 153 NW 2 m.)
Ph. 502/743-9158 Fax 502/743-5661 **Facilities:** 80 indoor stalls, holding pens, pasture, feed, outdoor arena, walker & camper parking. Late arrivals - CALL.

SULPHUR, 40070

Dwenger Nurse Mares, Ted & Nancy Dwenger
9549 Sulphur Rd. (I-71, exit 28. 32 m. NE of Louisville. Hwy 157, 3/10th m. off Hwy 42)
Ph. 502/743-9731 Louisville 502/222-7433 Mobile 502/552-2749 **Facilities:** 6 indoor stalls, 2 holding pens, pasture, hay, elec & water for campers can be arranged and trailer parking. Owner lives on farm.

Herd at River — Photo by: Jehnet Carlson

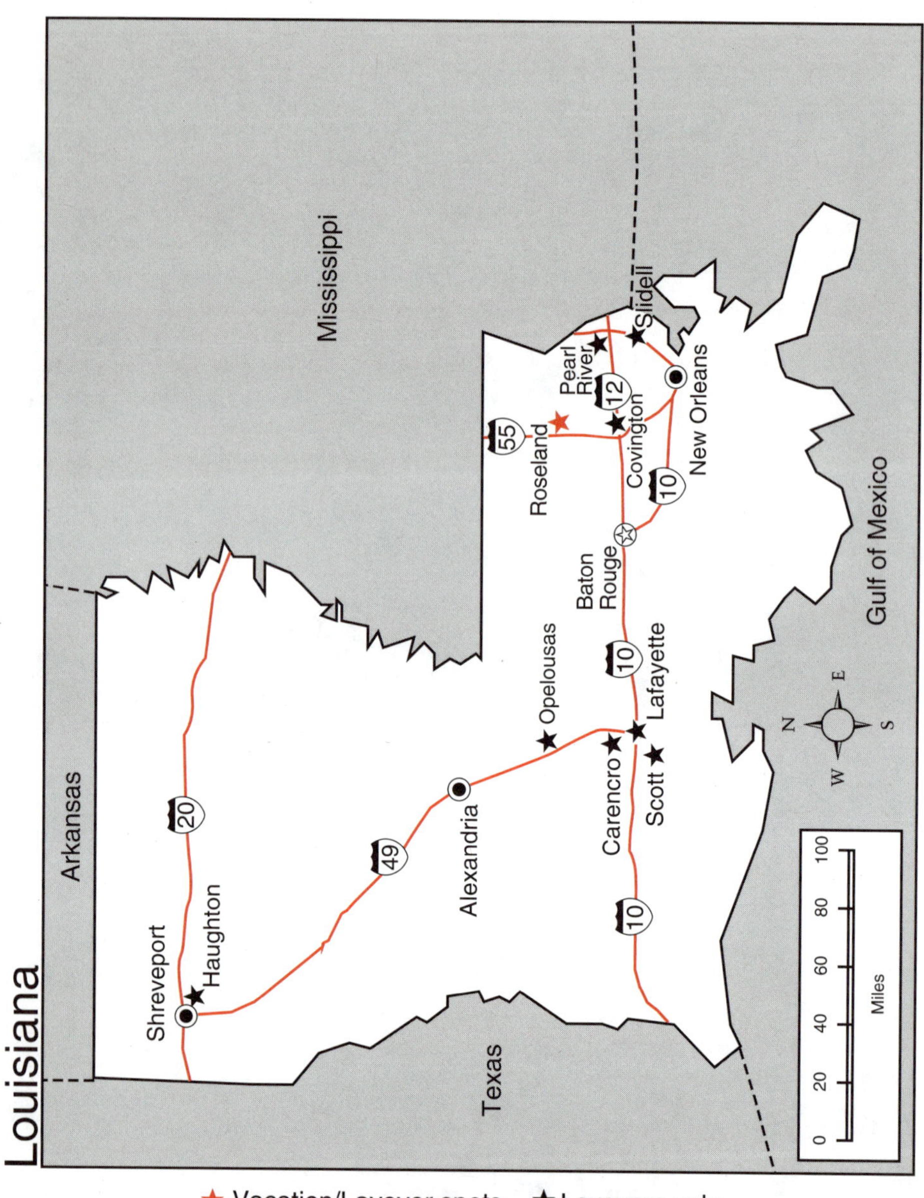

★ Vacation/Layover spots ★ Layovers only
State Capitol Hwy Junction cities

CURRENT NEGATIVE COGGINS, HEALTH CERTIFICATE & OWNERSHIP PAPERS REQUIRED - see page 2 for details

CARENCRO, 70520

Traders Rest Farm, Inc.
P.O. Box 156 (I-10, exit 100)
Ph. **1-800/544-6773** 337/234-2382 337/232-0631 **Facilities:** 150 indoor stalls, 27 pastures & 5 walkers.

COVINGTON, 70435

Tanglewood Stables
75548 Hwy 437 - Lee Rd. (Exit 1-10 North/190 North)
Ph. 985/892-4156 Fax 985/893-7931 Email:jmonju@bellsouth.net **Facilities:** 115 stalls, 15 indoor stalls, 3 pastures, feed, round pen, arena, picnic area & parking. Close to AAA motels & campgrounds. Call for directions & reservations. Owner/mgr. on premises. BRING ALL HEALTH PAPERS.

HAUGHTON, 71037

Double Rainbow Equestrian Center, Sig North & Raegan St. John, owners
1860 Adner Rd. (I-20, Louisiana Downs exit; E. on Hwy 80)
Ph. 318/949-9133 at Barn 1 318/949-9113 at Barn 4 **Facilities:** 100 indoor stalls, pasture, feed, outdoor arena, walker, training track & parking. Security lighting/owner on premises. Riding lessons: Hunter/Jumper/Western/Dressage. Clinics frequently held on grounds.

LAFAYETTE, 70507-5707

Lazy Hill Farm, Kyle Halter
1105 E. Pont Des Mouton Rd. (At I-10 & I-49 interchange. From I-49, exit 1/E. Pont Des Mouton Rd)
Ph. 337/234-8652 Fax 337/233-3143 Email:lazyhillfarm@prodigy.net Web:www.lazyhillfarm.com **Facilities:** 12x12 safe & secure indoor bedded stalls, hay avail., 60' round pen, wash rack & camper/trailer hookup or parking. Several hotels/motels & great Cajun restaurants within 1-2 m.

OPELOUSAS, 70570

Cedar Lane Farm, Laura Ryan
510 Judson Walsh Dr. (1/4 m. off I-49, exit 17)
Ph. 337/942-7755 (farm) 337/948-7719 (home) Fax 337/942-4436 Email:lauraryan@charter.com Web:lauraryan.com **Facilities:** 14x14 stalls w/attached paddocks, holding pens, pasture, feed avail., lighted dressage arena, wooded trails & camper hookup. Can accommodate stallions & mares w/foals.

CURRENT NEGATIVE COGGINS, HEALTH CERTIFICATE & OWNERSHIP PAPERS REQUIRED - *see page 2 for details*

PEARL RIVER, 70452

Carousel Riding Stables, Priscilla Bush
P.O. Box 369, 38103 Pine St. Ext. (Near junction of I-10/I-12/1-59)
Ph. 985/863-6100 Fax 985/863-5933 Email:Boldryder@aol.com **Facilities:** 10 indoor stalls w/paddock access, round pen, dressage & jumping arenas, elec hot walker and parking w/110 elec & water for campers.

ROSELAND, 70456

★ **Country Lane Bed & Breakfast, Leah Beth Simpson & Betty Ballow**
62058 Simpson Ln. (2 m. from I-55, exit Amite/Montpelier/47W. 20 min. N. of I-12)
For reservation inquiries Ph. Betty 985/748-3033 Leah Beth 985/748-8763
B&B 985/748-5789 Email:leahbeth@i-55.com or femmme@i-55.com **Facilities:** 8 indoor stalls, safely fenced pasture, 500 acres of trails adjoining property, horse trailer parking and 1 suite/4 bdrms for Bed & continental Breakfast. No smoking or pets inside. Dog pen, pool, cabana, BBQ pit, wildlife refuge, bird watchers paradise.

SCOTT, 70583

Dee's Farm, Kevin Domingue
407 Rue Des Babineaux (2 m. N. of I-10, exit 97)
Ph. 337/873-8350 **Facilities:** 25 indoor stalls, stallion stalls, pasture, feed avail., round pen, covered walker w/washrack, areas to ride & room for large rigs. Vet/farrier avail. Cajun restaurant, Texaco w/diesel, new Howard Johnson and KOA campground all at exit.

SLIDELL, 70461

Lewis Stables
80 Tortoise St. (1.5 m. from I-10, exit 266/Hwy 190)
Ph. 504/643-8025 Fax 504/643-6791 Email: lewistrl@cmq.net Website: lewistrailers.com **Facilities:** 130 indoor stalls, holding pens, arena, walker, feed & camper hookup. Trailer sales & repair. Major motels this exit.

MAKE RESERVATIONS FOR OVERNIGHT STABLING BEFORE YOU LEAVE ON THAT TRIP WITH YOUR HORSES!

Call or write to make stabling reservations as far ahead of time as possible. Find out what time you are required to check in and check out.

If you stay at a facility once, don't expect to make a return stop in a few days or a week or so without making reservations.

If you wait until 7 or 8 o'clock at night to start looking for a place to overnight, don't be surprised if you have trouble finding a facility that will put up your horses.

PLEASE BE CONSIDERATE.

Maine

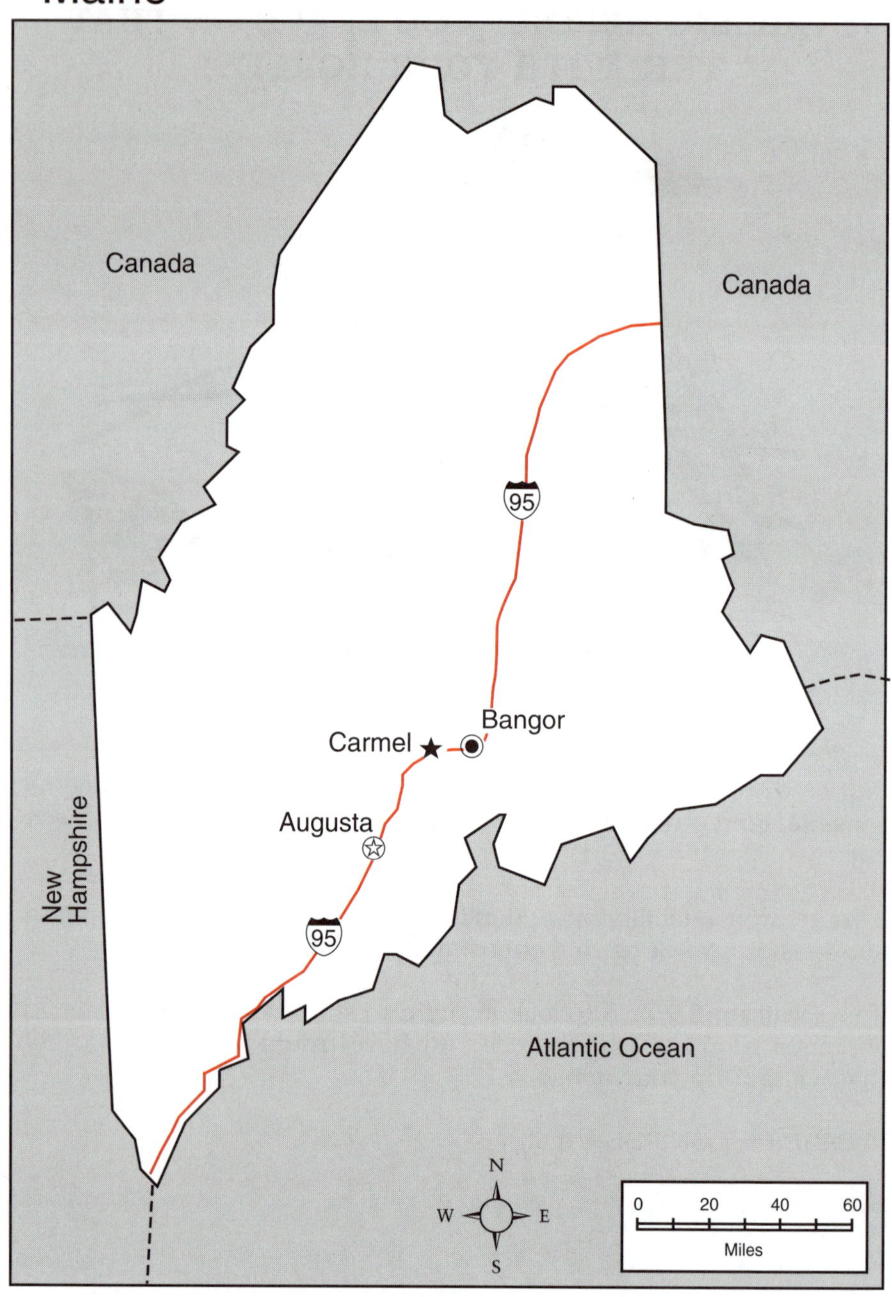

★ Vacation/Layover spots ★ Layovers only
☆ State Capitol ◉ Hwy Junction cities

CURRENT NEGATIVE COGGINS, HEALTH CERTIFICATE & OWNERSHIP PAPERS REQUIRED - see page 2 for details

CARMEL, 04419

Stepping Stone Farm, Kris Nicola
Rt. 2, Box 3340 (Cork Rd. S. I-95, exit 42. Call for directions)
Ph. 207/848-5310 Email:krisbabcock@hermon.net **Facilities:** 25 stalls, 8 paddocks, 4 pastures & plenty of trails on farm and nearby.

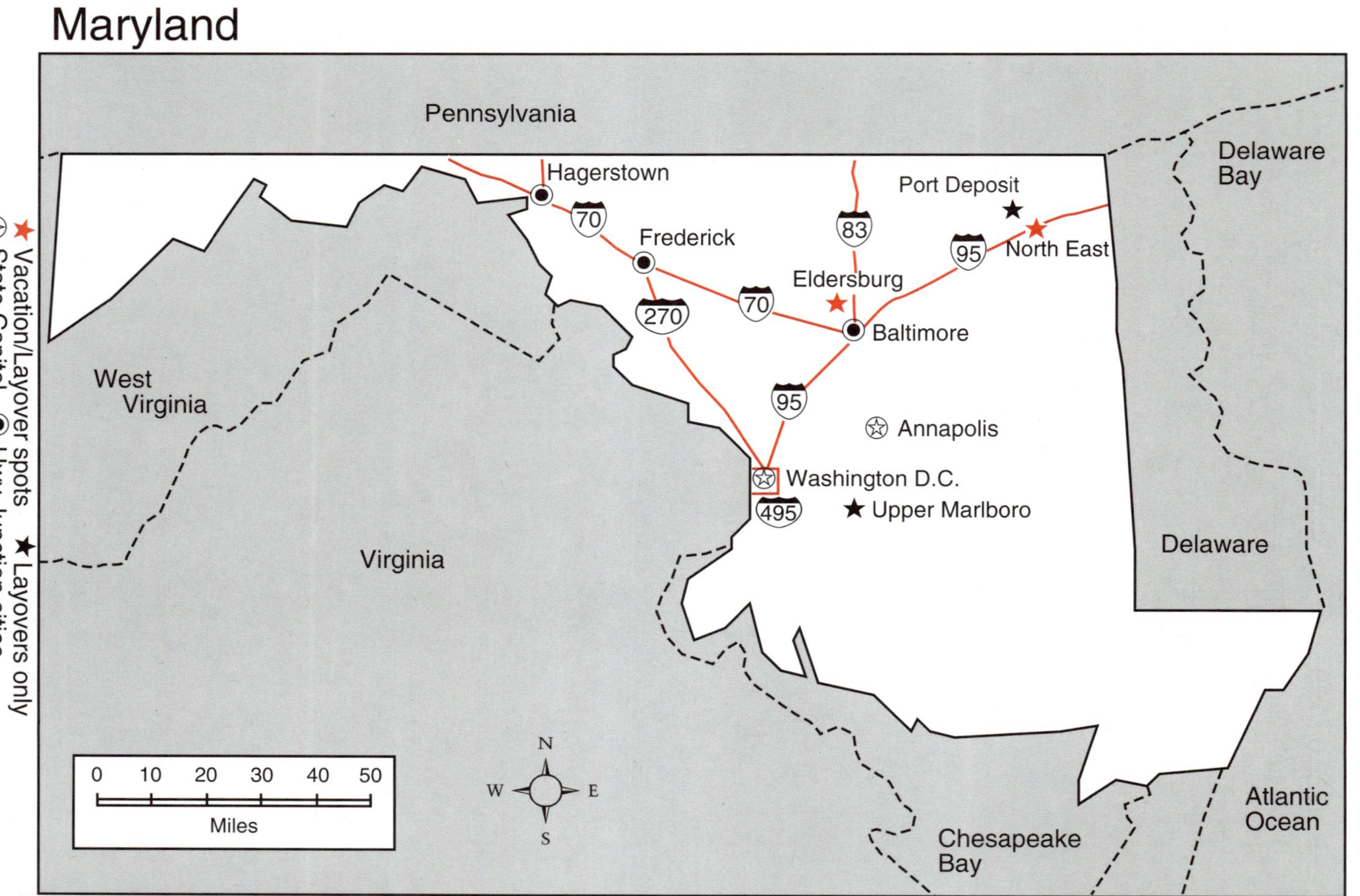
Maryland
Pennsylvania
Delaware Bay
Hagerstown
Port Deposit
70
83
Frederick
95
North East
Eldersburg
270
70
Baltimore
West Virginia
95
Annapolis
Washington D.C.
495
Upper Marlboro
Virginia
Delaware
N
W
E
S
0
10
20
30
40
50
Miles
Chesapeake Bay
Atlantic Ocean
Vacation/Layover spots
Layovers only
State Capitol
Hwy Junction cities

CURRENT NEGATIVE COGGINS, HEALTH CERTIFICATE & OWNERSHIP PAPERS REQUIRED - see page 2 for details

ELDERSBURG, 21784

★ **Americana Bed & Breakfast, Randi & Bob Wetzel**
2400 Constantine Dr. (NW of Baltimore)
Ph. **1-800/437-5770** Email:rplace@qis.net Web:www.americanabnb.com
Facilities: 4 stalls, 3 paddocks, 6 pastures, adjacent to thousands of acres of trails around a reservoir and 2 suites for B&B, one sleeps 2, other sleeps up to 4. No camping. Self care, bring own feed & hay. Complete meal package avail. See web page.

NORTH EAST, 21901

★ **Tailwinds Farm, Ted & JoAnn Dawson**
41 Tailwinds Lane, Rt. 272 (4 m. N. of I-95 at exit 100. 1 hr. from Philadelphia & Baltimore)
Ph. 410/658-8187 Web:www.fairwindsstables.com **Facilities:** 18-12x12 indoor stalls, feed/hay avail., ample grass turnout, indoor/outdoor arenas, parking for trailers and 2 rms for Bed & Breakfast. Call for reservations/rates. 10 min. to Fair Hill/5000 ac. of trails. Close to Chesapeake Bay, rivers, Plumpton Park Zoo.

PORT DEPOSIT, 21904

Anchor and Hope Farm, Edwin Merryman
P.O. Box 342 (Halfway between Philadelphia & Baltimore. 4-1/2 m. off I-95, exit 93/Port Deposit/Perryville)
Ph. 410/378-4081 **Facilities:** Indoor stalls, board-fenced paddocks, small & large turn-out pastures, feed, turf gallops & parking space. 20 min. from Fair Hill; 5 min. from motel.

UPPER MARLBORO, 20772

Prince George's Equestrian Center
14900 Pennsylvania Ave. (Exit 11A off Capital Beltway, I-495/95; proceed 7 m. SE on Pennsylvania Ave/Rt. 4. Exit at Upper Marlboro. Right off Rt. 301)
Ph. 301/952-7990 Fax 301/952-8167 Email:showpl@erols.com Web:www.show-placearena.com **Facilities:** 240 outdoor stalls, feed avail. thru local vendor & 20 RV hookups/no water.

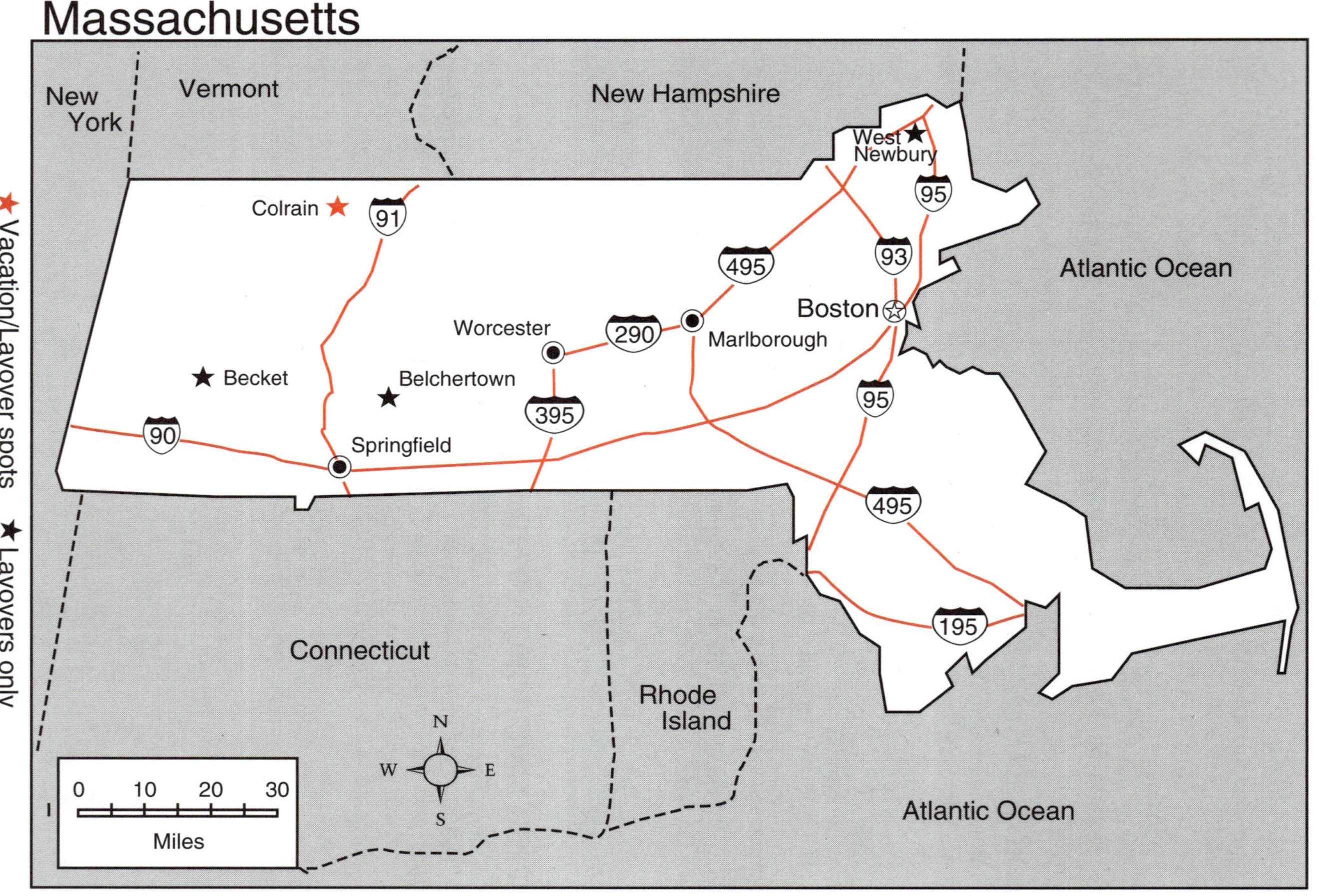
Massachusetts
New York
Vermont
New Hampshire
West Newbury
Colrain
Atlantic Ocean
Boston
Worcester
Marlborough
Becket
Belchertown
Springfield
Connecticut
Rhode Island
Atlantic Ocean
91
95
495
93
290
395
90
95
495
195
N
W
E
S
0
10
20
30
Miles
Vacation/Layover spots
Layovers only
State Capitol
Hwy Junction cities

CURRENT NEGATIVE COGGINS, HEALTH CERTIFICATE & OWNERSHIP PAPERS REQUIRED - *see page 2 for details*

BECKET, 01223

Toomey Tree Farm, Deborah Toomey
37 Mitchell Rd. Mail:37 Mitchell Rd., Chester MA 01011 (Western MA, halfway between exits 2 and 3 on MA Turnpike. 1/2 m. off US 20 on the Becket/Chester town line)
Ph. & Fax 413/623-6682 Email:dntoomey@juno.com **Facilities:** 4 stall barn, 2-50x100 paddocks, 1-100x100 paddock w/run-shed, 50x100 outdoor riding arena, miles of trails, camper parking/hookup avail. and overnight accommodations available w/advance notice.

BELCHERTOWN, 01007

Ingate Farms Equine Center and Bed & Breakfast
60 Lamson Ave. (Exit 19 off I-91N to Bay Rd. to S. Amherst line)
Ph. 413/253-0440 **1-888-INGATE B** (464-2832) **Facilities:** 10 indoor stalls, 6 holding pens, feed, indoor/outdoor arenas, miles of trails, camper hookup & 4 bdrms for Bed & Breakfast. Children over 8 yrs old. Reservations required.

COLRAIN, 01340

★ **High Pocket Farm, Bed & Breakfast...and Barn, Mark & Sarah McKusick**
38 Adams Place Rd. (20 min. from I-91 in Greenfield MA)
Ph. 413/624-8988 Fax 413/624-3363 Web:www.highpocket.com **Facilities:** 6 stall barn, pasture, 50' round pen, trails and B&B in 160 yr. old farmhouse. 3 bdrms w/baths, hot but/game room/daily guided trail ride/breakfast served daily at 8 a.m. Kitchen avail. for your own lunch/dinner prep. Smoking outside only. Pets ok in barn/dog house.

WEST NEWBURY, 01985

Rowland Meadow Farm, Jefferson & Lauren Rowland
P.O. Box 810 Location: 69 Crane Neck St. (5 m. off I-95 on Rt. 113)
Ph. 978/363-8128 Web:rowlandmeadowfarm.com **Facilities:** 8 indoor/4 outdoor stalls, holding pens, pasture, feed & small trailer parking. Call for rates. Truckstop nearby.

Michigan

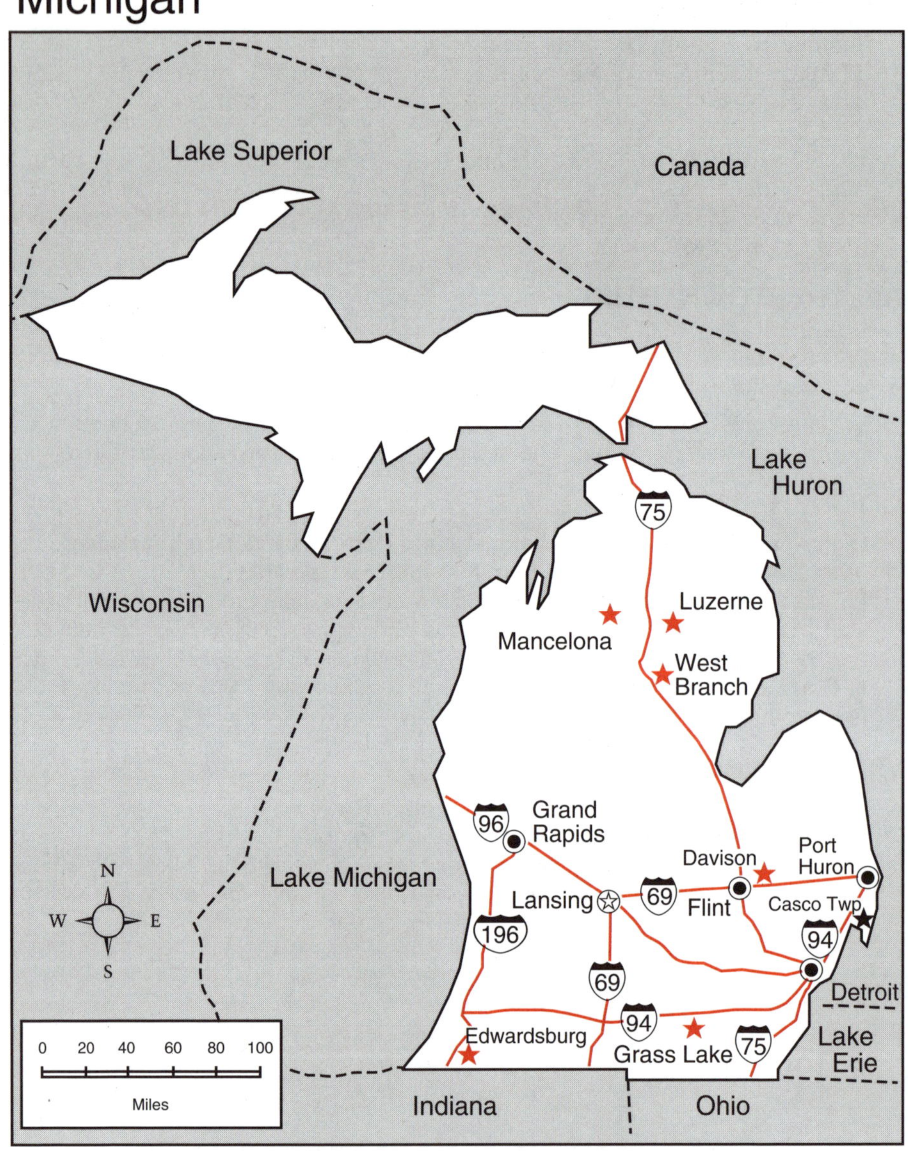

★ Vacation/Layover spots ★ Layovers only
State Capitol Hwy Junction cities

CURRENT NEGATIVE COGGINS, HEALTH CERTIFICATE & OWNERSHIP PAPERS REQUIRED - *see page 2 for details*

CASCO TWP, 48064

DL Ranch, Dave & Del Ledford
5860 Palms Rd. (Apx. 35 m. NE of Detroit; 25 m. SE of Port Huron; 6 m. E. of I-94 off Marine City exit. 1/10th m. N. of Palms Rd)
Ph. 810/765-7067 Email:ponyexpress1970@hotmail.com **Facilities:** 3-10x20 stalls, paddocks, pasture, feed, camper parking & hookup. Vet/blacksmith on call. Close to motels & restaurants.

DAVISON, 48423-8966

★ **Riverbank Farm, Colleen B. Pace**
8375 E. Coldwater Rd. (Just E. of Flint, on paved road, w/easy-off, easy-on to both I-69 & I-75. 1 hr. W. of the US/Canadian Blue Water Bridge)
Ph. 810/653-1440 Fax 810/658-9733 Email:colleenpace@onemain.com **Facilities:** Box stalls w/14x16 stall for larger horses, indoor/outdoor arenas, access to extensive trails along Flint River and full Bed & Breakfast in 1940's Tudor home w/bdrms. kitchen & visiting room. American country breakfast incl. Call for info packet.

EDWARDSBURG, 49112

★ **Morning Star Ranch & Retreat, Sam Walsh**
23285 US Hwy 12 (Minutes from IN Toll Rd./I-80/90. 25 min. from South Bend. 1-1/2 hr. from Chicago & 3 hr. from Detroit & Indianapolis)
Ph. 269/699-9568 Fax 269/699-8199 Email:info@morningstarrandr.com Web:www.morningstarrandr.com **Facilities:** 12 stall barn w/birthing stall & wash rack, paddocks, 140x70 indoor arena and 3 rooms w/private baths for Bed & Breakfast w/indoor swimming pool, hot tub & sauna; private patios overlook woods w/walking & riding trails. 2-bdrm guest house/sleeps 6.

GRASS LAKE, 49240

★ **Trailhead Stable, Julie Nelson**
12890 Trist Rd. (In the heart of the Waterloo Recreation Area, located 4 m. N. of I-94 between Ann Arbor & Jackson MI)
Ph. 517/522-4639 Fax 517/522-6201 Email:tjnelson@absolute-net.com Web:www.trailheadstable.com **Facilities:** 16-10x12 stalls, 2-20x12 stalls, hay/feed avail., round pen, outdoor arena, wash rack w/h&c water, bathroom, lounge, over 20 m. of marked horse trails w/maps, trailer/camper parking avail & rustic cabin/sleeps 8 for rent from DNR. No dogs. Cash or travelers checks.

LUZERNE, 48636

★ **Lost Creek Sky Ranch & Flyin' R Livery & Tack Shop, Debbie Coulon**
768 Mapes Rd. (Halfway between Luzerne & Mio, 1 m. N. of M72)
Ph. 989/826-1491 **Facilities:** 26 box stalls, picket, bring your own feed, show arena, trails in Huron Nat'l Forest, rustic camping w/porta johns, Lodge, full service restaurant & pizza. AuSable River w/ canoeing, fly fishing, etc. Many attrractions: pack trips, hay rides, western gift shop, etc.

CURRENT NEGATIVE COGGINS, HEALTH CERTIFICATE & OWNERSHIP PAPERS REQUIRED - *see page 2 for details*

MANCELONA, 49659

★ **Maple Grove Stables, Chyerl Gardner**
7252 N. Maple (Off US 131. Apx. 1 hr. from Traverse City, Petosky & Gaylord areas)
Ph. 231/587-5782 Email:cmancelona@bignet.net **Facilities:** Private location with 10 stalls, wash area, indoor arena, wash rack, separate holding pen for overnighters & ample parking for trailers. Quiet setting close to Jordan River Valley, near resorts & lakes..

WEST BRANCH, 48661

★ **Log Haven Bed, Breakfast & Barn, Gail Gotter**
1550 McGregor Rd. (I-75)
Ph & Fax. 989/685-3527 Email:gotter@m33access.com **Facilities:** 3 indoor box stalls w/turnout, paddock w/shelter & 1/2 ac. pasture, separate 1 ac. pasture, feed avail., trailer/camper parking, but no hookup, and new Bed & Breakfast w/3 rooms/private baths/country breakfast. Adjacent to State & Federal nat'l forest riding trails.

NOTES

Minnesota

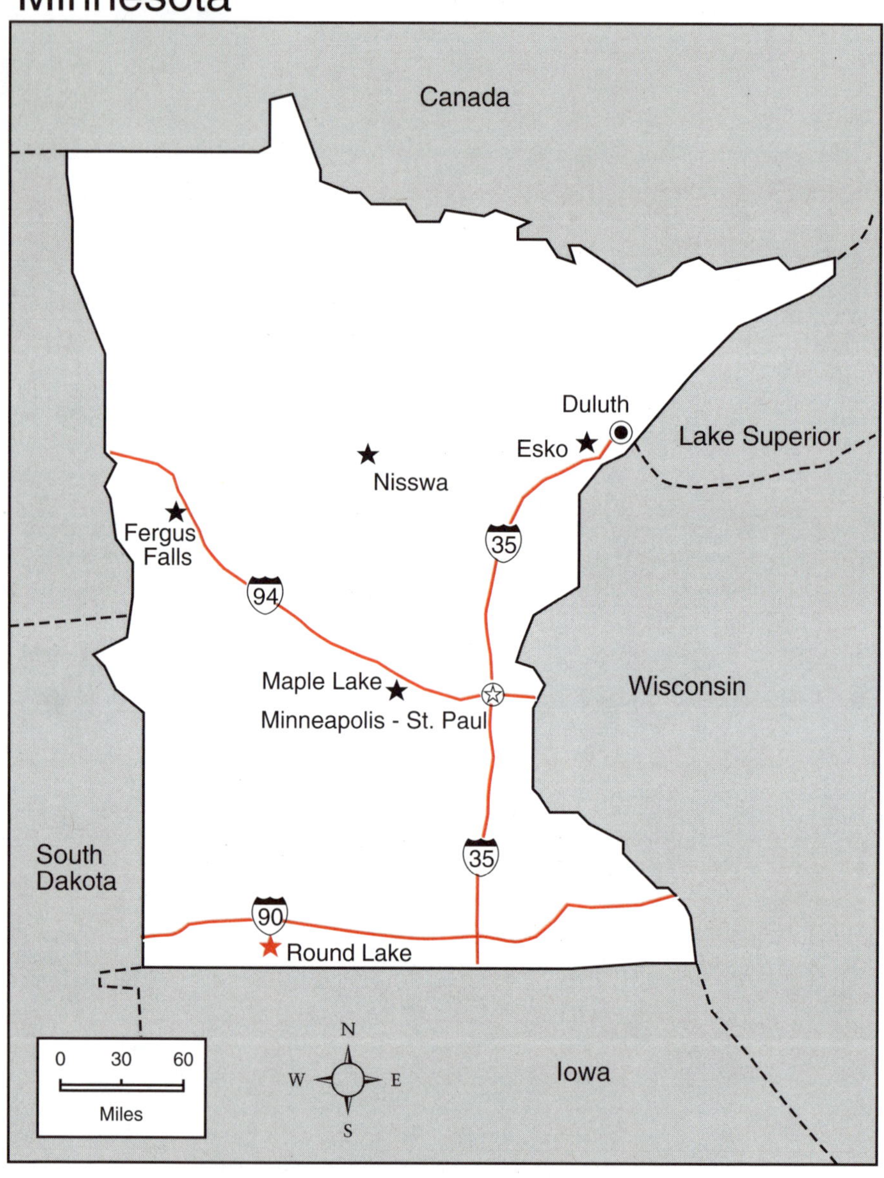

★ Vacation/Layover spots ★ Layovers only
✪ State Capitol ◉ Hwy Junction cities

CURRENT NEGATIVE COGGINS, HEALTH CERTIFICATE & OWNERSHIP PAPERS REQUIRED - *see page 2 for details*

ESKO, 55733

RiverRanch Arena, Bruce Larson/Dean Korach
41 Juntunen Rd. (15 m. W. of Duluth & only 2 m. off I-35, exit 242)
Ph. Barn 218/878-0055 Business 218/525-2270 218/722-1750
Email:brlarson@cpinternet.com **Facilities:** 31 large box stalls, heated barn, feed/hay/grain avail., indoor/outdoor arenas, 2 round pens, heated wash stalls & trailer parking. Farrier & vet on call. Restaurant/motel/Park 3 m..

FERGUS FALLS, 56537

River B Corriente Ranch, Brad or Cheri Brause
17345 - 125th Ave. (11 m. SW of I-94)
Ph. 218/736-5134 - answering machine/leave message Cheri work: 218/739-4662 **Facilities:** 7 indoor bedded stalls. Please call first. Motels/camper hookup in town. 9 p.m. arrival or call ahead.

MAPLE LAKE, 55358

Freedom Stables, Inc., Kevin & Laura Holen
2868 - 90th St. N.W. (I-94, exit 183. 7 m. S. on CR 8, E. on CR 106 2 m. to 90th, first place on left)
Ph. 320/963-3351 Fax 320/963-6616 Email:kevinholen@aol.com **Facilities:** 72 indoor stalls, 13 paddocks, numerous holding pens & pasture, feed incl., 70x200 indoor heated/100x200 outdoor arenas, 2 m. of trails on property, camper hookup & easy pull through parking, incl. semi's. Reservations requested. 24 hr. Vet/farrier avail. Pets welcome. Friendly staff.

NISSWA, 56468

Steve Vollmer
4716 Mission Rd. (At Tall Timbers on Hwy 371 at Mission Rd. intersection. 9 m. N. of Brainerd)
Ph. 218/963-4687 Fax 218/963-4687 **Facilities:** 4 indoor box stalls, 4 holding pens, feed & camper hookup. Harness & Saddle Shop on property.

ROUND LAKE, 56167

★ **Painted Prairie Farm, The Prairie House on Round Lake (B&B), Ralph & Virginia Schenck**
29344 St. Hwy 264 (4.4 m. S. of I-90 at Round Lake/Brewster exit; Hwy 264)
Ph. 507/945-8934 507/945-8922 **Facilities:** 24 indoor stalls, holding pens, pasture, feed, indoor/outdoor/jumping arenas, walker, trails, camper parking/elec/water for overnight stablers, 4 rooms for Bed & Breakfast (private & shared baths.)

Mississippi

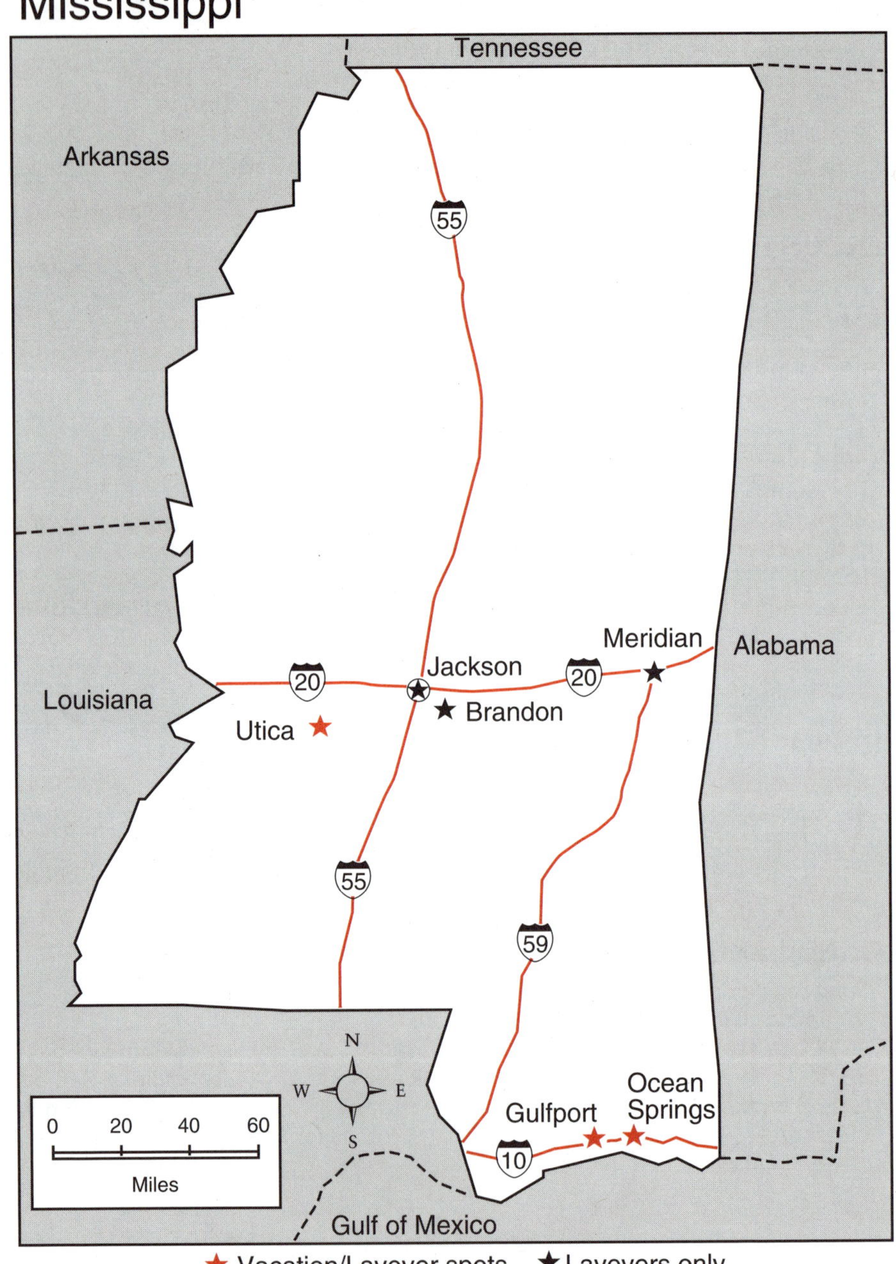

★ Vacation/Layover spots ★ Layovers only
☆ State Capitol ◉ Hwy Junction cities

CURRENT NEGATIVE COGGINS, HEALTH CERTIFICATE & OWNERSHIP PAPERS REQUIRED - see page 2 for details

BRANDON (Jackson area), 39042

Hilltop Painted Acres, John & Barbara Blough
607 North St. (I-20, exit 56 to Hwy 80)
Ph. 601/825-2094 **Facilities:** 10 indoor stalls, 8 holding pens, 25 acre pasture, camper hookup & bunkhouse w/shower. 48 hr. notice req. Parking for big rigs/rodeo animals. $10 per horse.

GULFPORT, 39503

★ **Shady Oaks Stables, Ronnie & Paige Bourgeois**
12726 Wolf River Rd. (I-10, exit 28, N. 3-1/2 m. from next 4-way stop)
Ph. 228/832-0435 Cell 228/326-3492 Email:boursos@bellsouth.net **Facilities:** 10 indoor stalls w/shavings, round pen, hay & feed racks & 2 camper hookups w/elec/ water/sewer. Restroom/shower facilities. Major motels within 7 m. Rates $20 per night for stalls. Vacation area - casinos, beaches & family fun within 15 min.

JACKSON, 39209

Dancing Hooves Stable, Dawn Clarke
1609 Carsley Rd. (Located in North Hinds Co. Within 10 m. of Clinton city limits & apx. 20 m. from Jackson)
Ph. 601/924-3140 Email:msdawn0957@aol.com **Facilities:** 40 ac. farm with 18 stall barn (12x10 & 12x12), foaling stalls, separate wooden paddocks for turnout, wash rack, round pen & arena. Never more than 16 horses boarded at any time. The Petrified Forest is within 10 m. of facility. Natchez Trace Trails - 45 min.

MERIDIAN, 39301

Fortunate Farms, Lauren Drummond
5725 Windsor Cir. Location: 4840 Arundel Rd. (3 m. S. of I-20/59 in Meridian)
Ph. Cell 601/917-8496 Home 601/681-6001 Barn 601/693-7705 Email:laurend@prodigy.net **Facilities:** Very close to I-20, new wider entrance. 20 stalls, paddocks, bedding incl., feed avail., outdoor arena w/jumps, grass dressage ring & some elec. avail. Please call for reservations

OCEAN SPRINGS, 39565

★ **The Horse Hotel, Julie Russell**
13027 Perigal Rd. (I-10, exit 50)
Ph. & Fax 228/818-5139 Email:Horsehotel8@aol.com **Facilities:** Indoor/outdoor stalls, shavings, pasture, round pen & walker. 6 new motels & feed store (8-5:30) within 2 m. Biloxi beaches & casinos, 10 m.; Gulf Islands Nat'l Seashore Park, 6 m.; DeSoto Nat'l Forest, Bigfoot riding trail, about 10 m.

CURRENT NEGATIVE COGGINS, HEALTH CERTIFICATE & OWNERSHIP PAPERS REQUIRED - *see page 2 for details*

UTICA, 39175

★ **Big Sand Campground, Inc., Sherril Strong**
3412 Reedtown Rd. (Between Jackson & Vicksburg. I-20, exit 1-C from Vicksburg. On Ross Rd., Claiborne Co)
Ph. 601/885-8068 Email:bigsandcamp@cs.com Web:bigsandcamp.tripod.com
Facilities: 6-12x12 stalls w/shavings, 2 pasture areas, large pipe arena, 26 RV sites w/water & elec., back-in & pull thru, restrooms, hot showers, bunkhouse w/linens, refrigerator, microwave, AC and trails. Borders Natchez Trace Pkwy & Natchez Trace Nat'l Scenic Trail.

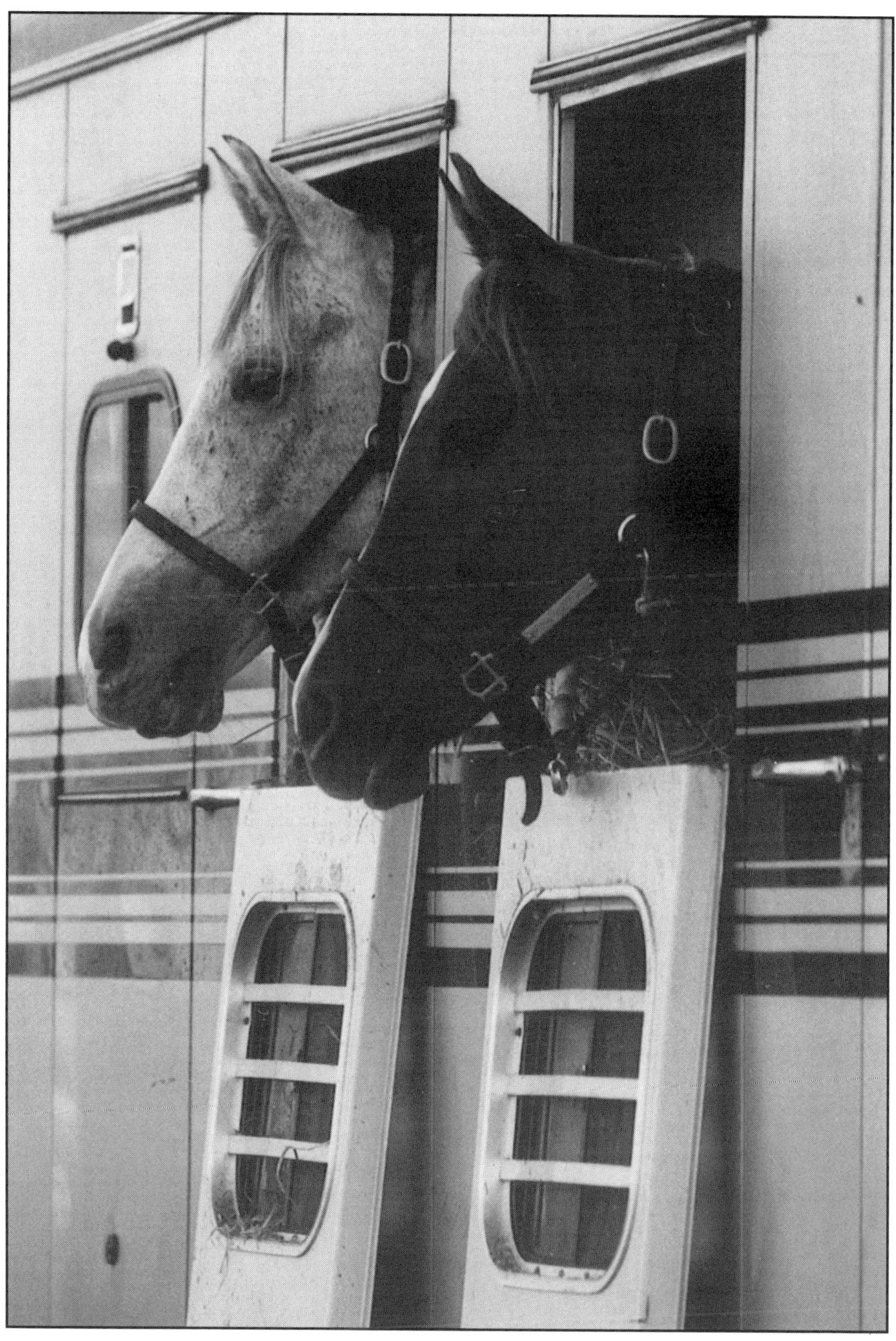

Break Time © Genie Stewart-Spears

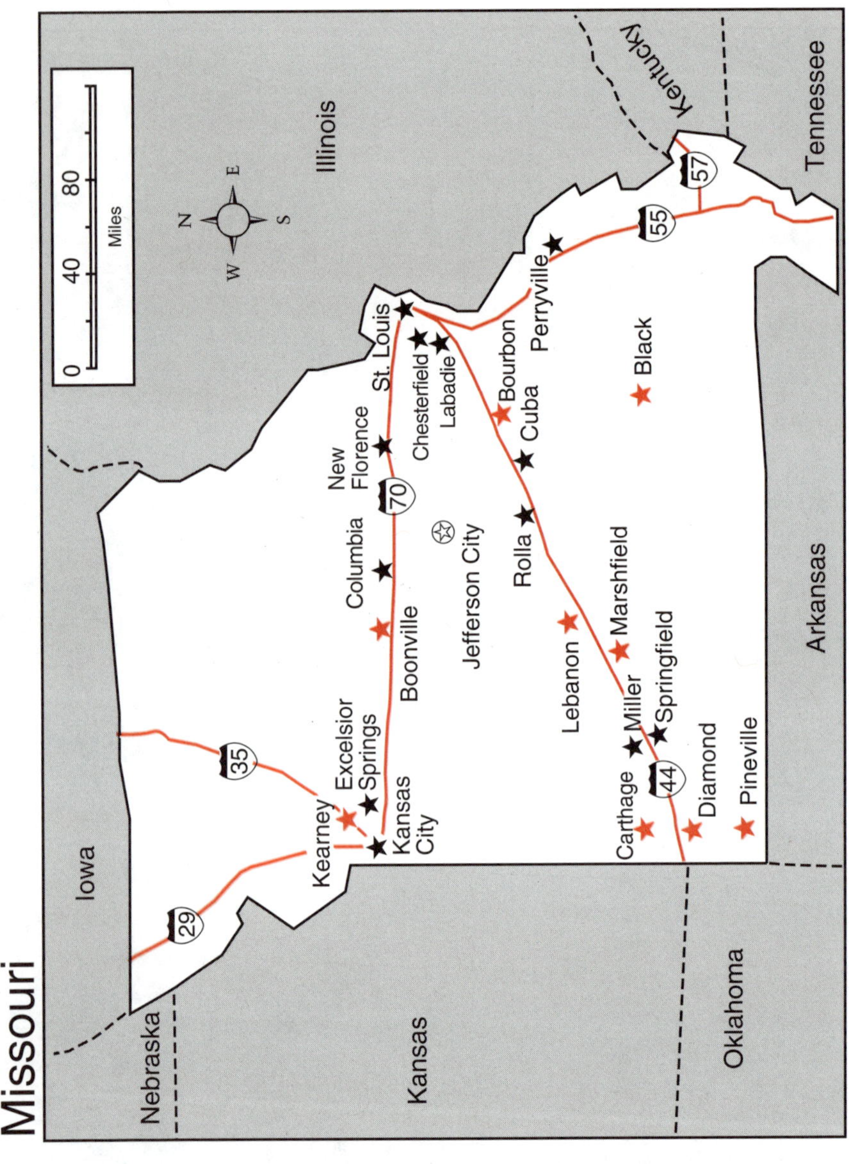

★ Vacation/Layover spots ★ Layovers only
⍟ State Capitol ◉ Hwy Junction cities

CURRENT NEGATIVE COGGINS, HEALTH CERTIFICATE & OWNERSHIP PAPERS REQUIRED - see page 2 for details

BLACK, 63625

★ **Valley Springs Foxtrotters & Brushy Creek Resort**
Rt. 1, Box 173 (Hwy J. In the heart of the Mark Twain Nat'l Forest, just outside of Black)
Ph. 573/269-4743 or 573/269-4600 Fax 573/269-4234 Email:vsfoxtrt@misn.com Web:www.missourifoxtrotter.com **Facilities:** 36 stalls, feed/hay, 150 m. of trails, elec & waer sites or primitive camping and cabins. Specializing in trail riding, packing trips, tee-pee rental, lodging, camping, log cabins, stall rentals, bath house & hot tub for campers.

BOONVILLE, 65233

★ **John & Kathy Little, Little's Four Oaks Farm**
22045 Boonville Rd. (I-70, exit 106 to Hwy 87)
Ph.660/882-8048
Email:fouroaks@starband.net
Web:www.littlesfouroaksfarm.com
Facilities: 10 stalls w/paddocks, 20 acres of pasture, hay/grain, round pen, 2 camper hookups and 2-3 rooms for Bed & Breakfast. Reservations req.

BOURBON, 65441

★ **Baileys Inn at Brazil Creek, Stacey Geddes**
6000 Hwy W (I-44 at Bourbon. 60 m. SW of St. Louis)
Ph. 573/732-2288 Fax 573/732-3288 Email:bailyinn@fidnet Web:baileysinn.com **Facilities:** Luxury three-suite inn with gourmet restaurant. 2 shaded 20x20 corrals on Brazil Creek. Situated on 120 acres on the Berryman Trail/fabulous riding trails.

BOURBON, 65441

★ **Meramec Farm, Cabins & Trail-Riding Vacations, Carol Springer and David Curtis**
208 Thickety Ford Rd. (I-44, exit 218; 9 m. S. on Hwy N, left on Thickety Ford to farm. 75 M. SW of St. Louis via I-44)
Ph. 573/732-4765 Email:mfarmbnb@fidnet.com Web:www.meramecfarm.com **Facilities:** 2 indoor stalls, 4 large pens & corral, 100 m. of trails, 2 hookups and 2 cabins w/kitchens/baths. Fishing, canoeing, wineries, caves & miles of trails. Brochure avail.

CARTHAGE, 64836

★ **Royal Oaks Arena/formerly Royalty Arena, Dick Fanning**
Mail: 10695 Dusty Ln. Location: 9895 Cork Ln. (Co. Rd. 100)
Ph. 417/358-1100 Email:royaloaksarena@yahoo.com **Facilities:** 200+ stalls, holding pens, feed can be provided, riding arena, wash racks, camper hookups & parking. Boarding stable, exhibition arena, restaurant.

CURRENT NEGATIVE COGGINS, HEALTH CERTIFICATE & OWNERSHIP PAPERS REQUIRED - see page 2 for details

CHESTERFIELD (St. Louis area), 63017

J.M. Pierce Stables Ltd.
2315 Baxter Rd. (2 m. S. of US 40 & Clarkson Rd. W. St. Louis Co.)
Ph. 314/394-4733 **Facilities:** Indoor stalls, indoor/outdoor arenas & hay/grain.

COLUMBIA, 65201

Rangeline Stables, Sandi Parker, owner
24 S. Rangeline Rd. (1 m. S. of I-70, exit 133 - Centralia Rt. Z exit)
Ph. 573/474-0018 or 573/474-0999 Email:sandiparker4@aol.com
Web:www.rangelinestables.com **Facilities:** 25-12x12 indoor rubber matted stalls, 8 outdoor paddocks, pasture avail., feed on request, indoor/outdoor arenas, hot-walker, trails and ample parking & hookup. Newest & nicest barn in the area.

COLUMBIA, 65202

Midway Exposition Center, C.W. Adams, mgr.
I-70 & Hwy 40, exit 121
Ph. 573/445-8338 **Facilities:** 425 indoor stalls, indoor/outdoor arenas and 50 camper hookups. Motel at same location (573/445-9565)

CUBA, 65453

Rex Bell Ranch
24265 Vinyard Rd. (Located on I-44. I-44, exit 203, 1/2 m. W. on the N. Service Rd)
Ph. 573/885-1166 **Facilities:** 26 large indoor stalls and indoor/outdoor arenas. Motels & restaurants 4 m.

CUBA, 65453

Blue Moon RV Park and Horse Motel
355 Hwy F (I-44, exit 203. 1/4 m. N. on Hwy F)
Ph. 573/885-3622 **1-877/440-CAMP(2267)** Fax 573/885-3752
Email:blmoonrv@fidnet.com **Facilities:** 5 indoor /6 outdoor stalls, turnout & camper hookups w/showers, restrooms, pool in season, pavilion, laundry & dump station. Vet/farrier on call.

DIAMOND, 64840

★ **Pear Tree Lane Stables, Harold Haskins**
20160 Hwy J (I-44, exit 18)
Ph. 417/325-4136 Fax 417/325-4137 Email:acofd@jscomm.net **Facilities:** 19 indoor/6 outdoor stalls, 12 holding pens, pasture, feed avail., indoor/outdoor arenas, walker, camper hookup & parking space for trailers. Vet on premises/farrier on call. Kennel for dogs & cats. Call for reservations/rates. Motels nearby.

EXCELSIOR SPRINGS - See Kansas City area

CURRENT NEGATIVE COGGINS, HEALTH CERTIFICATE & OWNERSHIP PAPERS REQUIRED - see page 2 for details

KANSAS CITY area

Dar-B-Ann Stables, Rebecca Potteiger
30023 NE 166th St., Excelsior Springs MO 64024-8437 (32 m. N. of Kansas City. I-35, exit 20 to Hwy 69 N. to 166th St.)
Ph. Fax 816/630-3332 Email:DarBAnnStables@cs.com **Facilities:** 10 indoor stalls, 3 large runs, indoor/outdoor arenas, wash rack, trails, parking space & elec. avail. for trailers. Call for reservations/rates. State Park and motel nearby. Cash or check only.

KANSAS CITY, 64138

Benjamin's Ranch
6401 E. 87th St. (located off I-435 & E. 87th St. exit)
Ph. 816/761-5055 or **1-800/43-RANCH Facilities:** 29 indoor stalls, paddocks, feed incl., exercise rings & elec. hookup only for campers/$10. Temporary boarding. Call for reservations. $20 per night/per horse.

KEARNEY, 64060

★ **Over the Hill Ranch, Inc., Bill & Connie Green**
P.O. Box 743 (5 m. from I-35. Call for directions. Jesse James hometown/historical James Farm 7 m; Watkins Mill & Smithville Lake nearby)
Ph. 816/628-5686 **Facilities:** 8-10x20 indoor stalls, 50 acres of pasture, 90x200 indoor arena, 1 camper hookup & B&B (no smoking)/ stay close to your horses in private guest house on premises. Owner is professional farrier/vet nearby. Call for res. Dogs allowed on leash. Visa & MC accepted.

LABADIE, 63055

Rhodes Riverside Ranch, An Equestrian Center, Julie & Keith Rhodes
112 Riverside (I-44 at Washington exit)
Ph. 636/451-5384 Fax 636/451-5326 Email:trplr@mindspring.com
Web:www.rhodesriversideranch.com **Facilities:** 10 indoor stalls, feed, arena, walker, trails & limited RV parking w/elec. Restrooms/shower. Proof of strangles vaccine, tetnus & rabies shots req. Non-refundable $20 deposit per stall due 7 workings days prior to arrival.

LEBANON, 65536

★ **Meadow View Ranch & Guesthouse, Heidi MacQueen**
27409 Missouri Dr. (Located in the Ozarks. Branson only 1-1/2 hr drive away)
Ph. 417/533-8133 Fax 417/533-7670 Email:atcMacqueen@yahoo.com
Facilities: 160 ac. ranch w/stalls, paddocks or pasture avail. Cabin, sleeps 4 w/1 bdrm, loft, 1 bath & fully equip. kitchen. First supply of Breakfast incl. Near Lake of the Ozarks, Bennett Spring SP, Mark Twain Nat'l Forest. Perfect for quiet time w/horses. No smoking.

CURRENT NEGATIVE COGGINS, HEALTH CERTIFICATE & OWNERSHIP PAPERS REQUIRED - see page 2 for details

MARSHFIELD, 65706

★ **Stevens Farm Inn, Walter & Sharon Stevens**
5484 Hwy 00 (Less than 1/4 m. from I-44, exit 96)
Ph. 417/859-6525 Email:pony1459@aol.com Web:www.usipp.com/ stevensfarm **Facilities:** 8 indoor stalls, 2 pens, indoor arena, walker and suite overlooking arena. Home can accommodate 8. Non-smoking rooms. Breakfast by request. Reservations req. Check in by 9 p.m.

MILLER, 65707

Brian & Penny Harrington
10950 Lawrence 2030 (8 m. N. of I-44 on Hwy 39, 1 m. W. on 2030)
Ph. 417/452-3873 **Facilities:** 10 indoor stalls, 6 paddocks, holding pens, pasture avail., feed avail., indoor/outdoor arenas, trails nearby, large parking lot w/hookups and B&B for 4. Call for reservations/rates. Parking space for trailers. Vet/farrier/equine dentist on call.

NEW FLORENCE, 63303

Circle B Ranch, Hal & Mary Battocletti
1298 Hwy J (9 m. off I-70, Hwy 19-Hermann/New Florence exiit S)
Ph. 573/252-4483 Cell 314/422-5039 Email:dixie66@ktis.net **Facilities:** 4 stalls w/adjoining runs, 2 holding pens, large pasture w/pond, trails, sweet feed/hay avail. for ad'l charge, camper parking w/elec & water. Motels avail. at I-70 exit or B&B & wineries abound in Hermann/8 m. Pets on leash. Cash only. Reservations required.

PERRYVILLE, 63775

Zeigler Stables, Kathy & Mike Zeigler
4997 Hwy T (3 m. from I-55, exit 129)
Ph. 573/547-7071 **Facilities:** 10 indoor 12x12 stalls, 12 paddocks, 7 acre pasture, feed avail. on request & camper hookup. Professional barn. $10 per head

PINEVILLE, 64856

★ **Ponderosa Trails & RV Park, Bert & Jean Pekul**
HCR 60, Box 278 (2 m. S. of Pineville off County K. 1-1/2 hr. from Branson; Eureka Springs short drive)
Ph. 417/223-4081 **1-888/644-6773** Fax 417/223-7073
Email:pndrosa@olemac.net Web:www.PonderosaTrails.net **Facilities:** 200 stalls, 108 water & electric hookups, showers & toliet facilities, dump station, arena, wash area and tack & gift shop. 600 acres of bluffs, woods, river and meadows to ride, plus 2100 acres of an adjoining state park. Canoeing/foat trips 1 m. Yearly art & craft fairs.

ROLLA, 65401

Green Acres Stables & Arena, Jerri Whitson
12555 Hwy 72 E. (Off I-44)
Ph. 573/341-3004 **Facilities:** 28 indoor stalls, round pen, feed/hay, indoor/outdoor arenas, trails & space for campers/trailers. Grooming salon. Other animals welcome. Call for reservations/rates. Motels nearby.

ST LOUIS area (see Waterloo, IL)

SPRINGFIELD, 65803

Schafer Brothers Equine Center, Brian & Marda Schafer
5853 West FR 94 (I-44, exit 75, 4 m. N. of Hwy 160. Apx. 40 m. from Branson)
Ph. 417/742-0704 Fax 417/742-0758 Email:MardaB417@aol.com **Facilities:** 28 indoor stalls, pasture, feed, indoor/outdoor arenas, walker, trailer parking avail. & Frisco Highline Trail. Emergency trailer pickup/Trailer cleaning & rebedding.

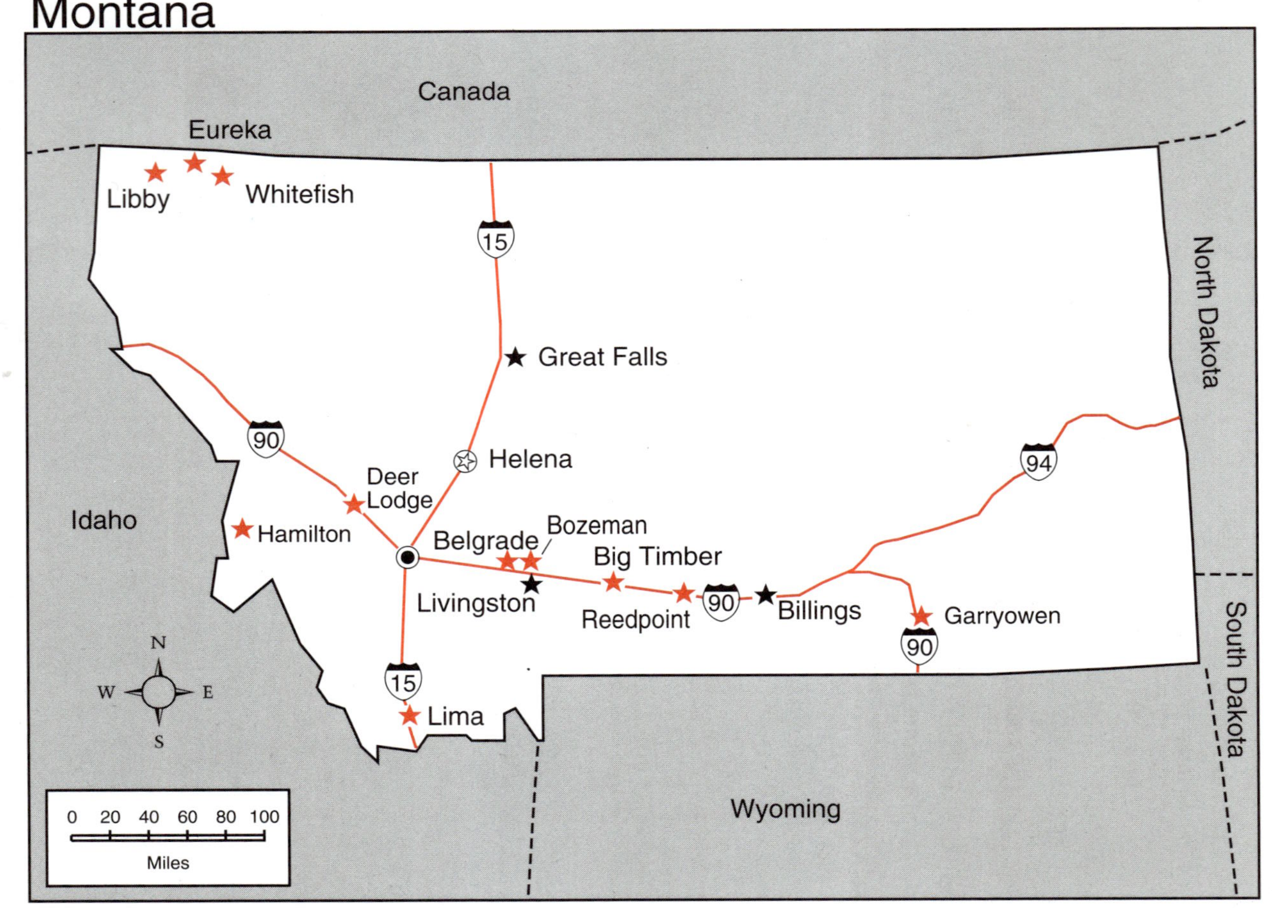

★ Vacation/Layover spots ★ Layovers only
State Capitol Hwy Junction cities

CURRENT NEGATIVE COGGINS, HEALTH CERTIFICATE & OWNERSHIP PAPERS REQUIRED - see page 2 for details

BELGRADE, 59714

★ **D J Bar Ranch, Jehnet Carlson & David Gannett**

5155 Round Mountain. Rd. (7 m. from I-90. Can fax or E-mail detailed map on request)
Ph. 406/388-7463 Fax 406/388-7443 Web:www.djbarranch.com
Email:info@djbarranch.com or mules@djbarranch.com **Facilities:** 3 box stalls w/runs, holding pens, pasture, 100x200 arena w/attached 100x200 pen w/loafing shed, camper hookup and log home sometimes during the off-season. $15 per night/per horse.

CURRENT NEGATIVE COGGINS, HEALTH CERTIFICATE & OWNERSHIP PAPERS REQUIRED - see page 2 for details

BIG TIMBER, 59011

★ **Carriage House Ranch, Sally DeStefano**
771 Hwy 191 N. (I-90, Big Timber exit to 191 N., 6.7 m. from Yellowstone River. In the Heart of Horse Whisperer Country)
Ph. 406/932-5339 Fax 406/932-5863 Email:chr@carriagehouseranch.com Web:www.carriagehouseranch.com **Facilities:** 10 indoor/70 outdoor stalls, 4 holding pens, pasture, hay, 100x225 indoor/outdoor arenas, 700 acres of trails, parking w/elec & water, family apt. and 3 bdrm B&B. On site management/fishing stream. Close to Crazy Mtn Horse access & trail head. Cafe. Dog kennels.

BILLINGS, 59107

L & D Livestock, Loren Larsen
P.O. Box 30474 Location: 3306 Becraft Ln. (Less than 1 m. froml-90, exit 455
Ph. 406/259-2011 or 406/425-1594
Email:debbiejlarsen@hotmail.com
Web:www.equinemotel.net **Facilities:** 14-12x22 indoor stalls, 18-12x48 shed row pens, Timothy hay incl., outdoor arena., camper hookup and queen-sized bed avail. Clean, safe barn & huge turn around area.

BOZEMAN, 59718

★ **Gallatin River Lodge, Steve & Christy Gamble**
9105 Thorpe Rd. (I-90, Belgrade exit S.)
Ph. 406/388-0148 **1-888/387-0148** Fax 406/388-6766
Web:www.grlodge.com Email:reservations@grlodge.com **Facilities:** 2 indoor/2 outdoor stalls, 4 holding pens, pasture, feed, outdoor arena/round pen, trailer parking and 6 guest suites w/all meals avail. Dining facilities for 50/dinner nightly/full bar service/open all year. Call for reservations/rates. Motels/campgrounds nearby.

CURRENT NEGATIVE COGGINS, HEALTH CERTIFICATE & OWNERSHIP PAPERS REQUIRED - see page 2 for details

DEER LODGE, 59722

★ **Mountain View Arena, Alex & Kayo Fraser**
255 Boulder Rd. (I-90, exit 184)
Ph. 406/846-1989 Email:horsebk@imine.net Web:www.drivehorses.com
Facilities: 30-12x12 indoor stalls, 72x235 indoor arena, dry camping & feed avail. Nat'l park and museum within 1 m. Driving lessons/training/clinics. Vet/motel/ cafes/truck stop/campground within 1000 ft.

EUREKA, 59917

★ **Ksanka Mountain Ranch & Guest Cabins, Bob or Ming Lovejoy**
3890 Indian Creek Rd. (Hwy 93 N., through town, E. on Burma Rd. 2 m., right on Indian Creek Rd)
Ph. 406/889-5683 406/889-5685 **1-866/682-2246**
Email:montana-cabins@montanasky.net Web:www.montana-cabins.com
Facilities: 12 indoor stalls, 8 w/paddocks, individual pipe panel corrals, post & rail fenced pasture, hay avail., indoor 90x190 arena, trails, space for self-contained units, fully furnished cabin w/many amenities & furnished apt. in barn w/kitchen. 3 night min. preferred..

GARRYOWEN, 59031

★ **7th Ranch RV Camp, Sandy Watts**
P.O. Box 117 (I-90, exit 514, 3 m. to Reno Creek Rd. Next to Custer's Little Big Horn Battlefield)
Ph. & Fax **1-800/371-7963** Email:wattsln@mcn.net Web:www.historicwest.com
Facilities: NEW! 8 stalls, 50' round training corral, large Linn Pipe & Post arena, full hook-up RV sites, tent & teepee sites, soft artesian water, washhouse, laundry, bunkhouse, historic tours & room to ride.

GREAT FALLS, 59404

Happy Trails Lodge, Katy MacDonald, contact
1401 N.W. Bypass (4 blocks from I-15)
Ph. 406/727-8387 - 24 hrs. **Facilities:** Indoor/outdoor stalls, holding pens, pasture, feed, arena, trails & one camper hookup.

HAMILTON, 59840-9744

★ **Deer Crossing Bed & Breakfast, Mary Lynch**
396 Hayes Creek Rd. (50 m. S. of Missoula; 1-1/2 m. W. of Hwy 93 on easily traveled country road)
Ph. 406/363-2232 **1-800/763-2232** Email:deercrossing@montana.com
Web:deercrossingmontana.com **Facilities:** 1 outdoor stall/1 holding pen, pasture, feed & access to Nat'l forest trails. Superb fly fishing/hiking/horseback riding. Luxury suites, gracious guest rooms & cozy cabins. Panoramic view of Bitterroot Valley.

CURRENT NEGATIVE COGGINS, HEALTH CERTIFICATE & OWNERSHIP PAPERS REQUIRED - see page 2 for details

LIBBY, 59923

★ **Trail 6 Ranch, LLC, Sue Vincent**
27506 US Hwy 2 S. (Easy access off Hwy 2 at milepost 60. 60 m. W. of Kalispell & 28 m. SE of Libby)
Ph. 406/293-8665 Email:Trail6Ranch@libby.org **Facilities:** 28 large box stalls, holding pens, round pen, pastures, hot walker, wash rack, trails (ride from ranch) & wildlife viewing, hay, feed, tack repair & big rig parking. Training & Lay up center. AQHA member. Many plans for 2003. Great vacation spot.

LIMA, 59739

★ **Centennial Outfitters, Mel & Chris Montgomery**
P.O. Box 92, Steel Bridge Ln. (3 m. N. of Lima off I-15. Easy access.)
Ph. 406/276-3463 **Facilities:** Pens, open pasture, round corral, feed avail., F.S. trails in Lima Peaks area & parking space. Cabin rental avail: full kitchen & bath, completely furnished, sleeps 4-6. Extra sleeping cabin for 2-3. Meals avail. by prior arrangement. Reservations please!

LIVINGSTON, 59047

Park County Fairgrounds
P.O. Box 146 (I-90W, exit 331; I-90E, exit 335. S. on Main, left on View Vista Dr.)
Ph. 406/222-4185 **Facilities:** 23 indoor/25 outdoor stalls, 10 pens, arena (hold-harmless claim required) and parking w/elec & water. Showers avail. between May 15 - Sept. 15.

REEDPOINT, 59069

★ **S Bar K Ranch, Joe Davis, Blanche Davis & Mary Berry**
P.O. Box 362 (2 m. off I-90, exit 392)
Ph. 406/326-2280 **Facilities:** Well-lighted barn w/4 stalls, holding pens, feed, round corral, 640 open acres for riding, camper parking w/elec & water and 2 bdrms for Bed & Breakfast. Trout fishing in Yellowstone River 1-1/2 m. Vet/farrier on call.

WHITEFISH, 59937

★ **Gaynor's Riverbend Ranch, Don Gaynor**
1992 K M Ranch Rd. (Just off Hwy 93; can be reached from either N. or S. of Whitefish. Call for specific directions.)
Ph. 406/862-3802 Email:riverbend@aboutmontana.net **Facilities:** 12 large indoor stalls/12 large outdoor paddocks, (paddock only $10; stall & paddock, $15), hay incl., 100x200 outdoor arena, trails adjacent to ranch, parking w/elec & water ($20) and 2 cabins w/kitchens/each sleep 6, ($75-150 per night depending on season & #) Pets ok. Credit cards accepted.

ETA'S INFORMATION SERVICE

The Information Service is for those who just need limited information. With one call, using your credit card, you can get the overnight stabling information you need. (Without a credit card, payment must be made in advance.)

With access to the Service, $19.95 per year, you can get the information you need (names and telephone numbers) for a one-time or a one or two-stop trip.

You can use the Service with or without the Directory. You must have a current Membership/Service Access No. to activate the Service. Always have this number available when you call ETA.

The Directory is published yearly and new layover listings which become available between printings will be added to and available through the Service.

Between the Directory and the Service, traveling and vacationing with your horse(s) is ***definitely easier, more convenient, less troublesome*** and ***practically worry-free***.

FOR MORE INFORMATION

Call 620/442-8131
Fax 620/442-8215

Email: eta@hit.net
Or visit our Web Site
www.overnightstabling.com

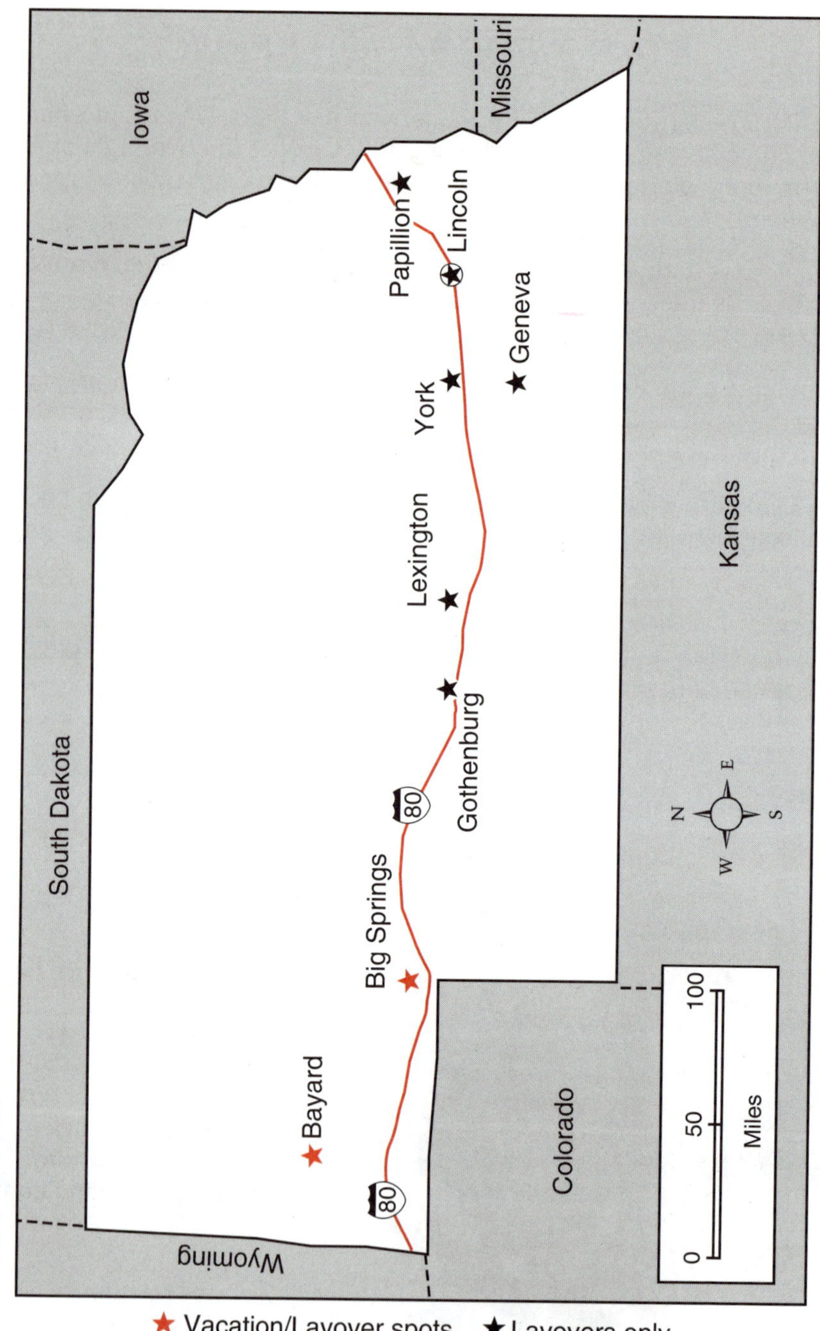

★ Vacation/Layover spots ★ Layovers only
State Capitol Hwy Junction cities

CURRENT NEGATIVE COGGINS, HEALTH CERTIFICATE & OWNERSHIP PAPERS REQUIRED - see page 2 for details

BAYARD, 69334

★ **Flying Bee Beefmaster Ranch LLC, Conrad & Louise Kinnaman**
6755 Cty. Rd. 42 (5 m. S. of Hwy 92 at McGrew on Cty. Rd. 34; 1/2 m. E. on Cty. Rd. 42. 20 m. SE of Scottsbluff)
Ph. **1-888/534-2341** Email:flyingbee@bbc.net Web:www.flyingbee-ranch.com **Facilities:** 7 indoor/18 outdoor stalls, 2 box stalls w/runs, 6 holding pens, hay avail., RV/camper spaces (w/wo hookups), picnic area w/BBQ grill and B&B cabin, sleeps 6 w/full bath/kitchen/AC. Scenic trails, vacation spots nearby. Call for reservations/brochures.

BIG SPRINGS, 69112

★ **HQH Stables & Campground**
1625 Rd. 203 (5 m. off I-80 & 1 m. off US Hwy 30)
Ph. **1-877/241-8653** Fax 308/889-3538 Email:lorie@lakemac.net **Facilities:** 7 indoor/5 outdoor stalls, holding pens, outdoor round pen/arena, walker, 110 ac. riding area, camper hookup w/lite breakfast. Parking space for trailer. Call for reservations/rates. Motels nearby.

GENEVA, 68361

J Bar D Ranch, John W. Wilkins
P.O. Box 73 Location: 1404 N. Hwy 18 (S. of I-80)
Ph. 402/759-3222 **Facilities:** 46 stalls, 20 holding pens, 70x120 indoor arena, 2 camper hookups and 2 bdrm apt. w/ living room & kitchen.

GOTHENBURG, 69138

Pony Express Stables c/o Tim Miller
2700 Lakeview Dr., Lot LL (I-80, exit 211. N. Hwy 47)
Ph. 308/537-7758 Cell 308/529-2676 **Facilities:** Indoor/outdoor stalls, holding pens, hay, arena, camper hookups and an apt. for 2-4 w/refrigerator & stove. Motel nearby.

LEXINGTON, 68850

Horse Motel, Dennis or Cyndi Ocken
204 W. River Rd. (I-80, exit 237. S. 1/4 m., W. 1 m.)
Ph. 308/324-6303 **Facilities:** 8 indoor stalls, holding pens, prefer owner provide own feed, arena, trails & camper hookup. Motels within 1 m.

LEXINGTON, 68850

Plum Creek Veterinary Clinic, Dr. Ken Reynolds D.V.M.
43248 Hwy 283 (I-80, 1.5 m. S. of Lexington Interchange. Hwy 283)
Ph. 308/324-2016 - clinic Residence 308/324-2023 **Facilities:** 8 indoor stalls, if avail., w/rubber flooring, 2 holding pens & camper hookup.

CURRENT NEGATIVE COGGINS, HEALTH CERTIFICATE & OWNERSHIP PAPERS REQUIRED - see page 2 for details

LINCOLN, 68522

Pioneer Stables
3145 Coddington Ave. (I-80, exit Hwy 77 S)
Ph. 402/477-5509 **Facilities:** 15 indoor stalls, feed, indoor/outdoor arenas, access to trails in Pioneer Park and parking w/elec. Stallions okay. Call ahead to make sure stalls avail.

PAPILLION, 68046-5763

Rafter "C" Horse Motel, Dolly Crandall
11701 S. 72 St. (1-80 & Hwy 370)
Ph. 402/331-9468 or 402/690-2963 **Facilities:** 6 stalls, 1 holding pen & camper hookup. Dogs welcome. Call for prices & reservations.

YORK, 68467

Diamond B, Inc., Diane Buss
1605 Road L (N. of I-80)
Ph. 402/362-5439 Email:diamondb@alltel.net **Facilities:** 20 indoor stalls, 6+ holding pens, indoor/outdoor arenas and parking w/elec. & water. Bed & bath on premises for 2 adults April thru Sept. Circle drive, vet on premises & other animals welcome. Call to reserve with credit card & get directions. Motels within 6 m..

NOTES

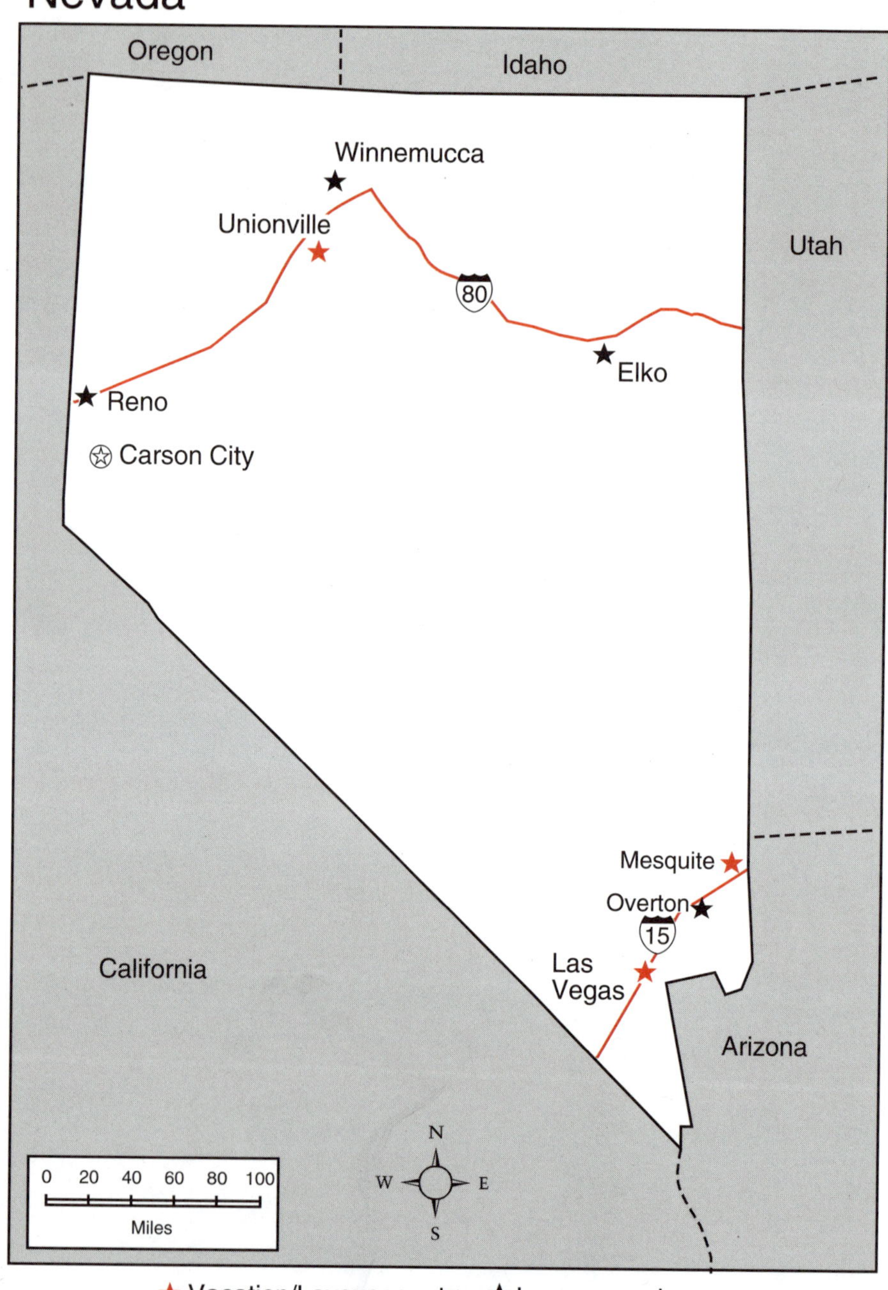
Nevada
Oregon
Idaho
Winnemucca
Unionville
80
Utah
Elko
Reno
Carson City
Mesquite
Overton
15
Las Vegas
California
Arizona
N
W
E
S
0 20 40 60 80 100
Miles
Vacation/Layover spots
Layovers only
State Capitol
Hwy Junction cities

CURRENT NEGATIVE COGGINS, HEALTH CERTIFICATE & OWNERSHIP PAPERS REQUIRED - see page 2 for details

ELKO, 89803

Suzie Creek Arabians
P.O. Box 1360 (I-80 , Hunter exit/292, 3 m. S.)
Ph. 775/738-8631 Email:suzck@ctnis.com Facilities: 14 indoor stalls, 6 outdoor holding pens, provide your own feed & hay, indoor/outdoor arenas & lots of trails.

LAS VEGAS, 89123

★ **Beckridge Ranch, Dick & Gina Beck**
8375 Gilespie St. (I-15, exit 33)
Ph. **1-800/704-8127** Email:beckridgeranch@sprintmail.com **Facilities:** 7 indoor/10 outdoor stalls, round pen, hay, outdoor arena, trails in neighborhood & on desert, 2 camper hookups and apt. w/2 bdrms, bath & kitchen. New RV Park and Hotel & Casino within blocks.

LAS VEGAS, 89129

★ **Valerie Punelli**
5837 El Capitan Way (NW Las Vegas, US Hwy 95, exit 90B/Ann Rd. 2 m. W.)
Ph. 702/645-2350 646-1859 499-4295 **Facilities:** 4 stalls w/runs, 8 outdoor stalls, alfalfa avail. for ad'l fee, lighted arena, hot walker, wash rack & access to desert trails. Call for reservations/rates. Cash only.

LAS VEGAS, 89139

★ **Bamberry Stables, Don & Debbie Bamberry**
7475 Rogers (SW Las Vegas. I-15S, exit 33/Blue Diamond/Pahrump exit)
Ph. 702/361-6620 - Let it ring **Facilities:** Safe, individual pens & access to arena, alfalfa avail. for add'l fee. Located just minutes from the Strip in quiet neighborhood. Motels nearby. Cash only. Call for reservations.

MESQUITE, 89027

★ **Sweet Annie's Bed, Breakfast & Boarding**
1376 Sea Pines (2 m. off I-15)
Ph. 702/346-1373 Cell 702/300-8199 **Facilities:** 2 large outdoor holding pens w/shade, hay incl. and Bed & Breakfast/1 king bedroom, no smoking. Casinos & hotels in town.

OVERTON, 89040

Tanglewood Ranch Horse Motel & Boarding
585 N. Moapa Valley Blvd. (Off I-15, exit 93. 10 m. to ranch)
Ph **1-888/387-8656** 702/397-8654 Call anytime Email:tanglewood@comnett.net **Facilities:** 10-20x20/4-16x16 outdoor stalls, 2 acre turnout, hay cubes, lighted arena, (avail. for clinics, shows, etc.), BLM land surrounding ranch & parking avail. Monthly gymkhanas and 4D barrel races. Best Western right across the field from us.

CURRENT NEGATIVE COGGINS, HEALTH CERTIFICATE & OWNERSHIP PAPERS REQUIRED - *see page 2 for details*

RENO, 89506

Long Ears Long Walk Ranch, Nancy L. Jackson
3205 Indian Ln. (N. of I-80. Hwy 395 to exit 73/Golden Valley Rd.)
Ph. 775/677-7046 **Facilities:** Indoor & outdoor stalls, feed avail., 3 arenas and open trails. Can park R.V. or horse trailers overnight. Specializing in Mules & Tennessee Walking Horses.

RENO, 89511

Meacham Ranch, Monty Meacham
2150 Greentree Lane (Exit 61 off Hwy 395. West on Holcomb Ln., N. on Greentree)
Ph. 775/851-3456 Fax 775/851-1098 **Facilities:** 35 indoor stalls, indoor/outdoor arenas & parking for horse trailers.

RENO, 89512

Reno Livestock Event Center
1350 N. Wells Ave. (I-80, exit Wells Ave. N)
Ph. 775/688-5751 775/232-2791 Web:www.renolaketahoe.com **Facilities:** 660 indoor stalls w/rubber mats, holding pens, indoor/outdoor arenas, camper hookup & parking. Shavings avail. for $6/bag. $19 per night for box stalls; $10 per night for 5 nights; $11 per night for corrals. Motel 6, Days Inn, Holiday Inn within 2 blocks.

UNIONVILLE, 89418

★ **Old Pioneer Garden, Lew & Mitzi Jones, Innkeepers**
2805 Unionville Rd. (17 m. off I-80)
Ph. 775/538-7585 Web:www.virtualcities.com/NV/old pioneer **Facilities:** 3 indoor stalls, pasture, feed at cost, unlimited trails & a very fine Bed & Breakfast.

WINNEMUCCA, 89446

Towne Farms, Pete Towne
P.O. Box 953 Location: 3500 Youngberg (7 m. off I-80, S. Call for map or directions)
Ph. 775/623-4625 Email:townefarms@hotmail.com Web:www.townefarms.com **Facilities:** 7+ stalls, holding pens, feed, 2 arenas & camper hookup. Call for reservations & your needs.

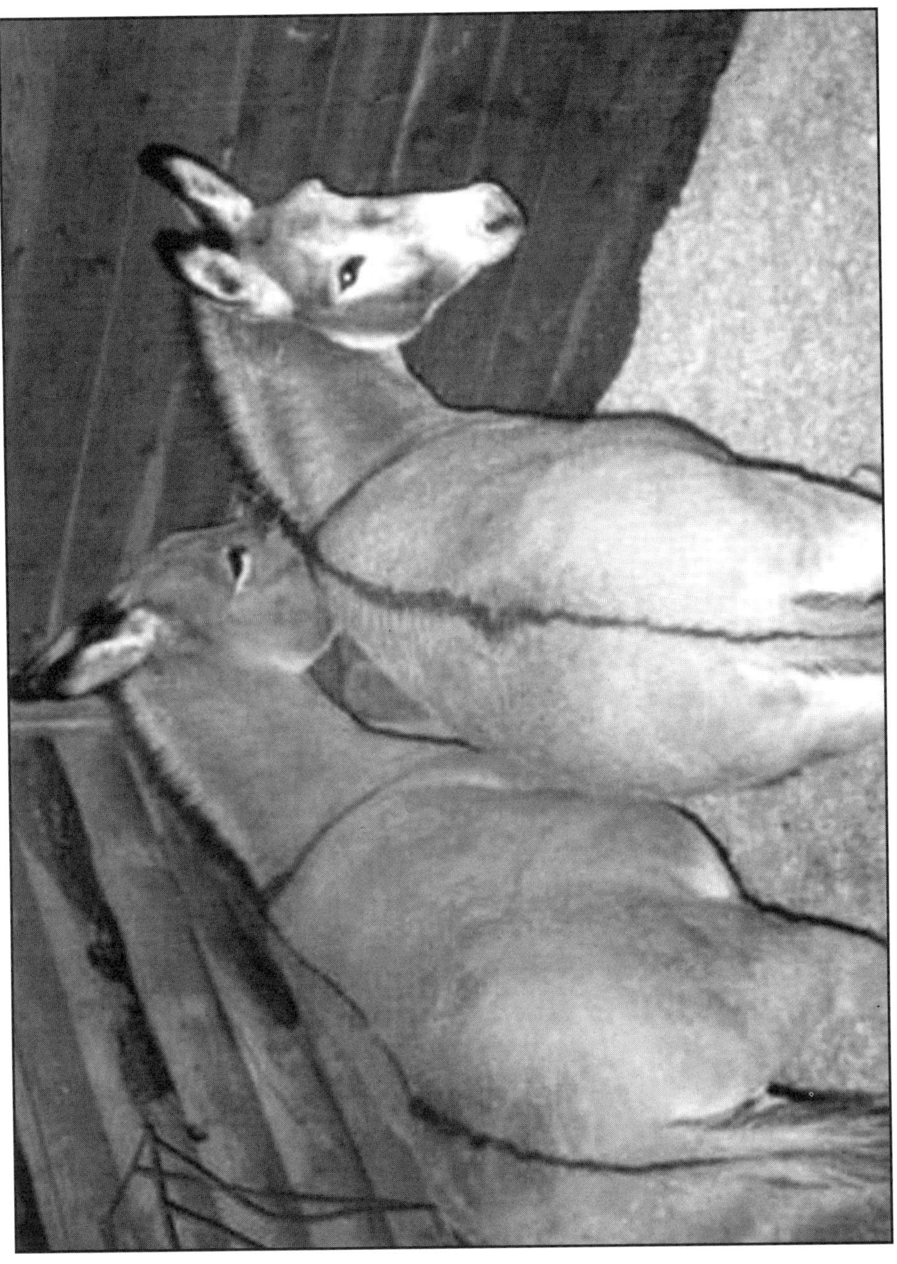

Donkey's Cross Photo by: Jehnet Carlson

New Hampshire

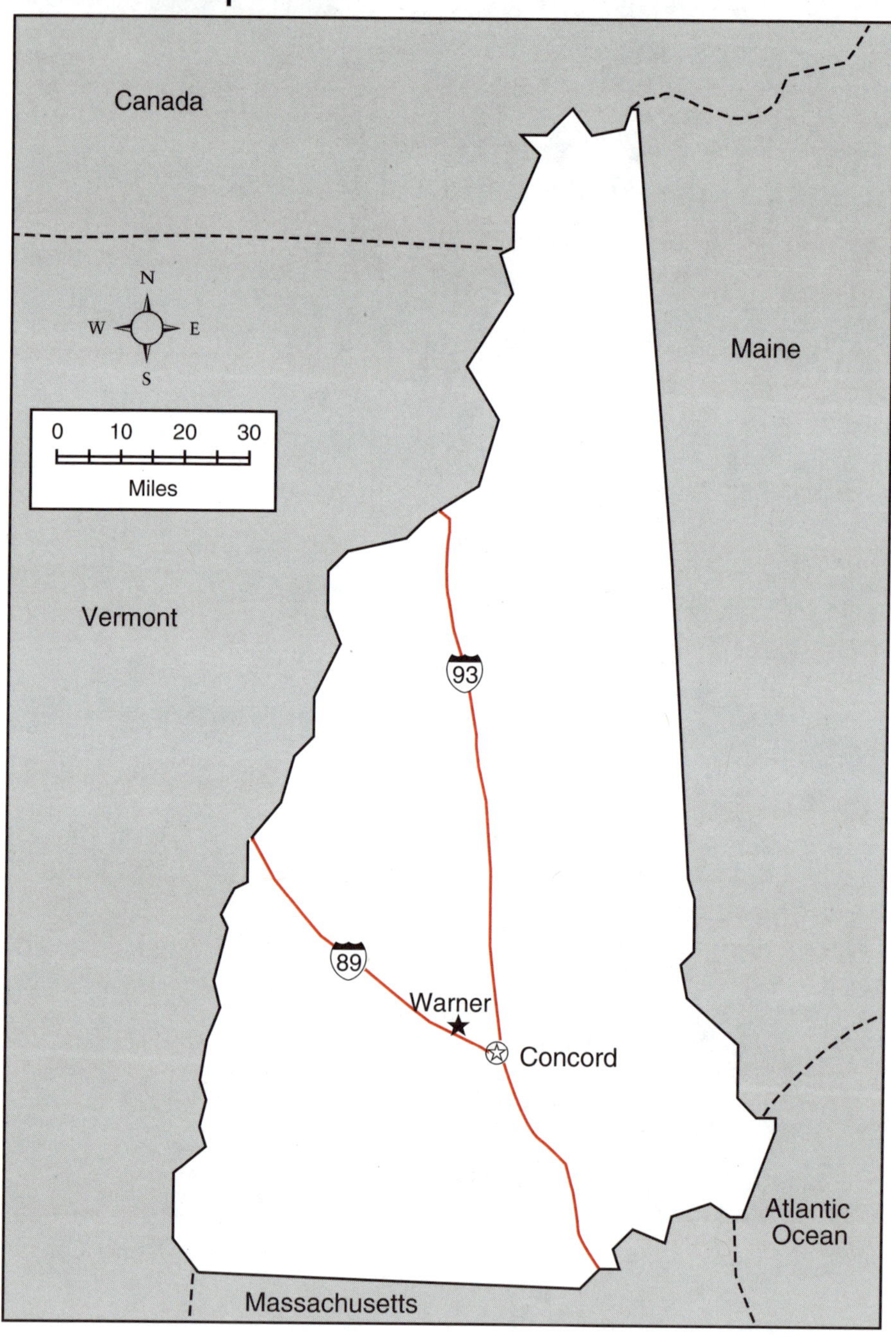

CURRENT NEGATIVE COGGINS, HEALTH CERTIFICATE & OWNERSHIP PAPERS REQUIRED - *see page 2 for details*

WARNER, 03278

Double Clear Farm, Cathy Aranosian
6 Poverty Plains Rd. (Off I-89)
Ph. 603/456-2392 or 603/456-2474 Email:cathf28@aol.com **Facilities:** 20 stall barn, w/indoor riding ring, outdoor show jumping course (gates, barrels, liver-pools, coops, planks, lattice, panels, roll tops), enclosed outdoor ring, round pen & wash rack.

New Mexico

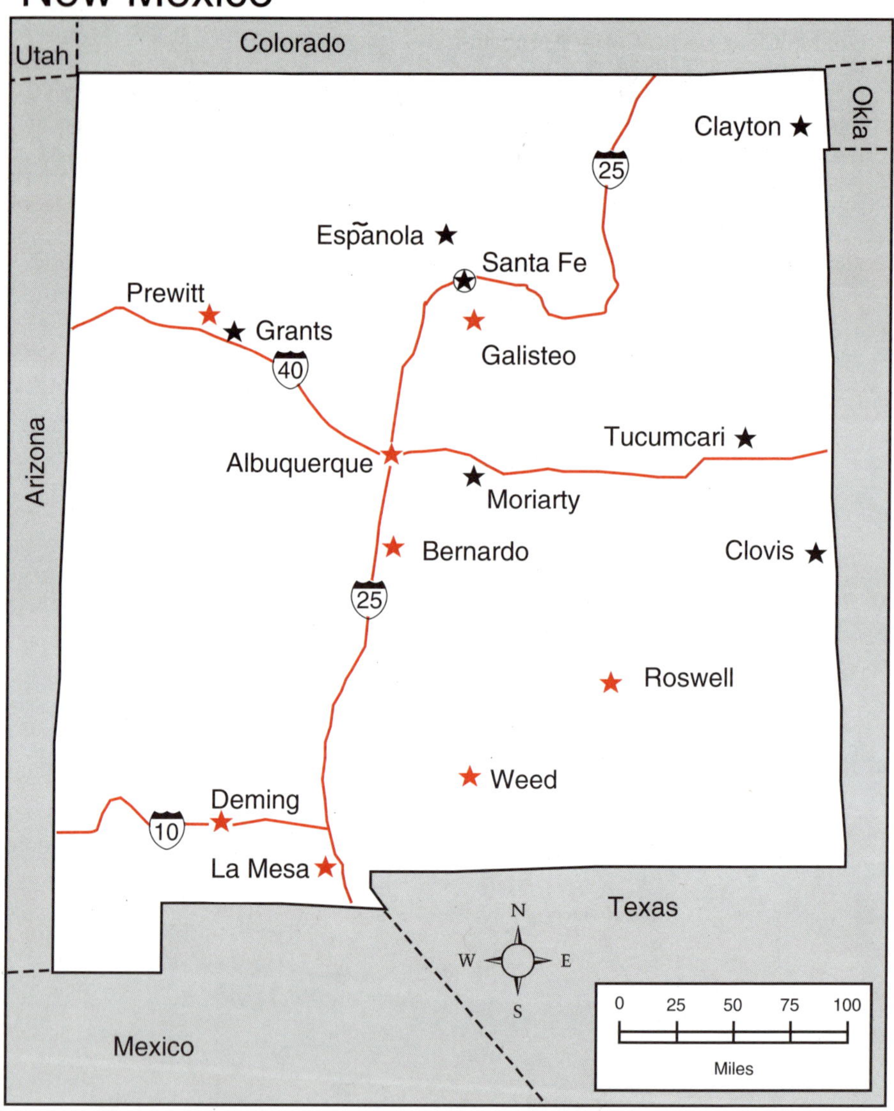

★ Vacation/Layover spots ★ Layovers only
State Capitol Hwy Junction cities

CURRENT NEGATIVE COGGINS, HEALTH CERTIFICATE & OWNERSHIP PAPERS REQUIRED - *see page 2 for details*

ALBUQUERQUE

★ **Cedar Crest Country Cottage & Stables, Donald Romero**
P.O. Box 621, Cedar Crest NM 87008 Location: 47 Snowline Rd. (4 m. N. of I-40 on Hwy 14. 15 min. E. of Albuquerque)
Ph. 505/281-5197 Fax 505/281-1915 Email:dnacccc@aol.com
Web:www.cedarcrestcottage.com
Facilities: 2 covered stalls, 4 outdoor stalls & 3 bdrm country home w/self-sufficient kitchen. No smoking or pets indoors. Restaurants & grocery store nearby. In the Sandia Mtns., adjacent to Cibola Nat'l Forest. Mountain ranch setting.

ALBUQUERQUE, 87105

★ **Spur Stables**
2029 Lakeview Rd. SW (S. of I-40 on I-25, exit 220, W. 2-1/2 m. to Isleta Blvd., S. 1 m. to Lakeview, W. 1/4 m.)
Ph. **1-800/305-1851** 505/873-1997 Fax 505/877-4335 Email:stables@nmia.com Web:www.spurstables.com **Facilities:** 7 indoor/6 outdoor stalls, 17 stalls w/runs, 3 holding pens, arena, walker, trails, camper hookup & guest house. Vet on call. Reservations req.

ALBUQUERQUE, 87114

Rio Grande Stables, Mary-Elizabeth Fain
1251 Bona Terra Loop Mail:5711 Vulcan Vista Dr. N.E., Albuquerque 87111 (Located in beautiful North Valley)
Ph. 505/235-1627
Email:mfain@vscat.com **Facilities:** First class 32-horse facility includes indoor/outdoor stalls, pastures, round pen, arena, wash rack, trailer parking, and on site barn mgr. Quality hay incl. w/fee. Direct access to miles of trails next to the Rio Grande River & thru village of Corrales..

ALBUQUERQUE, 87123

Town-n-Country Feed & Stables
15600 Central S.E. (Exit 170 off of I-40, E. of Albuquerque)
Ph. 505/296-6711 **Facilities:** Outdoor stalls, holding pens, arena, feed & trails. Motels nearby.

CURRENT NEGATIVE COGGINS, HEALTH CERTIFICATE & OWNERSHIP PAPERS REQUIRED - *see page 2 for details*

BERNARDO

★ **Kiva RV Park & Horse Motel, Diane & Robert Wiltshire**
21 Old Hwy 60 W., Bosque NM 87006 (I-25, exit 175, Bernado/Mountainair. Easy on/off)
Ph. 505/861-0691 Email:kivarv@juno.com **Facilities:** 8 indoor 10x12 stalls, 2 outdoor stalls, 3 holding pens, feed/hay, 2 hunter-type jumps arenas, trails, 26 full camper hookups and camper for rent/sleeps 2 adults. Showers & restrooms. Any animals welcome w/health certificates.

CLAYTON, 88415

Oney's, Charley Oney
Rt. 1, Box 87 (823 Curren St. by golf course)
Ph. 505/374-9009 505/374-7919 505/374-2413 **Facilities:** 10 indoor stalls w/outdoor runs, 5 holding pens and camper parking w/elec.

CLOVIS, 88101

"Amigo Del Caballo" Horse Motel & Cattle Rest, Bob Meisenheimer
945 Curry Rd. E. (3 m. W. of the TX/NM border on Hwys 60, 70 & 84)
Ph. 505/742-1033 **Facilities:** 7 indoor pipe stalls w/runs & shoe fly system to control flies, holding pens, 5 acre pasture, roping arena & 2 RV hookups w/elect & water. Owners live on premises. Motels within 4 m.

DEMING, 88030

★ **Diamond Arrow Ranch, Leslie B. Fleming, DVM**
15535 Palomas Rd. SE (From W: I-10, exit 85 E. From E: I-10, exit 102 W)
Ph. 505/546-1115 or 505/544-0076 **Facilities:** 6 outdoor stalls, 3 holding pens, pasture, trails & camper hookup. Clean your own stall. Owners are Vet & farrier.

ESPANOLA, 87532

Roy-El Morgan Farm
1301 N. McCurdy Rd. (25 m. N. of Santa Fe on US 285/84)
Ph. & Fax 505/753/3696 Email:dseybold@cybermesa.com **Facilities:** 6 outdoor pens, some indoor stalls & outdoor arena. Motels & RV park nearby. Call for reservations/rates.

GALISTEO (Santa Fe area), 87540

★ **The Galisteo Inn**
9 La Vega (Hwy 41, exit La Vega in Galisteo)
Ph. 505/466-8200 Fax 505/466-4008 Email:Galisteoin@aol.com
Web:www.galisteoinn.com **Facilities:** 2 outdoor hobing pens, feed and 11 rooms w/Bed & Breakfast in over 200 yr. old hacienda. Swimming pool, massage, hot tub, dry heat sauna, complimentary breakfast, fine dining restaurant, mtn. bikes & horseback riding. Adults & older children. Smoking outside only.

CURRENT NEGATIVE COGGINS, HEALTH CERTIFICATE & OWNERSHIP PAPERS REQUIRED - see page 2 for details

GRANTS, 87020

Pete Lucero
2032 Zuni Canyon Rd. (I-40, exit 81, S. 1/4 m. to Zuni Canyon Rd.)
Ph. 505/876-1000 **Facilities:** 6 indoor stalls, 10 outdoor stalls, hay & grain, arena, walker, trails and camper parking w/elec. & water. Cutting cattle & roping calves avail.

LA MESA, 88044

★ **Armstrong Equine Services**
Rt. 1, Box 303-B (3 m. W. of I-10, Vado exit/155. 15 m. S. of Las Cruces; 25 m. N. of El Paso)
Ph. 505/233-2208 **Facilities:** 40 bedded port-a-stalls, 21 w/runs, arena, walker, exercise area and water/elec for campers. $20/night. Owners live on premises. Motels nearby.

MORIARTY, 87035

Cheryl Feder
160 Martin Rd. (I-40, exit 194. 36 m. E. of Albuquerque. Call for directions)
Ph. 505/832-6380 **Facilities:** 3 indoor stalls, 4 outdoor stalls, under barn, with 36' runs & arena. Overnighters only.

MORIARTY, 87035

Rockin Horse Ranch, Tona Wright
P.O. Box 2790 (Exit 196 off I-40, turn N., go 4.5 m. to CR 6A, turn right, 1st drive on right)
Ph. 505/832-6619 - Patty Wright **Facilities:** 10 indoor/10 outdoor w/cover stalls, holding pens, hay & indoor/outdoor arenas.

PREWITT, 87045

★ **Bluewater Lake Lodge, R.V. & Horse Motel**
3415 Lake Route (I-40, exit 63/Hwy 412, 7 m. S)
Ph. & Fax 505/285-4312 **Facilities:** 5 holding pens, feed, trails, 6 full hookups & 3 hookups w/water & elec. R.V. & Horse Motel open Summer of 2003. Lodge under construction. Bluewater Lake State Park next door.

SANTA FE, 87502

Northern New Mexico Horsemen's Association
P.O. Box 4124 (NNMHA Arena-Rodeo-Fair Grounds on Rodeo Rd.)
Ph. 505/471-6654 or 505/466-6280 Web:www.horse-talk.com/nnmha **Facilities:** 150 outdoor stalls & camping-no hookups. Must provide own care.

SANTA FE, 87507

Nix Farm
1095 Nix Ln. (I-25, exit 282, N.)
Ph. 505/471-8630 Email:rgenenix.aol.com **Facilities:** 6 stalls w/corrals, feed, arena, 4 holding pens & camper hookup avail. Call in advance.

CURRENT NEGATIVE COGGINS, HEALTH CERTIFICATE & OWNERSHIP PAPERS REQUIRED - see page 2 for details

TUCUMCARI, 88401

Haller's Western Drive Stables, Jim & Marlene Haller
P.O. Box 1072 (I-40, exit 331/Camino del Coronado. Close to Hwy 54 & Rt. 66 Motels/restaurants nearby)
Ph. 505/461-0274 505/487-8824 Email:mjhallerstables@shipleysystems.com
Facilities: Overnight or weekly. All pipe pens & stalls, 12x18 covered pens, boxed & bedded stalls & stallion stalls, paddocks, holding pens, exercise area & elec. for campers. All-weather driveway. Reservations preferred. 10 p.m. arrival or call. Owners live on premises.

TUCUMCARI, 88401

Heggelund Quarter Horses, Van Heggelund
P.O. Box 601 Location: 1400 E. Main
Ph. 505/461-3605 Web:www.quarter-horses.info **Facilities:** 10 indoor/15 outdoor stalls, holding pens, pasture, feed, arena, walker, indoor wash rack & camper hookup. Close to motels. Reservations appreciated.

WEED, 88354

★ **Bed and Breakfast & Spa at Raven Wind Ranch, Ravenwild LLC**
1234 NM Hwy 24 (12 mile marker on NM Hwy 24. Off US 82)
Ph.505/687-3073 Fax 505/687-2039 Email:mail@ravenwindranch.com
Web:ravenwindranch.com **Facilities:** 4-10x12 stalls, 2-32x20 holding pens, 75 ac. of pasture, bring your own feed, 60' round pen, trails in adjacent Nat'l Forest and Bed & Breakfast w/2 large rooms, kitchenette, 2 meals. Must stay at B&B. Hot tub/spa. Massage therapist. 2-bdrm cottage night/week.

DIRECTORY USER PROFILE

SURVEY PROFILE

A survey card was sent to 463 current users of the Nationwide Overnight Stabling Directory & Equestrian Vacation Guide, selected at random from every state. The card was postage paid for return of the survey card. There was a 35% return from our users, with 71% of the respondents making comments - 66% were comments of praise, 19% gave personal and informative comments, 14% gave helpful suggestions and less than 1% made negative comments.

WHERE USERS LIVE

Users live in every state in the United States, plus Canada. 65% live in rural areas, and 80% live in cities of less than 25,000 populations. 82% own their own homes.

USERS DEMOGRAPHICS

Of our respondents, 55% were female and 45% were male, with 80% being in the premium buying age of 31 to 60.

For education, occupation and income: 89% have had some college, or are college graduates (59%.) 47% are business owners or work in professional capacities, 31% work in horse-related occupations, 30% work in government or education, and 10% are retired. 81% earn more than $30,000, the breakdown being $30-50,000, 29%; $50-100,000, 29%; and 23% over $100,000.

USERS & THEIR HORSES

98% own horses, with 89% owning two or more. 34% own Quarter Horses, 14% own Thoroughbreds, 11% own Arabians, 11% own Appaloosas, and nearly every other breed is represented (30%,) i.e. Warmblood, Paint, Clydesdale, Paso Finos, Morgan, Draft, Miniature, etc.

Areas of interest/activity of our users: 23% trailriding, 21% competition, 20% pleasure, 19% showing, 13% dressage, 10% breeding, 8% hunter/jumpers, 8% ranching & rodeos and 3% driving.

90% of the respondents have traveled in the last year. Their reasons for travel include: 48% for competition, 39% for pleasure, 30% moving and 22% for training, sales & breeding. The length of an average trip 2-3 days (47%), 19% traveled only one time; 80% traveled 2 or more times; and 25% traveled 10 or more times during the year.

USERS AND THE NATIONWIDE OVERNIGHT STABLING DIRECTORY

80% of ETA's users keep their copy of the Directory 2 or more years; each copy of the Directory is used by 3 or more people; and they like the Directory.

HOW USERS FEEL ABOUT THE NATIONWIDE OVERNIGHT STABLING DIRECTORY & EQUESTRIAN VACATION GUIDE

"I've found the stabling accommodations very nice and the people very friendly and helpful."

"Most helpful! Makes traveling with our horses overnight much safer & more comfortable."

"It is a life saver. I can't believe after hauling horses professionally over-the-road for 9 years, I just recently found this book. It's wonderful."

"Excellent! Extremely helpful! Good resource!"

"Like your service. We enjoy hosting new people."

"The Directory was EXCELLENT in helping me plan my trip from CT to CA - over 3500 miles! I could not have done without the Directory. My trip was very successful - and I was a sole traveler with one horse."

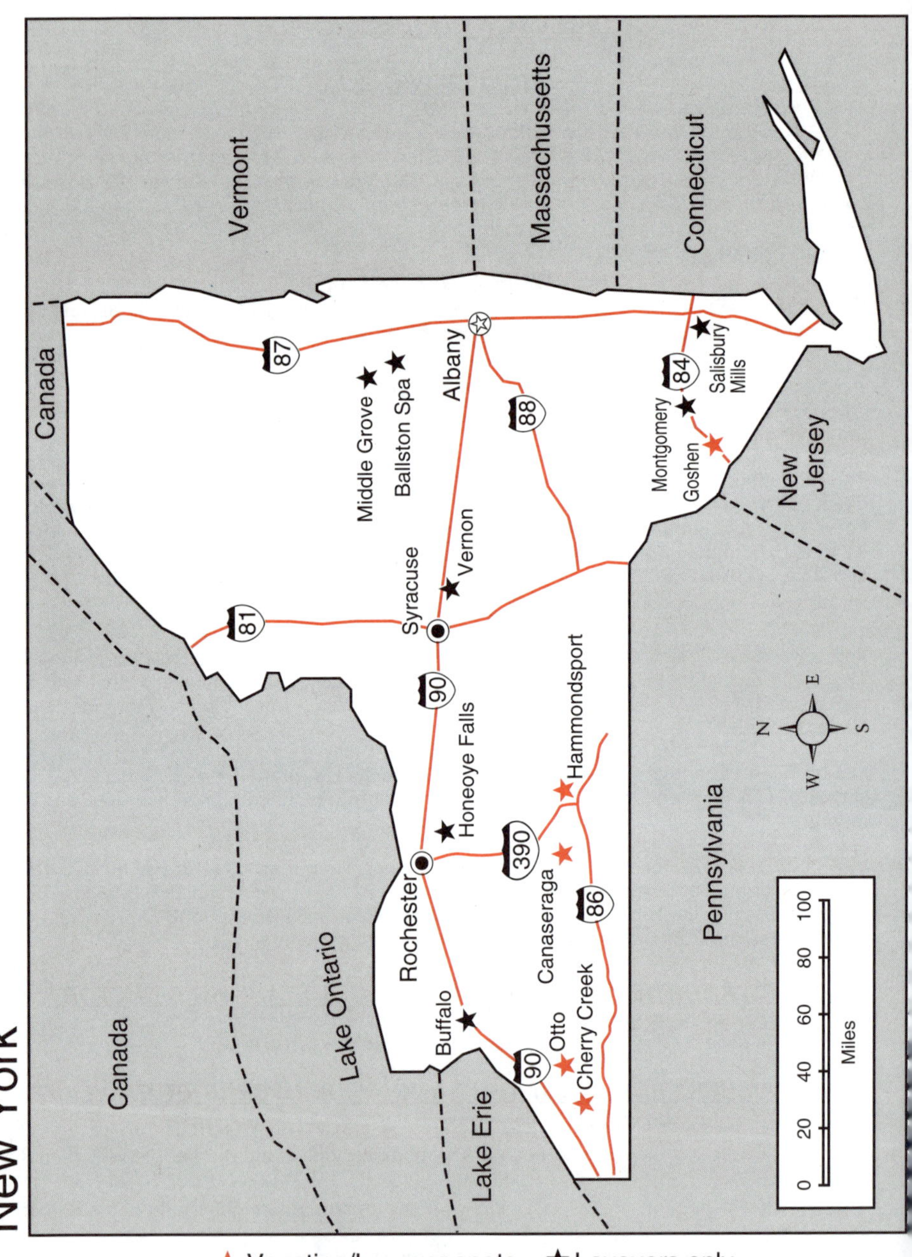

★ Vacation/Layover spots ★ Layovers only
State Capitol Hwy Junction cities

CURRENT NEGATIVE COGGINS, HEALTH CERTIFICATE & OWNERSHIP PAPERS REQUIRED - see page 2 for details

BALLSTON SPA, 12020

Pine Meadow Farm, Celeste Othmer Brown
161 White Rd. (I-87, exit 12. Rt. 87 N. Just minutes from Saratoga Springs))
Ph. 518/884-0723 Fax 518/884-0567 Web:www.pinemeadowfarm.com **Facilities:** 28 stalls, pasture, 70x180 indoor/2 extensive outdoor arenas, parking w/elec. for campers and limited guest rooms - call for availability. Bring own buckets & feed. Facility has been completely renovated - new fencing every amenity for horse & rider.

BUFFALO, 14216

Buffalo Equestrian Center
950 Amherst St. (In Buffalo, 15 min. from I-90)
Ph. 716/877-9295 **Facilities:** 110 indoor stalls. In before 6 p.m. Call for reservations.

CANASERAGA, 14822

★ **Brookdale Farms, James Freiner**
10387 Freiner Rd. (12 m. from both I-86 & I-390. 4 m. from Rt. 36 and 1 m. from Rt. 70)
Ph. 607/545-8650 Fax 607/324-0515 Email:jfreiner@dctmail.com **Facilities:** 6 box stalls, 2 large pastures, indoor exercise area, groomed trails and electrical hookups.

CHERRY CREEK, 14723

★ **Foxe Farmhouse Bed & Barn, Carol Lorenc**
1880 Thornton Rd. (S. of I-90. Co. Rt. 66 off NYS Rt. 60. Near Cockaigne Ski Center)
Ph. 716/962-3412 Email:lorencfoxefarm@madbbs.com Web:www.foxefarmhouse.com **Facilities:** 4-12x12 box stalls, pasture w/run-in shed, miles of trails through 3000 acres, and 3 rooms for Bed & Breakfast in renovated farmhouse. In the heart of Amish country.

GOSHEN, 10924

★ **Silent Farm, John & Mary Quick, owners**
35 Axworthy Ln. (NY Thruway to Rt. 17, exit 124, Rt. 207)
Ph. 845/294-0846 Fax 845/294-0844 Email:silentfarm@pioneeris.net Web:silentfarm.com **Facilities:** 50 indoor stalls, holding pens, pasture, feed, lighted arenas, trails, camper parking w/elec & water, 4 rooms for Bed & Breakfast and 1 bdrm cottage. Dogs, cats & children welcome. Late arrivals no problem.

HAMMONDSPORT, 14840

★ **Donameer Farm, Neal Esposito/Cynthia Harrison**
P.O. Box 355 (I-86, exit 40/Savona, 4 m. from exit)
Ph. & Fax 607/569-2115 Email:donameer@empacc.net **Facilities:** 10-12x12 covered stalls, 15 acres pasture fenced into 8 turnouts, 20+ m. of trails & dirt roads, 12 hookups, 30 amp w/water and 1-rm efficiency cottage. Sugar Hill St. Park 5 m. Well-behaved dogs okay. Open June 1 - October 15.

CURRENT NEGATIVE COGGINS, HEALTH CERTIFICATE & OWNERSHIP PAPERS REQUIRED - see page 2 for details

HONEOYE FALLS, 14472

Equestrian Village
44 Sheldon Rd. (10 m. from Rochester. 5 m. S. of NY Thruway, exit 46)
Ph. 585/624-5250 Email:kathykissinger@hotmail.com **Facilities:** Bed & Breakfast w/3 bdrms for Equestrians traveling with their horses. Paddocks w/protected lean-tos & auto waterers, feed, pasture and parking space for trailers. Visit our website at equestrianvillage.com

MIDDLE GROVE, 12850

Braken Farm, Dolores Arste
6326 Barkersville Rd. (Off Rt. 29, Mosherville. 15 m. E. of Johnstown, I-90, exit 28; 15 m. W. of Saratoga Springs, I-87, exit 15).
Ph. 518/882-6485 Fax 845/818-3871 Email:darste@emi.com **Facilities:** 10 stalls, pasture, feed, indoor/outdoor arena, elec. hookup only, space for camper & horse trailer parking. Motels neary..

MONTGOMERY, 12549

Highland Farm, Yvonne Turchiarelli
2101 Rt. 17K (I-84, exit 5; 8 m. W. on Rt. 17K)
Ph. 914/361-2204 **Facilities:** 24 indoor stalls, 8 turnouts, pasture, paddocks, feed/hay & trailer parking. Quiet atmosphere, immaculate barn. Vet nearby. $25 per night.

OTTO, 14766

★ **Recreation Ranch Estate (R&R), Alice Ferguson, owner/mgr.**
P.O. Box 139, 8940 Lange Rd. (Hwy 86, exit 16 - Hwys 394/242/353, Lovers Lane to CR 12. I-90, exit Hwy 219, 8 m. W. on Lindberg/Hinman Hollow/Maple to 12)
Ph. 716/257-5663 Fax 716/257-5664 Email:info@rrduderanch.com
Web:www.rrduderanch.com **Facilities:** 27 stalls, 5 holding pens, 7 pastures, Blue Seal feed, arena, elec. for campers, 13 m. of trails, 5 rooms for Bed & Breakfast in 100 yr. old farm home & cabins. Ideal for conditioning. Year round facility. Camping/fishing/rental horses/winter activities.

SALISBURY MILLS, 12577

Old Oak Farm, Mark Gisselbrecht
P.O. Box 171 Location: 333 Woodcock Mountain Rd. (I-84, exit 7. I-87, between exits 16 & 17)
Ph. 845/496-2894 Email:cowboy1@frontiernet.net **Facilities:** 4 outdoor/several indoor stalls, hay/grain, grass arena, access to trails & camper parking. Hotel info avail. Cash only. 24 hrs. notice required.

VERNON, 13476

Morning Star Farm, Deborah Martin
4101 State Rt. 26 (I-90, exit 33)
Ph. 315/829-3454 **Facilities:** 30 indoor stalls, pasture, feed, trails & parking. Late arrival OK.

NOTES

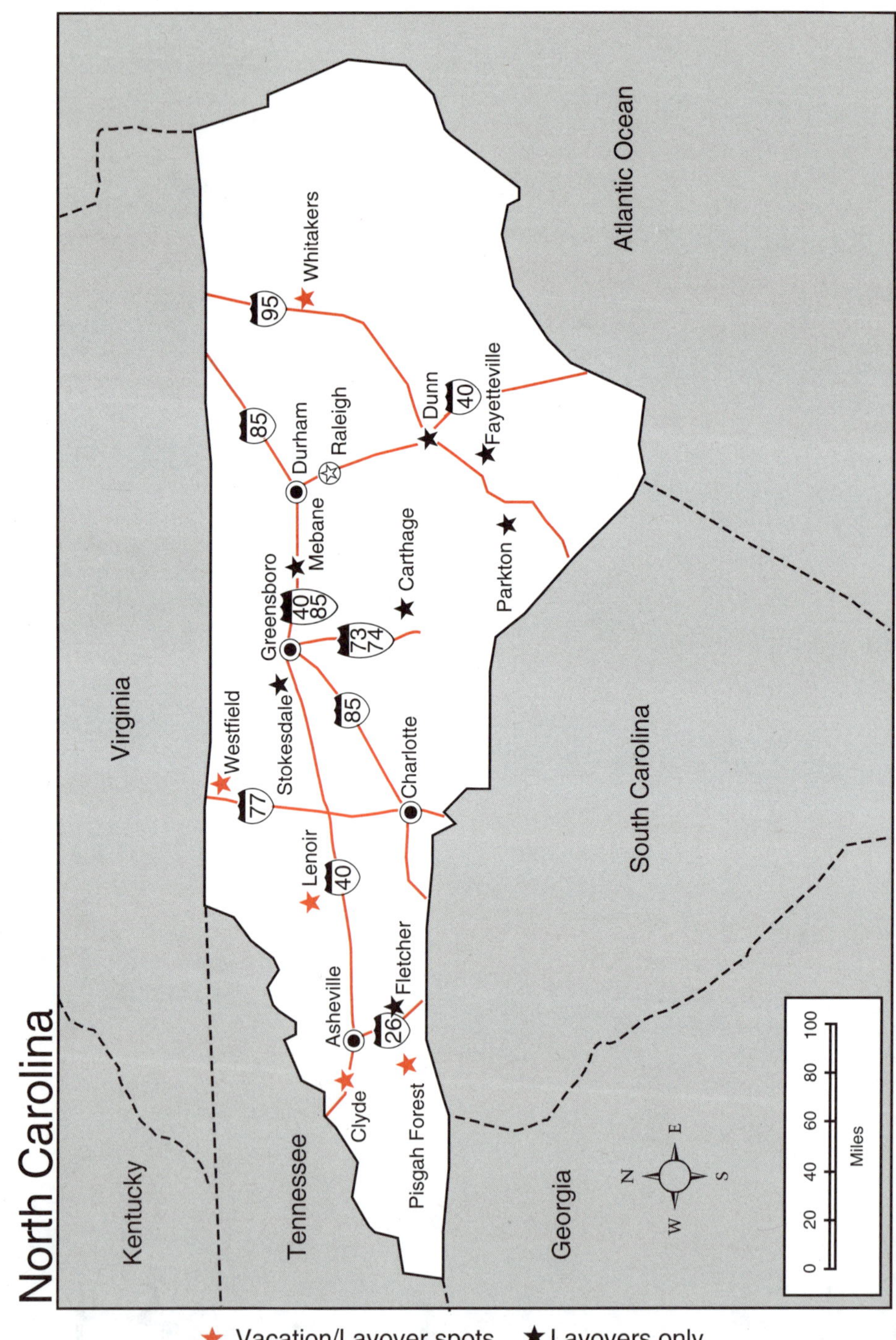

★ Vacation/Layover spots ★ Layovers only
State Capitol Hwy Junction cities

CURRENT NEGATIVE COGGINS, HEALTH CERTIFICATE & OWNERSHIP PAPERS REQUIRED - see page 2 for details

CARTHAGE, 28327

The Crowsnest at Briargait Farm, KarenStavermann
417 Farm Life School Rd. (6 m. E. off US 1. 1 hr. S. of Raleigh & 10 min. from Walter Moss Foundation in Southern Pines)
Ph. 910/947-3051 Email:crowsnest11@hotmail.com **Facilities:** 2 stall barn home w/private entrance to 1-bdrm/sleeps 2 w/private bath, 2 pastures w/run-in sheds, feed avail., round pen & trails. Vet/farrier on call. Call in advance for reservations/rates.

CLYDE, 28721

★ **Best Haven Farm, Marty & Karen Best**
1028 Lost Cove Rd. Location: 95 Glades Rd. (I-40, exit 24. N. on Hwy 209. Apx. 5 m. from I-40, 15 m. from Smokies Park)
Ph. 828/627-2076 - barn Home 828/627-3044 **Facilities:** 12 indoor stalls, holding pens, pasture, grain/hay, outdoor arena, next to Great Smokies Nat'l Park trails & parking space for campers. Farrier avail. Call for reservations.

DUNN, 28334

Aysgarth Stables, Faith & Ted Bradshaw
129 Bumpas Creek Access (4 m. W. off I-95, exit 71)
Ph. 910/892-4030 **Facilities:** 6 stall barn, turnout paddocks, wash stall, tractor/trailer parking and Bed & Breakfast on site. Electric gates for security. Dog kennels on site. Much more, call for details & reservations.

DUNN, 28334

Town's End, Dean Wiley
7785 Burnett Rd. (I-95, exit 65. 2 m. W. on Hwy 82)
Ph. 910/980-1804 **Facilities:** 30 indoor stalls, 2 holding pens, feed, lighted arena & very good trails.

FAYETTEVILLE, 28301

Flying "C" Ranch, Greg Combs & Mary Jo Cobett
2132 Evans Dairy Rd. (1 m. from I-95, exit 49. 50 m. N. of the South/North Carolina border. Easy access)
Ph.910/483-6583 Email:gcombs@wireweb.net **Facilities:** 30 ac. ranch dedicated to overnight stabling. New facility includes 12x12 stalls, 60x80 paddocks, 2-10 ac pastures w/Horse Guard fencing, 15 m. of trails across from facility & bunk house at stable w/shower. Numerous hotels avail.

FLETCHER, 28732

Kadora Farms, Jerry Laughter
260 Williams Rd. (I-26, exit 9, on Hwy 280)
Ph. 828/687-1958 Email:kadora1@juno.com **Facilities:** 5 indoor stalls, 3 holding pens, hay & grain, outdoor ring & parking only. Call for reservations.

CURRENT NEGATIVE COGGINS, HEALTH CERTIFICATE & OWNERSHIP PAPERS REQUIRED - *see page 2 for details*

LENOIR, 28645

★ **Horseplay Ranch**
1154 Woodrow Pl. (NW of I-40. Less than 2 m. off Hwy 64/90; 6 m. from Lenoir)
Ph. 828/757-9114 - best to call after dark or leave message
Email:eve28645@aol.com **Facilities:** Indoor/outdoor stalls, portable stall areas, feed store w/hay & arena nearby, many trails, beautiful/primitive camping (9 indoor stalls here) w/picnic tables, camper parking (pond & hand pump only,) primitive log cabin, fishing, BBQ grill, camp fire area.

MEBANE, 27302

Brindabella Farms LLC, Enid R. Kafer
3720 Mebane Oaks Rd. (I-40/85, exit 154/Mebane Oaks Rd. On edge of Chapel Hill & the research triangle)
Ph. 919/304-3473 Fax 919/304/3424 Email:enidkafer@mindspring.com Web:www.brindabellahorses.com Pager **1-800/458-2397** **Facilities:** 10 covered/3 open corrals, 10-stall mare barn, round pen, dressage arena, grassed arena, forest trails, 10 ac. conditioning track, parking for trailers & kennels for dogs. Ad'l visitor barn under construction. Vets on call. Res. preferred. MC/Visa accepted.

PARKTON, 28371

NSE Stables
342 Canady Rd. (I-95N, exit 33, left on Hwy 301 N. 5.8 m. left on Canady. I-95S, exit 41 to 301S. From 301/95 split, go 2.2 m., right on Canady))
Ph. 910/858-2545 Pager 910/437-7486 **Facilities:** 24-12x12 stalls, 7 holding pens, 5 pastures, lunge pen, arenas w/hunt course & dressage, H&C wash area and groom's room for rent. Equine vet owned.

PISGAH FOREST, 28768

★ **The Walk Inn, Kathy Case**
Mail: 1083 Wilson Rd. Location: 157 Little River Campground Rd. (I-26, exit 9, Asheville Airport/WNC Agricultural Center. Hwy 280 West. Call for directions)
Ph. 828/884-WALK Fax 828/862-5518 Email:kcase@citcom.net
Web:www.TheWalkInn.com **Facilities:** A Bed & Breakfast accommodating 3 couples and 6 horses. 12x12 stalls & turnout in grass area. Ride from the property to Dupont State Forest or haul to Pisgah Nat'l Forest or Biltmore Estate. Full hookups avail., tent camping. Cattle panels avail. for horses.

STOKESDALE, 27357

Windy Knoll Farm - Horse & Rider Accommodations
494 Lemons Rd. (Hwy 220 & Hwy 68)
Ph. 336/643-7582 **Facilities:** 4 indoor stalls. Call for rates/reservations (pets must be crated.)

CURRENT NEGATIVE COGGINS, HEALTH CERTIFICATE & OWNERSHIP PAPERS REQUIRED - *see page 2 for details*

WESTFIELD, 27053

★ **Forbes Farm**

2879 Horseshoe Rd. (20 min. off Hwy 52/I-74 - new alternate rt. from I-77 to 85. Call & we will fax or mail directions traveling N. or S.)

Ph. 336/351-3941 Fax 336/351-3949 **Facilities:** 5 indoor stalls, 4 shelters w/grass turnouts, rubber fencing, 2 holding pens, pasture, arena, mowed trails & accommodations in 2 self-contained double log cabins & a double annex; ea. sleeps 3. Supper & continental breakfast. Pets welcome. Ideal for longer stay.

WHITAKERS (Rocky Mount area)

★ **Creekside Horse Complex, Vickie & Thorp Baker**

2505 Creekridge Dr., Rocky Mount NC 27804 Location: 4236 Massengale Rd., Whitakers (3 m. off I-95, exit 145)

Ph. 252/443-3145 - stables Home 252/443-6770 **Facilities:** 23 indoor stalls, 11 holding pens, 5 pastures, feed incl., lunge-ring, & indoor arena, 106 acres of trails, 2 spaces avail. for campers & guest house.

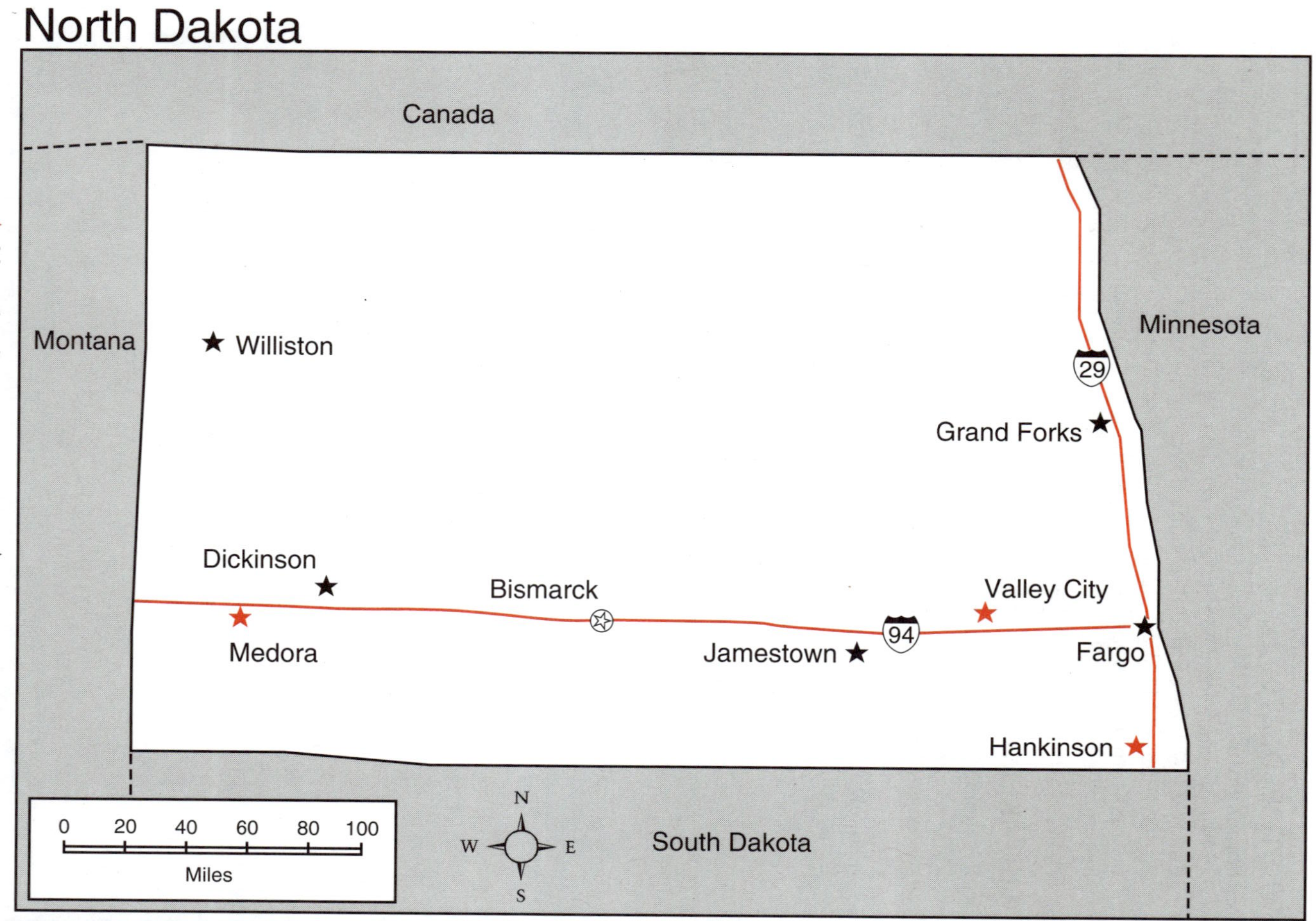

★ Vacation/Layover spots ★ Layovers only
State Capitol ◉ Hwy Junction cities

CURRENT NEGATIVE COGGINS, HEALTH CERTIFICATE & OWNERSHIP PAPERS REQUIRED - *see page 2 for details*

DICKINSON, 58601

North Forty
11042 - 32nd "R" St. SW (I-94 to Hwy 22, N. 4 m., E. 1/2 m)
Ph. 701/227-1915 or 701/483-4886 **Facilities:** 15 indoor stalls, holding pens, pasture, hay/water, close to Badlands trails, parking space w/elec & room to park horse trailers. Motels and B&B in Dickinson.

FARGO, 58104

Breezy Manor Equestrian Centre, Buel Sonderland
6340 77 St. S. (3 m. W. of I-29, exit 60; 4 m. S. of I-94, exit 346A)
Ph. 701/277-9517 or 701/280-0073 Web:www.breezymanor.org **Facilities:** 64stalls, 6 holding pens, feed, 80x200 heated indoor arena, 5 m. of trails and 3 elec. hookups.

GRAND FORKS 58201

Kusters Wagon Wheel Stables, Myron & Joyce Kuster
5100 47th Ave. S. (1 m. S, 3/4 m. W. of I-29, exit 138)
Ph. 701/772-6526 **Facilities:** Indoor stalls, hay & oats incl. and indoor/outdoor arenas avail.

N O R T H D A K O T A

CURRENT NEGATIVE COGGINS, HEALTH CERTIFICATE & OWNERSHIP PAPERS REQUIRED - see page 2 for details

HANKINSON, 58041

★ **Huufda Hotel, Kevin & Marie Crago**
9410 - 171 Ave. S.E. (1/4 m. E. of exit 8, I-29. 50 m. S. of Fargo)
Ph. 701/242-9898 **Facilities:** 8 box stalls, 4-16x20 stalls w/outdoor runs, 4 holding pens, feed incl., arena, round pen, trails in Nat'l Grasslands - 8 m., 2 camper hookups and 2 rooms for Bed & Breakfast. 8 m. from Dakota Magic Casino w/new 64 room hotel. Specializing in TN Walking Horses.

JAMESTOWN, 58401

American West, Linda Levin/Thomas Sagaser
3523 79th Ave. S.E. (I-94 & US Hwy 281)
Ph. 701/252-0452 701/252-2792 **Facilities:** 12 indoor/4 outdoor stalls, holding pens, feed & large vehicle parking. B&B nearby.

MEDORA, 58645

★ **Medora Boarding Stables, Lyle Glass, mgr.**
P.O. Box 198 (1/2 m. off I-94, exit 24 & 27)
Ph. **1-800/633-6721** 701/623-4444 Email:medora@medora.com
Web:www.medora.com **Facilities:** 24-12x30 half-covered pens w/water, hay, rodeo arena, washrack & limited parking for RV's. Trails in Badlands & Theodore Roosevelt Nat'l Park. Reservations recommended. Security lights. Historic restored cowtown.

VALLEY CITY, 58072

★ **North Dakota Winter Show Complex, Dale Hildebrant, Mgr.**
P.O. Box 846 (I-94, exit 292 N)
Ph. **1-800/437-0218** 701/845-3914 Email:ndws@rrnet.com Web:www.ndws.org
Facilities: 300 indoor stalls, holding pens, hay & bedding, indoor arena and 30 camper spaces w/elec. Hours: 8 to 3:30 Central. Arrive by 3:30 p.m. or make prior arrangements. Open March thru November.

WILLISTON, 58801

Bob Roles
P.O. Box 1154 (Hwy 2 & Hwy 85 N. 5 m. N., 1 m. W)
Ph. 701/572-2905 **Facilities:** 11 indoor, heated stalls, 10 indoor, unheated stalls, hay/oats, indoor arenas & walker. Motels & camper hookups in town.

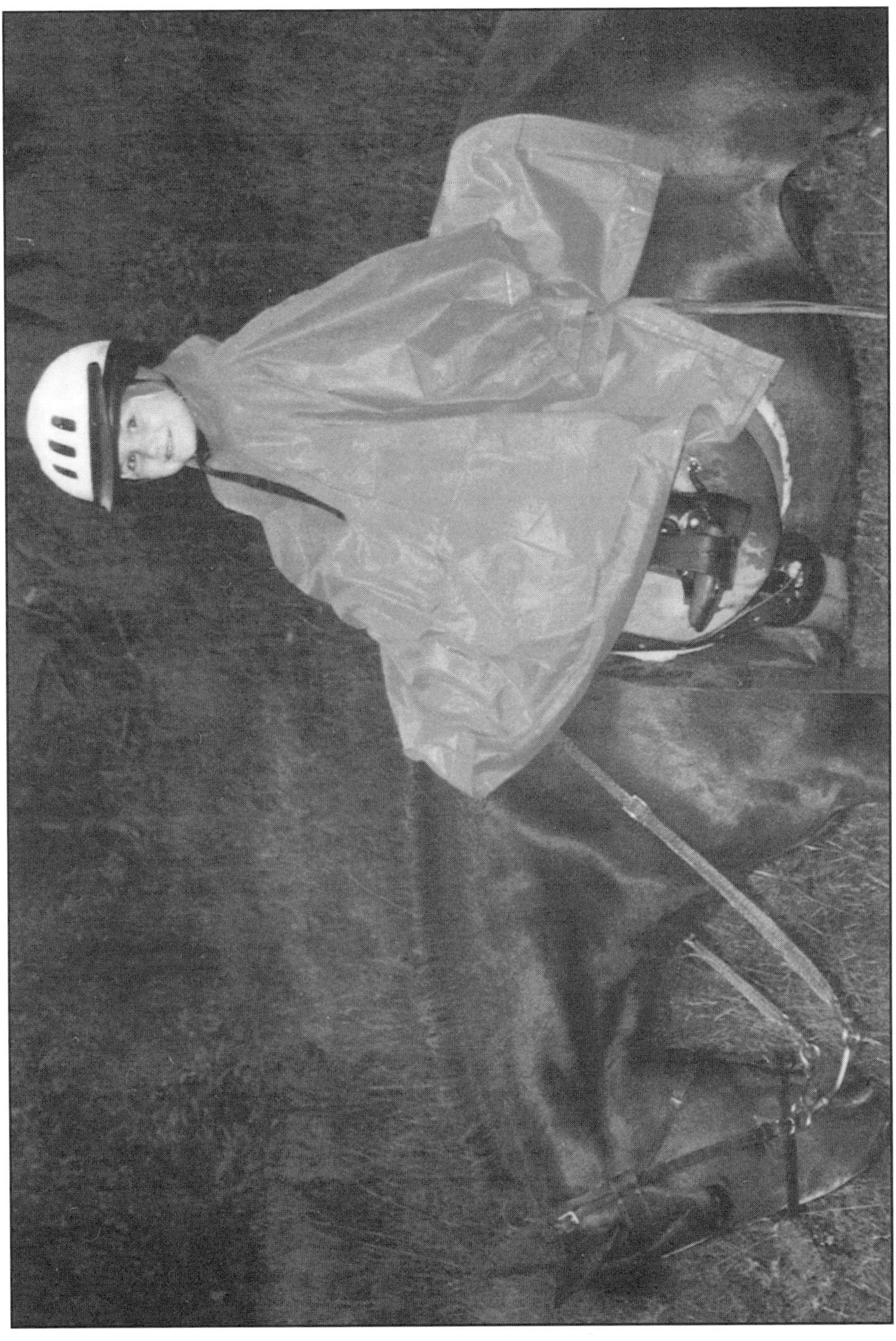

Aim in Rain Gear

Photo by: Kris Robards

Ohio

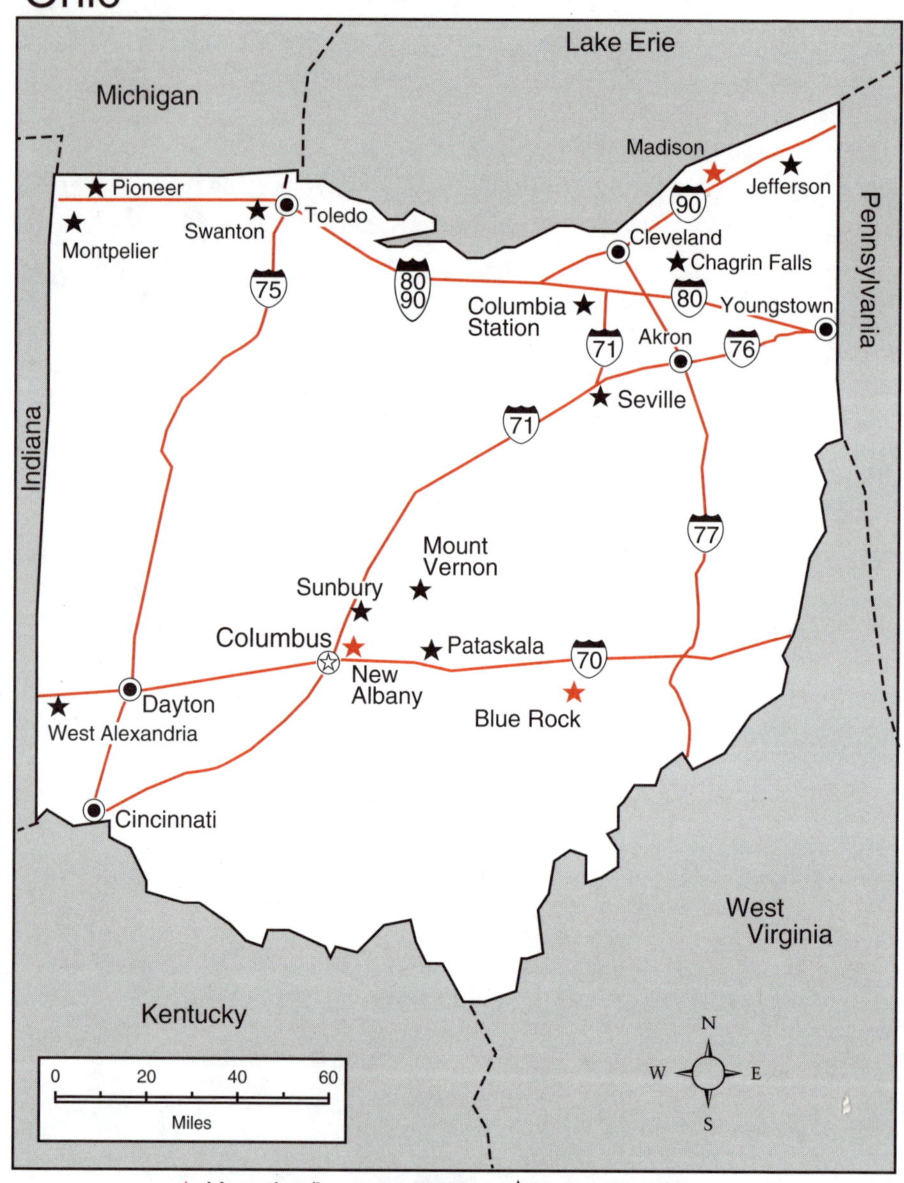

★ Vacation/Layover spots ★ Layovers only
State Capitol Hwy Junction cities

CURRENT NEGATIVE COGGINS, HEALTH CERTIFICATE & OWNERSHIP PAPERS REQUIRED - *see page 2 for details*

BLUE ROCK, 43720

★ **McNutt Farm II Outdoorsman Lodge & Horse Motel**
6120 Cutler Lake Rd. (11 m. SE of Zanesville. Off I-70, exit 155S/SR 60S. 35 m. SW of I-77, Cambridge exit. All blacktop roads)
Ph. 740/674-4555 **Facilities:** Stalls for your horse ($10 ea.) & lodging for you ($40 ea.) For longer stays (vacationing), call for fees. Vet/farrier on call. Call for reservations/details. Pets $5 ea. 9 AM check out/extra$ after 9 AM. Check in 5 to 7 PM.

CHAGRIN FALLS, 44023

Saddlebrook Farm, Patti Carleton
17650 Auburn Rd. (Rts. 422 & 44. Off I-480)
Ph. 440/543-9253 **Facilities:** 18 stalls, 12x12 & 16x16 paddocks, pasture, feed, indoor/outdoor arenas and 4 rooms for Bed & Breakfast. Reservations required.

COLUMBIA STATION, 44028

Dinglewood Farm, Mary Sollan
18650 S. Boone St. (I-71, W. on Rt. 82 I-80, Strongville exit 10 to Rt. 42 S. to Rt. 82, W. to Boone)
Ph. 440/236-3624 Email:dinglewood@aol.com **Facilities:** 2 indoor stalls, round pen, pasture, hay (grass/timothy) & arena. Camper hookup no avail. Advance Reservations.

JEFFERSON, 44047

Grand Haven Stable
1946 E. Union Rd. (Between Cleveland & Erie. S. of I-90. 2 m. from SR 11 at Rt. 307 exit)
Ph.440/858-2164 Email:grandhvn@suite224.net
Web:www.grandhavenstable.com **Facilities:** 38 indoor/66 outdoor covered stalls, holding pens, if avail., bedding & hay provided, 1 indoor/1 outdoor/warmup arenas, seasonal trails, camper parking, 20 new hookups w/elec. and 1 or 2 rooms usually avail.

MADISON, 44057

★ **Shillelagh Farm, Paul Hanahan**
4541 Turney Rd. (I-90, 30 m. E. of Cleveland, 50 m. W. of Erie PA)
Ph. 440/259-5550 Email:hanahan@alltel.net **Facilities:** 9 indoor stalls, outdoor turnout, outdoor arena, wash rack w/hot&cold water & camper hookup. $20/night/horse.

MONTPELIER, 43543

Scottfarm Boarding Stables, Kerren Scott
11222 Co. Rd. N. 30 (I-80/90, exit 2 at Holiday City. Call for directions)
Ph. 419/485-3508 Email:scottfarm123@hotmail.com **Facilities:** 10 stalls, automatic waterers, 7 acre pasture field w/automatic waterer, heated wash bay, 60x120 indoor/70x120 outdoor arenas, round pen, 2 tack rooms, restroom facility w/shower, heated office w/observation window & elec. hookup avail..

CURRENT NEGATIVE COGGINS, HEALTH CERTIFICATE & OWNERSHIP PAPERS REQUIRED - see page 2 for details

MOUNT VERNON, 43050

Giddy Up Stables, Keitha Smith
8980 Tucker Rd. (NE of Columbus on US 36)
Ph. 740/397-6237 Email:GiddyUpStables@aol.com
Web:www.members.tripod.com/piderwoman **Facilities:** 11-12x12 & 12x14 box stalls, round pen, 5 pastures, paddock and/or outdoor training arena & can provide feed/hay. Small, quiet, peaceful facility in the pretty rolling hills SW of Mt. Vernon.

MOUNT VERNON, 43050

Willow Brook Farm Stables, Ray Wortman
9450 Dunham Rd. (W. of Mt. Vernon)
Ph. 740/397-7153 Email:gww564@infinet.com
Web:www.willowbfs.com **Facilities:** Small Quiet Horse Boarding facility. Overnight guests welcome. 10-11x12 matted stalls w/sawdust bedding, paddocks, pastures, feed, hay, tack room, storage & elecric hookups.

NEW ALBANY, 43054

★ **Herald House Bed & Breakfast and Stables, Connie & Nelson Mercier**
11681 Johnstown Rd., St. Rt. 62 (I-71 N. to Rt. 161 Express to New Albany/Johnstown exit. E. on St. Rt. 62)
Ph. 614/939-0322 Email:conmer592@cs.com **Facilities:** 3 indoor stalls, fenced pasture, parking space and 2 private rooms with full/continental breakfast. Non-smoking/non-alcohol facility. Call for reservations. Arrive by 9 p.m. or call. MUST HAVE VALID CREDIT CARD.

PATASKALA, 43062

Hawk's Nest Farm
8056 Outville Rd. (2 m. N. of I-70, exit 122. Rt. 158.)
Ph. 330/336-8104 **Facilities:** 6-8 indoor stalls, pasture & feed avail., trails, 1 camper hookup, & bunkhouse avail. Dogs welcome. No stallions. Requirements: Depart by 9 a.m.; arrive no earlier than 4 p.m.

CURRENT NEGATIVE COGGINS, HEALTH CERTIFICATE & OWNERSHIP PAPERS REQUIRED - see page 2 for details

PIONEER, 43554-9770

Silver Creek Tack & Saddle Repair, Paul & Edna Goble
19-484 St. Rt. 15 (5-1/2 m. N. of OH Turnpike exit. 13.2 m. at OH-MI line)
Ph. 419/737-3214 **Facilities:** 6 indoor stalls, 3 pastures w/sheds, feed avail. & camper parking w/elec

SEVILLE, 44273

Flowers' Fabled Stables, Denny & Kay Flowers
2 m. from I-71 & I-76 interchange. Call for directions.
Ph. 330/887-5482 **Facilities:** 4-6 indoor box stalls, round pen, turn-out pastures & trails. Certified equine massage therapy.

SUNBURY, 43074

L & M Vacation Boarding, John H. Steen
9224 ESR 37 (20 m. N. of Columbus off I-71, exit 131)
Ph.740/965-9971 Fax 614/416-9246 Email:jsteen@xo.com **Facilities:** 2 stalls, holding pens, pasture, full feed & 60' corral if required.

SWANTON, 43558

Post & Rail Stable, Inc., Bonnie Cicora, owner
10362 St. Hwy 64 (I-80/I-90, Airport exit)
Ph. 419/826-9934 **Facilities:** 40 indoor stalls, 4 round pens, 2 pastures, feed, indoor arena, walker, wash rack & camper hookup. 10 p.m. arrival or call.

WEST ALEXANDRIA, 45381

Surecare Farm, Scott & Barb Stockslager
7089 St. Rt. 35E (8 m. S. of I-70)
Ph. 937/839-4186 Fax 937/839-1138 Email:surecare@infinet. Equines & Canines stop in for a good nights sleep & bring your owner. **Facilities:** 3 indoor stalls, paddock, pastures, feed/hay, parking & hookup for camper/trailer and Bed & Continental Breakfast for 2. Vet on call. Call for reservations/accommodations.

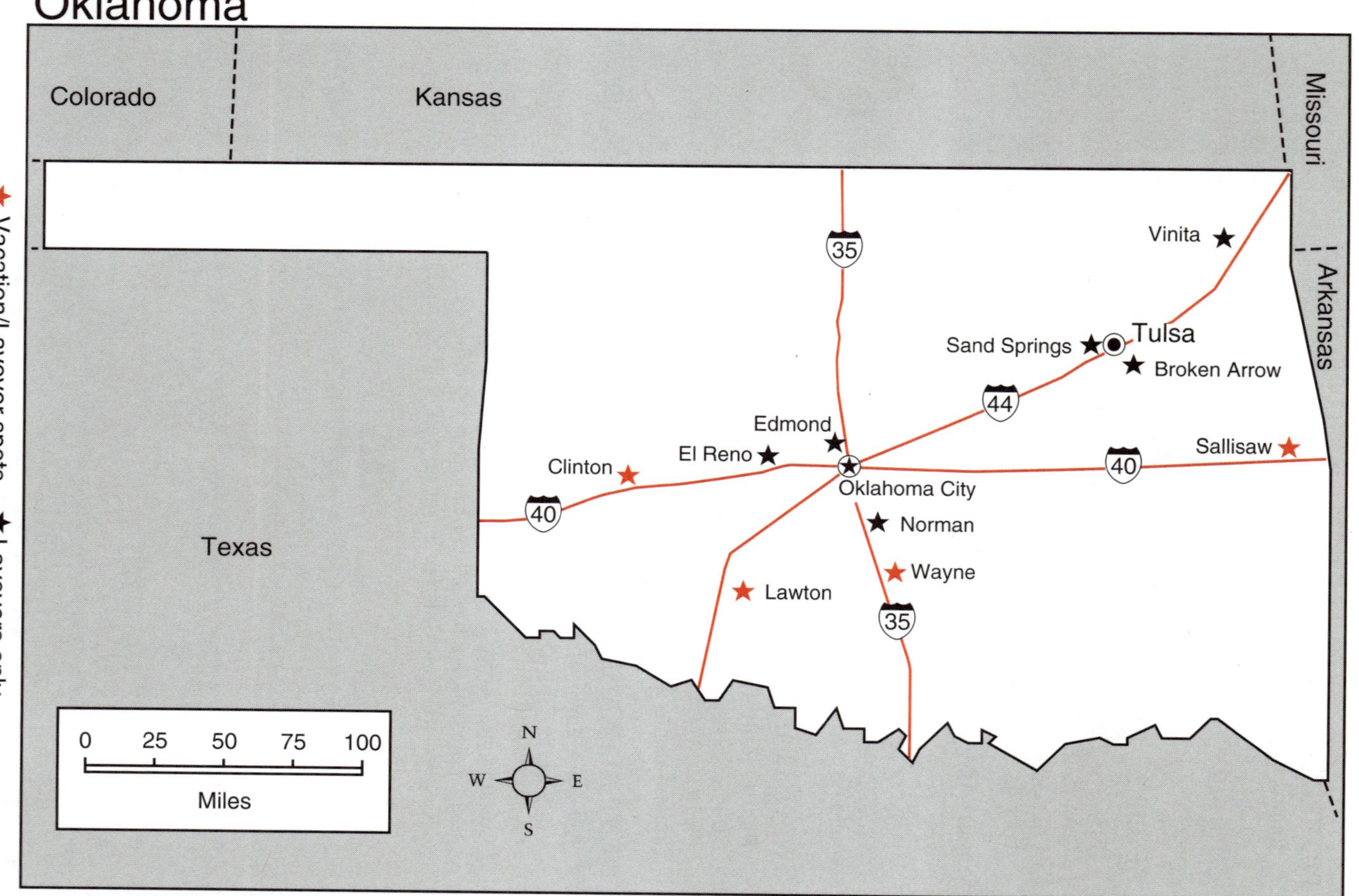

★ Vacation/Layover spots ★ Layovers only
✪ State Capitol ◉ Hwy Junction cities

CURRENT NEGATIVE COGGINS, HEALTH CERTIFICATE & OWNERSHIP PAPERS REQUIRED - see page 2 for details

CLINTON, 73601

★ **E. J. Roberts**
P.O. Box 1323 (I-40, Hwy 183 N.)
Ph. 580/323-1987 580/323-0483 580/445-7258 **Facilities:** 8 indoor stalls, holding pens, pasture, feed, outdoor arena, trails, large vehicle parking w/elec. Practice cattle avail.

EDMOND, 73034

Tommy's Ranch, Tommy Farnsworth
4300 Tommy's Ranch Dr. (17 m. N. of I-40 & 9 m. N. of I-44. E. of I-35, exit 146/Waterloo Rd)
Ph. 405/216-8669 405/844-6452 Cell 405/473-4976
Email:Tommy@Tommysranch.com Owner email:TommyFarnsworth@aol.com Web:www.tommysranch.com **Facilities:** Stalls, RV Hookups (20, 30 & 50 amps), water, elec., sewer, Cable TV and 12x20 guest cottages w/private bathrooms. Coming in summer of 2003: Public restrooms, showers & hot tub w/view.

EL RENO

Little Bit Farm, David & T. J. Meschberger
1405 N. Fort Reno Rd., Calumet, OK 73014 (Location: I 40, Exit 119. 1/2 m. N. to Ft. Reno exit, 1 m. W., 1/2 m. N. on W. side)
Ph. 405/262-7504 **Facilities:** 20-12x12 indoor steel stalls, 150x150 dry pen w/barn & water and 150x200 holding pen. Can accommodate big rigs. Vet/farrier avail.

LAWTON, 73501

★ **Pool Arena & Stables**
HC 30, Box 853 (I-44, exit 45. 5 m. W. to Hwy 58, 6 m. N.)
Ph. 580/492-4856 **Facilities:** 24 indoor stalls, 6 holding pens, pasture, feed, indoor/outdoor arenas, walker, heated washrack, trails, camper hookup & parking. Public bathrooms & shower. Vet on grounds/farrier on call. Lakes. Mountains, Widlife Refuge nearby.

NORMAN, 73072

Burr Oak Farms
1250 E. Burr Oak Rd. (Off I-35, exit 104)
Ph. 816/304/5015 Fax 405/288-2202 **Facilities:** 18 indoor stalls, 4 holding pens & pasture avail.

OKLAHOMA CITY, 73105

Oklahoma City Equine Clinic, Dee M. Gragg, DVM
400 N.E. 70th (10 min. from either the State Fairgrounds or Remington Park Racetrack; just off I-44 & Broadway Extension in OKC)
Ph. 405/843-1099 Fax 405/843-1143 Email:ocec@swbell.net **Facilities:** A full service equine veterinary clinic on 24 acres. Adjacent to the vet facility are approximately 100 stalls avail. for lay-overs plus indoor/2 outdoor arenas.

CURRENT NEGATIVE COGGINS, HEALTH CERTIFICATE & OWNERSHIP PAPERS REQUIRED - see page 2 for details

OKLAHOMA CITY, 73111

Ridgecrest Equestrian Center, Debbie Alseth
6800 N. Miramar (Near I-35, Wilshire exit, directly off Westbound I-44 Service Rd. between Wilshire & M.L. King exits)
Ph. 405/478-1166 **Facilities:** 20 large indoor stalls w/shavings & Nelson waterers, paddock turn-out & indoor/outdoor arenas.

OKLAHOMA CITY, 73139

Edward Cook
8400 S. Walker (Easy access at crossroads of I-35/I-40/I-240)
Ph. 405/634-1787 **Facilities:** New barn, fireproofed & insulated w/cement walkways. 7 indoor/2 outdoor stalls, 5 holding pens, feed, arena & walker. Clean & safe environment. Motels within 1 m.

OKLAHOMA CITY, 73150

BARN - Bed & Breakfast, Kenn & Donna Robinson
11200 SE 44th Pl. (I-40, exit 162/Anderson Rd.)
Ph. **1-877/733-2443** Email:horseldy@earthlink.net
Web:home.earthlink.net/~horseldy **Facilities:** 8 stalls w/shavings & large pipe runs, turn-out paddock w/riding arena and Bed & Continental Breakfast room in barn, private bath w/shower. Campers/RV's welcome; hookup w/elec/water. Kennel avail. Close to motels/restaurants etc. Reservation preferred

SALLISAW, 74955

★ **Future Book Farm, Renee & Ron Lazarus**
Rt. 2, Box 43-E1 (I-40, exit 308 @ Hwy 59)
Ph. 918/776-0876 **Facilities:** 34 stalls, 50 acres of pasture/paddocks, exercise areas, grain/hay, trailer parking & stocked lake. Other animals OK. Blue Ribbon Downs race track, restaurants, motels, state park & RV hookups nearby. Call for reservations.

CURRENT NEGATIVE COGGINS, HEALTH CERTIFICATE & OWNERSHIP PAPERS REQUIRED - see page 2 for details

SAND SPRINGS, 74063

Flying G Equestrian Center, Arron Spradling
P.O. Box 364 (Hwy 412, exit Sand Springs/Sapulpa, West Hwy 51)
Ph. 918/245-8854 Barn 918/951-8246 **Facilities:** 22 stalls, holding pens, pasture, feed, indoor/outdoor arenas, round pen, trails & large vehicle parking. 8 p.m. arrival or call.

TULSA area (Broken Arrow), 74011

Aberdeen Farms, Inc., Nancy Hoyle
4300 S. Butternut Ave., Broken Arrow
Ph. 918/665-6464 Email: dbayer@hoyleyellowpages.com **Facilities:** Stalls & paddocks avail. and 2 outdoor/1 indoor arenas.

VINITA, 74301

Double D Ranch, Paul & Deanne Brown
447954 E. Hwy 60 (7 m. off I-44. Take Afton exit/302, W/S on Hwy 60/69 for 10 m. Or take Vinita exit / 289, E/N on Hwy 60/69 for 7 m.)
Ph. 918/256-6268 **Facilities:** 80 acre ranch. 40 indoor stalls, turnout pens, feed/hay, indoor riding arena, indoor wash rack & trailer parking on premises. Camper parking OK if self-contained. Ranch breeds & sells pure Polish Arabians. $15 per horse, extended stays avail. Motel within 7 m.

VINITA, 74301

Southwind, Marilyn & Bridget Proulx
446355 E. Hwy 60 (Eastbound: I-44, Vinita exit 289, 5.3 m.; Westbound: I-44, Afton exit 302, 11.5 m.)
Ph. 918/256-2660 Bridget 918/256-5478 Fax 918/256-8708
Email:southwind@junct.com **Facilities:** 5 stalls, turn-outs, camper hookup & large parking area. Pets welcome. Motels nearby. Call for rates.

WAYNE, 73095

★ **Trails End Horse Motel, Pamela Monroe**
28601 Hwy 59 Mail: P.O. Box 292 Location: 1-35 & Hwy 59 (Just 1/4 m. E. of I-35 on Hwy 59 at exit 86. 30 m. S. of Oklahoma City)
Ph. **1-800/957-3366** Cell 405/834-8222 Fax 405/449-1304
Email:pam@trailsendusa.com **Facilities:** 18 - 20 ft. indoor stalls, pasture, hay/grain avail., round pens, indoor workout area. 300 acres w/miles of trails, RV hookups and Bed & Breakfast/non-smoking. Great fishing. Primitive campsites w/horse pens.

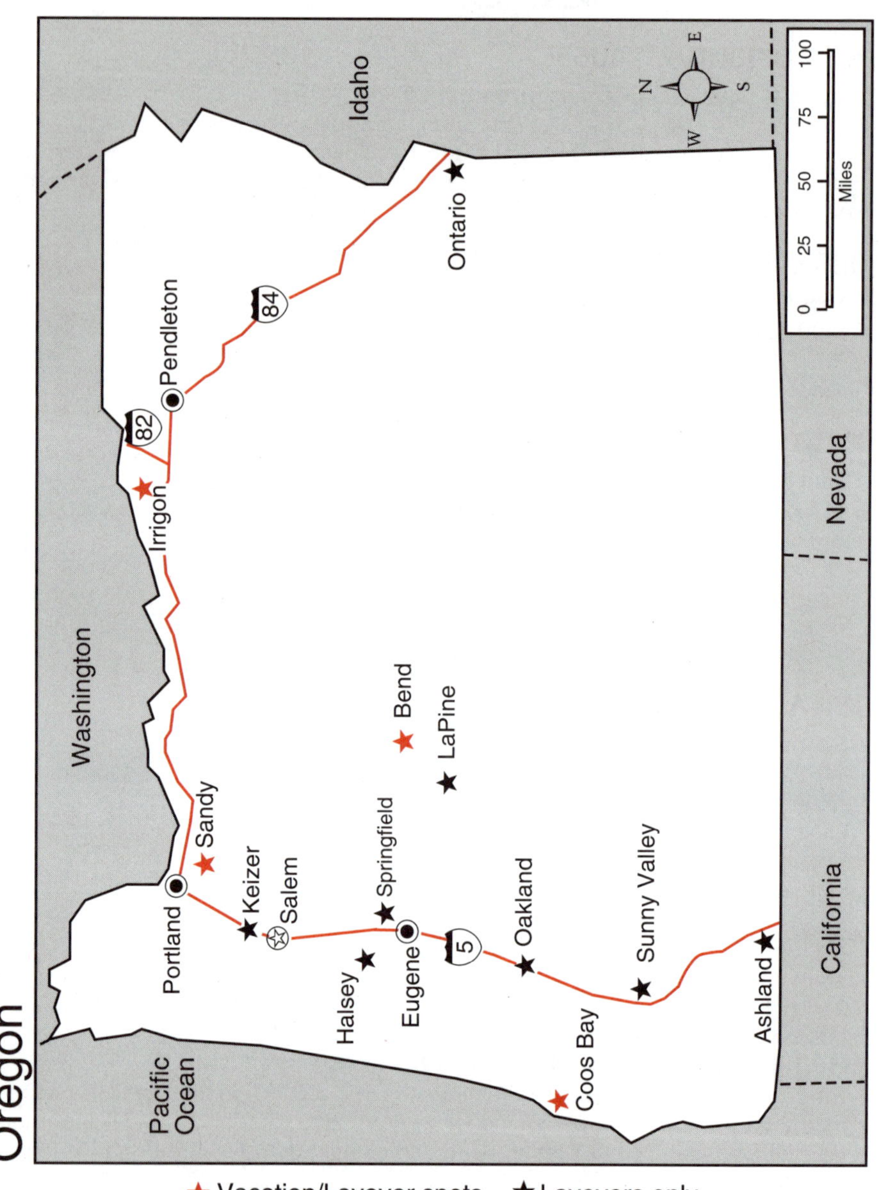

★ Vacation/Layover spots ★ Layovers only
⚝ State Capitol ◉ Hwy Junction cities

CURRENT NEGATIVE COGGINS, HEALTH CERTIFICATE & OWNERSHIP PAPERS REQUIRED - see page 2 for details

ASHLAND, 97520

B-G Valley View Stables, Virginia J. Blair
263 Wilson Rd. (I-5, exit 19)
Ph. 541/482-1772 **Facilities:** 8-12x12 box stalls w/12x32 runs, hay/grain/bedding, 70x120 indoor arena, H/C horse shower & parking. No smoking/no loose dogs. Smoke alarms/fire sensors. Reservations req. Stables close at 10 p.m. MUST have ALL health/vaccination papers incl. Stangles/Potomic Fever.

BEND, 97701

★ **Hawkview Ranch, Karen Bish**
24166 Dodds Rd. (1.7 m. off Rt. 20)
Ph. 541/388-1410 rates/availability Email:karen_bish@bendnet.com **Facilities:** 7 stalls w/paddocks, pasture, feed, 100x250 arena, round pen, free BLM trails access from ranch and guest bdrms for Bed & Breakfast. Nightly/weekly/monthly rates. Panoramic views of the Three Sisters Mts & Mt. Bachelor - experience high desert country.

COOS BAY, 97420

★ **Family Four Stables, James & Peggie Henriksen**
662 Family Four Dr. (7 m. S. of Coos Bay; 12 m. W. of Coquille; 15 m. N. of Bandon)
Ph. 541/267-5301 Fax 541/269-7059 **Facilities:** 50 indoor stalls, holding pens, pasture, full line of hay & grain, arena, walker, trails, elec. for campers & parking for horse trailers. 24 hr. notice required. Call for info on motels.

HALSEY, 97348

Pioneer Stables, Willow Coberly
32744 Hwy 228 (I-5, exit 216. 1/2 m. W. of Hwy 228 & Falk Rd)
Ph. 541/369-3622 Fax 541/369-3634 Email:pioneerstables@rtinet.com **Facilities:** Overnight Stabling. Complete & Full care boarding by the month-week-day. Training & lessons. Covered turn-outs, 60x156 indoor arena. 12x12 rubber matted stalls & hot water wash rack. 1/2 m. from Best Western Hotel.

IRRIGON, 97844

★ **Columbia River Equestrian Center, Julie Errend**
81968 Pleasant View Rd. (Hwy 730 and the Morrow/Umatilla County Line)
Ph. 541/922-2704 Fax 541/922-9500 Email:samlivst@oregontrail.net **Facilities:** 10 stall show barn, outdoor corrals, round pen, 100x150 indoor arena, Columbia River Trails to ride and parking w/elec. Vet/farrier on call. Call for reservations/rates. Motels nearby.

KEIZER, 97307

Keizer Equestrian Center, L.L.C.
P.O. Box 21085 (I-5, exit 260, W. on Chemawa, right on Radiant 1 m.)
Ph. 503/463-5197 Pager 503/540-7054 Web:www.KeizerEquestrian.com **Facilities:** 40-12x12 indoor stalls, round pen, various pastures, hay & grain extra, 80x156 indoor/100x300 outdoor arenas, wash rack & parking space for trailers. By appointment only.

CURRENT NEGATIVE COGGINS, HEALTH CERTIFICATE & OWNERSHIP PAPERS REQUIRED - see page 2 for details

LaPINE, 97739

J and B Acres
52097 Pine Forest Dr. (3-1/2 m. from Hwy 97 N. of LaPine, 5 m. from Hwy 31 jct)
Ph. 541/536-5833 Email:jandbacres@coinet.com **Facilities:** Outdoor fenced pens, grass hay/alfalfa avail. & parking for self-contained trailers. Dogs okay.

OAKLAND, 97462

"RIDE & REST" Horse Motel, Ron & Norma Groves
500 Metz Hill Rd. (I-5, exit 142. 1/4 m. W. on Metz Hill Rd., 1st driveway on left)
Ph. 541/459-9220 Email:grovesrn@mcsi.net **Facilities:** 17 indoor stalls, indoor lighted arena/outdoor arena & camper hookup. Large truck turn-around. Emergency pickup. Vet within 1 m., on call.

ONTARIO, 97914

Malheur County Fairgrounds, Attn: Janeen
795 NW 9th St. (I-84 & Hwy 20/26)
Ph. 541/823-2581 or 541/823-2997 - even. **Facilities:** 100 box stalls & elec. for campers/RV's.

SANDY, 97055

★ **Burnt Spur Ranch Equine Bed & Breakfast, Linda & John Keeter**
42100 SE Locksmith Ln. (2 m. E. of Sandy near Hwy 26)
Ph. 503/668-9716 **Facilities:** 6 indoor stalls, holding pens, 96x144 outdoor arena, pasture, walker, feed, trails & elec/water for campers.
Bed & Breakfast within 3 m., motel 2 m.

SPRINGFIELD, 97478

Pacific Equestrian Center, Larry Spielman
3525 Garden Ave. (Just off I-5, exit 194A)
Ph. Office 541/746-6564 Barn 541/744-9104 Call office first. Fax 541/741-8878 **Facilities:** 78 indoor stalls, 3 holding pens, feed - extra, 100x200 indoor arena & camper hookup/electricity only.

SUNNY VALLEY, 97497

T & R Stables, Tom & Rose Johnston
359 Old Stage Rd. (1/2 m. off I-5, exit 71. 15 m. N. of Grants Pass)
Ph. 541/474-2516 Email:gypsyrlj@aol.com **Facilities:** 6-12x14 stalls w/50' runs, many miles of BLM trails & KOA across the road. Open 6 a.m. to 10 p.m. Vet on call. NO STALLIONS.

Outdoor Camping
to
Luxurious
Pampering
STAKE
YER CLAIM...
for a dream
vacation
DO-IT-
YOURSELF
VACATIONS

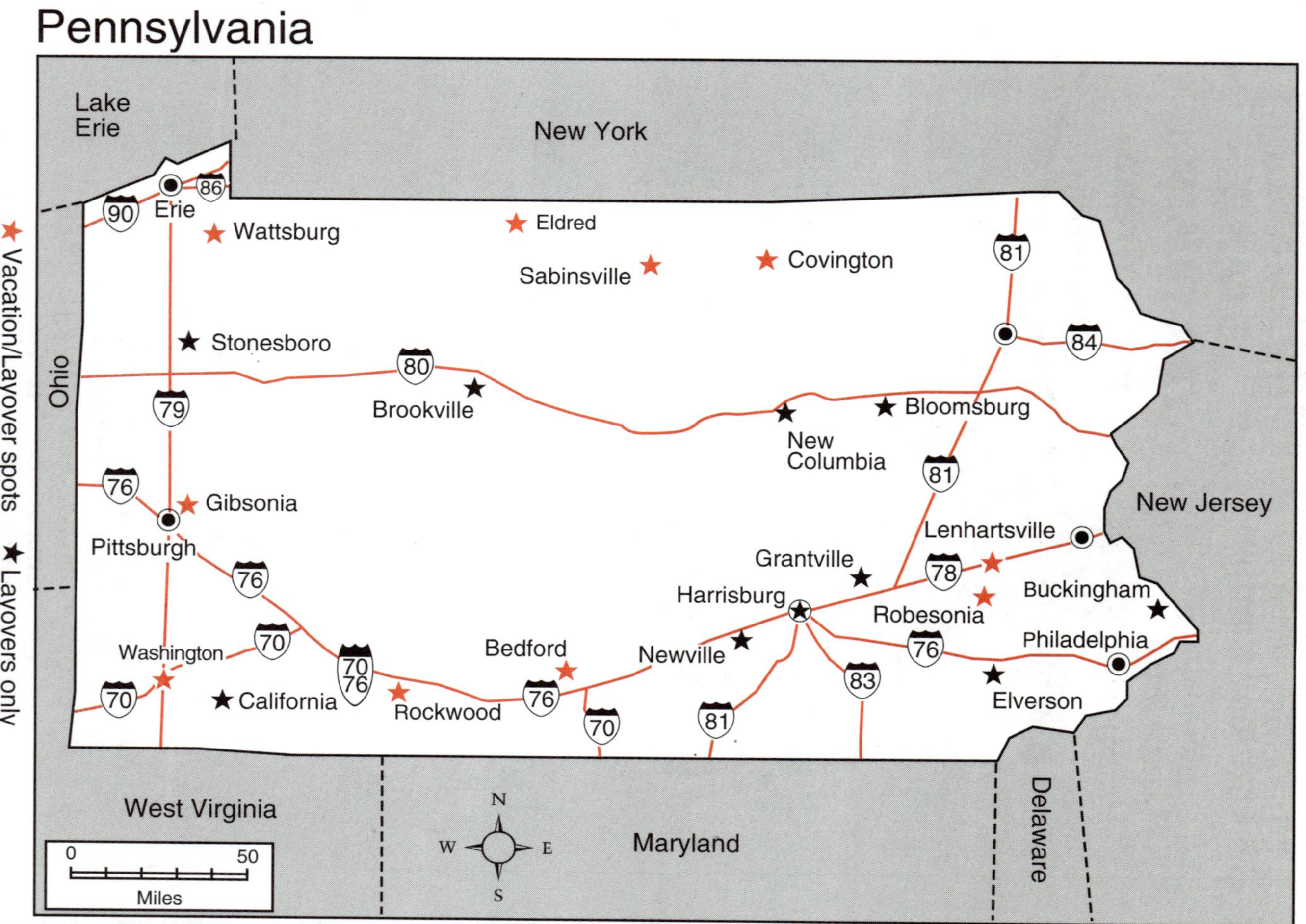
Pennsylvania
Lake Erie
New York
New Jersey
Delaware
Maryland
West Virginia
Ohio
Erie
Wattsburg
Eldred
Sabinsville
Covington
Stonesboro
Brookville
Bloomsburg
New Columbia
Gibsonia
Pittsburgh
Washington
California
Rockwood
Bedford
Newville
Harrisburg
Grantville
Lenhartsville
Robesonia
Buckingham
Philadelphia
Elverson
90
86
79
80
84
81
78
76
83
70
N
E
S
W
0
50
Miles
Vacation/Layover spots
Layovers only
State Capitol
Hwy Junction cities

CURRENT NEGATIVE COGGINS, HEALTH CERTIFICATE & OWNERSHIP PAPERS REQUIRED - see page 2 for details

BEDFORD, 15522

★ **"The Silhouette," Jack Monsour**
1120 Oppenheimer Rd. (4 m. N. of exit 11, PA Turnpike)
Ph. 814/623-8243 Web:www.bedfordcounty.net/monsour
Email:monsour@bedford.net
Facilities: 3 stalls, 2 holding pens, 25 ac. of pasture, hay avail., 400 acres of trails, camper hookup w/parking & elec. and a Vacation Home/sleeps 9. Monsour Sheep Farm. Raise & train Registered Morgan horses. No smoking in house/no pets on farm. Call for reservations.

BLOOMSBURG, 17815-6901

Engelwood Paint Horses & Animal Chiropractic Clinic, Neil & Janine Engelman
35 Horse Farm Rd. (I-80, Bloomsburg exit 236-Lightstreet/Rte 487. 30 min. from I-81)
Ph. Residence 570/387-0510 Barn 570/387-6655 Email:engelwood@bwkip.com Web:www.engelwood.com **Facilities:** Private show facility. 38-12x12 stalls, 2-30x30 rehab stalls, four-rail wooden fence, individual grass turnouts, grain/hay, auto waterers & exercise areas. Equine chiropractic, acupuncture, massage & dental services avail. Bring your own buckets. $25 per night.

BROOKVILLE, 15825

Seneca Trail Horses, John McAninch
RR 8, Box 64 (I-80 & Rt. 28S, exit 78)
Ph. 814/849-8135 **Facilities:** 6-10x12 box stalls, round pen, pasture & feed avail., 60x60 indoor arena, trails & parking.

BUCKINGHAM, 18912

Mill Creek Farm Enterprises, Inc.
P.O. Box 816 Location:2348 Quarry Rd. (Rt. 202)
Ph. 215/794-5495 **Facilities:** 13 indoor stalls, paddocks, ample pasture, feed, trails & rooms.

CALIFORNIA, 15423

Horse Heaven Stable, Gayle & Fred Mull, Jr.
44 Kaukonen Dr. (2 m. off I-70, exit Rt. 43/California)
Ph. 724/938-3023 **Facilities:** 10 indoor stalls, holding pens, pasture, feed, indoor/outdoor arenas, trails, parking w/elec. and an apt. for 2-4 people. 9 p.m. arrival or call.

COVINGTON, 16917

★ **Tanglewood Camping**
P.O. Box 35 Location: RR 1, Box 64A (5 m. off Rt. 15, S. of Mansfield)
Ph. 570/549-8299 Email:tnglewod@ptd.net Web:tanglewoodcamping.com
Facilities: Pasture, trails adjoining Camp in State Forest & water & elec for campers. Primarily a campground w/space for horses. Local guides avail. Primitive tent sites/modern restrooms/hot shower/dumping station/lake/paddle-boats. Camping cabins/lodge and more.

CURRENT NEGATIVE COGGINS, HEALTH CERTIFICATE & OWNERSHIP PAPERS REQUIRED - *see page 2 for details*

ELDRED, 16731

★ **Big Loop Lodge, Sharon Tennies, Mgr.**
640 Artline Rd. (Located on 1700 ac. of wooded hills on the NY/PA state line, apx. 20 min. SE of Olean NY)
Ph. 814/225-4406 Email:manager@bigloop.com Web:www.bigloop.com
Facilities: Large barn w/6 box stalls/6 tie stalls & tack storage area. Small barn w/5 box stalls. Feed/bedding avail. with advance reservations, parking for trucks/trailers & spacious lodge for up to 15. 12 m. of logging roads & trails avail. Variety of wildlife.

ELVERSON, 19520

Windspot Farm, Susan H. Roberts
21 Bollinger Rd. (10 minutes from Morgantown exit PA Turnpike)
Ph. 610/286-9765 **Facilities:** 4 indoor stalls, guest turnout pasture, hay & feed avail. for sale & 5 min. to Hack trails.. Can accommodate stallions. Call for reservations. Motels 5 min. away.

GIBSONIA, 15044

★ **Sun & Cricket Bed & Breakfast, Tara & John Bradley-Steck, owner/operators**
1 Tara Lane (5 m. from I-76/PA Tpk.; 12 m. from I-79)
Ph. 724/444-6300 Web:www.sunandcricket.com **Facilities:** 5 indoor stalls, 1/4 acre grass pasture, hay provided, trails and 2 suites for B&B. No smoking. No pets w/o prior approval. Reservations & deposit req. Restaurants nearby. Close to major interstates.

GRANTVILLE, 17028

Wind Ridge Stable, Thomas & Victoria Bowman
1091 Ridge Rd. (I-81, exit 80)
Ph. 717/469-0448 Email:bowmanv@juno.com **Facilities:** 5 indoor stalls, feed avail. & parking for horse trailers. Call for reservations/rates. Motels nearby.

HARRISBURG, 17112

Pony Express
546 N. Fairville Ave. (1 m. N. of I-81, exit 77)
Ph. 717/652-6177 **Facilities:** 10 stalls, feed incl., trails & parking. Rooms and camping avail. Near Hershey Park & Penn Nat'l Racetrack..

LENHARTSVILLE, 19534

★ **BreezeWood Stables, Christina Muller**
89 Long Rd. (Just outside of town off I-78, about 1 hr. E. of Harrisburg)
Ph. 610/756-3197 Email:BreezeWoodStables@hotmail.com **Facilities:** 36 indoor stalls, 8 pastures for turnout, hay/pellets, 40x120 lighted indoor riding/outdoor riding arenas, indoor riding track, round pen, 2 heated lounges, 10 grooming bays, 3 h&c wash stalls and accommodations for 5 people. Easy trailer access.

NEW COLUMBIA, 17856

Feather Hill Stables
210 Feather Hill Ln. (25 m. S. of Williamsport on Rt. 15. 1 m. S. of I-80)
Ph. 570/568-8222 Fax 570/568-8227 **Facilities:** 27 indoor stalls, 5 holding pens, pasture, feed, indoor/outdoor arenas, walker & trails nearby.

NEWVILLE, 17241

Breezy Mac Farm, Michael & Shelley George, owners
23 Stamy Rd. (I-81, exit 11, Rt. 233 W.)
Ph. 717/776-5026 Email:michaelgeorge776@hotmail.com **Facilities:** 7 stalls, holding pens, pasture, feed, trails & elec/water/parking. Arrive by 7:30 p.m. or call.

ROBESONIA, 19551

★ **Gruber Homestead, Russell & Mary Getz**
1576 Milestone Rd. (422 to Robesonia, 3 m. N. on Bernville Rd., right onto Milestone)
Ph. 610/488-1905 Fax 610/488-6285 **Facilities:** 2 indoor stalls for 1-2 guests staying at Gruber Homestead Settler's Cabin. 3 m. from Blue Marsh Lake Recreation Area w/over 30 m. of trails. Call for reservations/rates. The Settler's Cabin is a restored 18th centurh log cabin.

ROCKWOOD, 15557

★ **Laurel Echo Farm Vacation Bed & Breakfast, Paul & Carol Pyle, owners**
174 Crossroad (PA Turnpike, I-70/76, exit 10. Hwy 281 S. 6 m.)
Ph. **1-888/655-5335** 814/926-2760 Fax 814/443-4313 **Facilities:** 4 stalls, feed, trails, room for parking and Bed & Breakfast. Late arrivals - call. In the Laurel Highlands of western Pennsylvania.

SABINSVILLE, 16943

★ **Endless Mountains Bed & Breakfast, Hope Johnson**
465 RR #1 (St. Rt. 349, 5 m. N. of Rt. 6 at Gaines PA)
Ph. & Fax 814/628-2244 Web:www.endlessmountainsbed and breakfast.com Email:johnsonhe@earthlink.net **Facilities:** Circa 1860's barn has 5 oak box stalls w/2 turn-out paddocks, oak board fenced pastures, 1 w/run-in shed & 8 m. from Pine Creek Trail at PA's grand canyon. Will rent camper/RV space. B&B w/5 bdrms & 1 suite/sleeps 8. Visit quaint & charming historic Wellsboro..

STONEBORO, 16153

Silvermist, Barbara Scheer
1986 Harrisville Rd. (10 min. from I-79 & I-80. From I-79, exit 121/Franklin-Mercer. Cal for directions)
Ph. 814/786-0024 Fax 814/786-9164 Email:bscher@stargate.net **Facilities:** 4 stalls, 2 paddocks, 80 acres of pastures and guest house w/full kitchen, bath & living room overlooking beautiful scenic pastoral setting. Guests can enjoy full generous breakfast..

CURRENT NEGATIVE COGGINS, HEALTH CERTIFICATE & OWNERSHIP PAPERS REQUIRED - *see page 2 for details*

WASHINGTON, 15301

★ **Maple Lane Stables, Helene Brand**
634 McKee Rd. (Exit 11 off I-70)
Ph. 724/225-2286 Fax 724/225-6805 Email:helene@pulsenet.com **Facilities:** 14 indoor stalls, indoor/outdoor arenas, wash stall & 100 acres of trails. Vet/blacksmith avail. Motels & other conveniences at exit 12.

WATTSBURG, 16442

★ **Ridgeview Farm, Ed & Sue Snippert**
12190 Hill Rd. (10 m. S. of I-90 Erie, exit 29/St. Rt. 8 Call for exact directions)
Ph. 814/739-9662 814/739-0342 Email:snippss#att.net **Facilities:** New facility. 12-box stall barn, attached 70x120 indoor arena, hay & grain, wash rack, lounge overlooks arena, 2 fenced paddocks, large parking area for big trailers & hookups avail.

NOTES

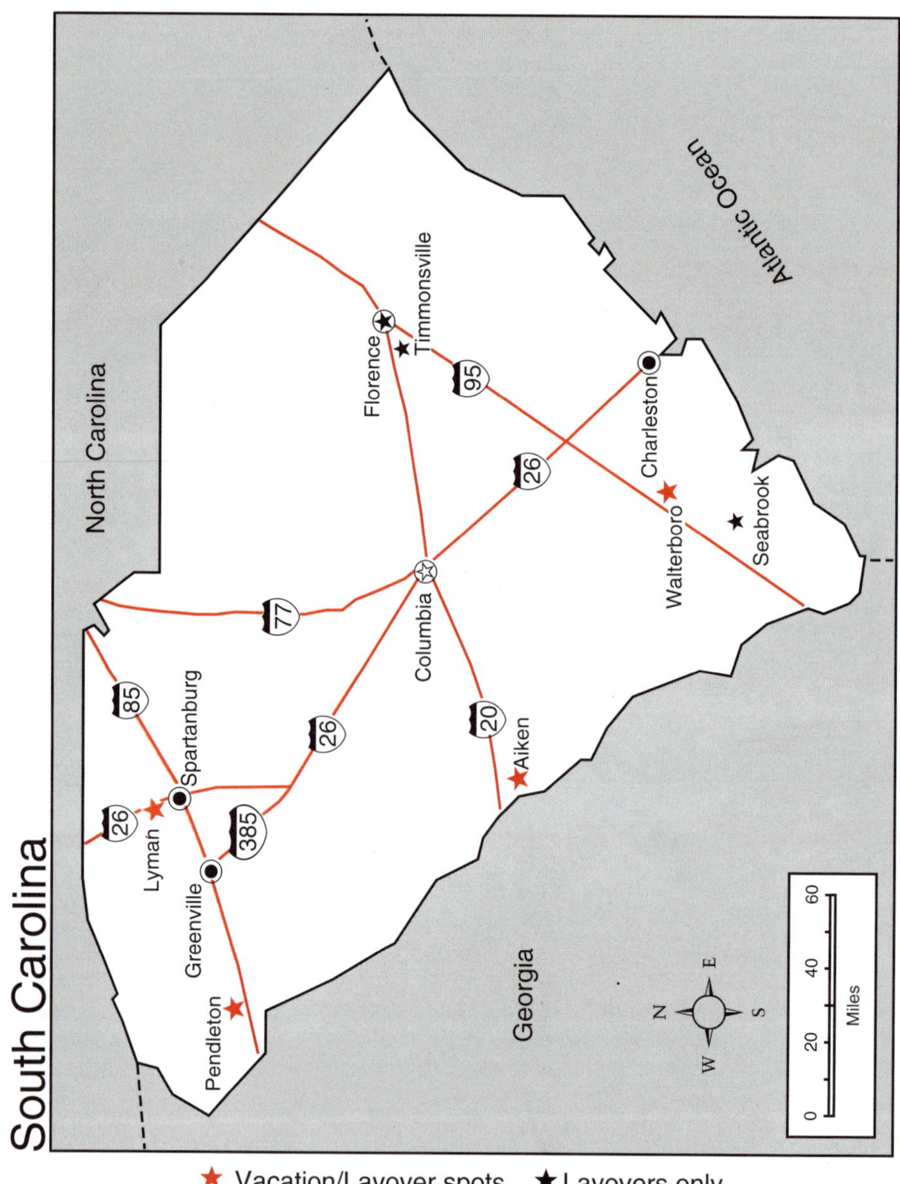
South Carolina
North Carolina
Georgia
Atlantic Ocean
Pendleton
Greenville
Lyman
Spartanburg
Columbia
Aiken
Florence
Timmonsville
Charleston
Walterboro
Seabrook
26
385
85
77
20
95
N
S
E
W
0
20
40
60
Miles
Vacation/Layover spots
Layovers only
State Capitol
Hwy Junction cities

CURRENT NEGATIVE COGGINS, HEALTH CERTIFICATE & OWNERSHIP PAPERS REQUIRED - *see page 2 for details*

AIKEN, 29803

★ **First Flight Stable, Anne B. Torreyson**
708 Cardinal Dr. Location: 187 Chime Bell Church Rd. (30 min. S. of I-20 or 15 min. S. of downtown, 2 m. W. of Rt. 19/Whiskey Rd.)
Ph. 803/648-9642 Email:abtstable@aol.com **Facilities:** Center aisle barn, paved, rubber matting and up to 5 stalls avail. plus large grassy paddocks, pen for turnout/lunging, heated/AC tack & feed rooms and wash stall w/h&c water In hunt country w/four hunts. Area well known for it's Hunt Week, and golf.

AIKEN, 29803

★ **TOWN & COUNTRY INN Bed-Breakfast-Barn, David & Marlene Jones, Innkeepers**
2340 Sizemore Circle (I-20 to Hwy 19/exit 18S. 10 m. through Aiken, right on Sizemore)
Ph. 803/642-0270 Call for brochure Fax 803/642-1299
Email:tcinn@duesouth.net Web:www.towncountrybb.com **Facilities:** 5 indoor stalls, 3 acre pasture, round pen, riding at nearby Hitchcock Woods and Bed & Breakfast w/5 lg bdrms w/private baths. 20x40 in-ground pool. Aiken is Thoroughbred Country, home of the Aiken Triple Crown & Thoroughbred Racing Hall of Fame.

FLORENCE, 29501

Florence Horse Center, Jack Belew
3508 Cherrywood Rd. (5 min. from I-95 & US 52. Call for directions)
Ph. 843/679-5502 or 843/667-0951 Fax 843/679-3129
Email:jack@easternx.com **Facilities:** 37-12x12 box stalls, paddocks, ring, dressage ring, jumps and truck/trailer parking. Western & English dressage & hunter training for horse and rider. Reservations required.
25 motels within 5 min.

LYMAN, 29365

★ **Scotsgrove Farm**
39 Hillcrest St. (Can access from I-85 or I-26. Call for directions)
Ph. 864/877-9392 **Facilities:** 16 stalls, 6 paddocks, pasture, 150x250 sand arena, extensive trails, camper parking w/elec. and Bed & Breakfast - 3 rooms each w/private bath. Fox hunting in season.

PENDLETON, 29670

★ **Hound Hollow Farm, Becky Tolson**
123 Old Sanders Rd. (I-85, exit 21, in direction of Liberty/Hwy 178)
Ph. 864/224-8205 or 864/375-0051 **Facilities:** 8 indoor stalls w/rubber matts/auto fly system, 2 holding pens w/turnout pen, 8 acres of pasture, feed, 100x200 riding ring, 60' round pen & 5 min. trail ride to hundreds of acres of public trails. Numerous B&Bs & hotels in area - info upon request.

CURRENT NEGATIVE COGGINS, HEALTH CERTIFICATE & OWNERSHIP PAPERS REQUIRED - see page 2 for details

SEABROOK, 29940

Beaufort Equestrian Center
163 Keane's Neck Rd. (8 min. off I-95, Beaufort exit/Hwy 21; 2 min. from Hwy 17)
Ph. 843/846-4765 **Facilities:** 22 indoor stalls, 9 pastures & 10% pellets incl..

TIMMONSVILLE, 29161

Glenview Farm, Doris Rabon
1540 Center Rd. (I-95, exit 153. 1 m. E. on left)
Ph. 843/346-2908 **Facilities:** 47 indoor stalls.

WALTERBORO, 29488

★ **Double D Arena - Quarter Horses by Double D, Tommie Derry**
1256 Rodeo Dr. (I-95, exit 53 or 57. 5 m. off interstate, easy access)
Ph. 843/893-3894 Fax 843/893-2588 Email:horsesrme@yahoo.com **Facilities:** 2 barns w/8 stalls ea., holding pen, 35 acres of pasture, 175x250 arena, 4-horse walker, 7 hookups w/elec & water and dump station. Reservations preferred. Must contain dogs/cats. Provide transportation. Farrier/vet on call. Wash room/feed room/tack room.

WALTERBORO, 29488

Double L Farm, Lynn Huggins
1932 Henderson Hwy (3-1/2 m. from exit 53, I-95. Easy on/easy off)
Ph. 843/538-2581 or Barn 843/538-4170 Mobile 843/866-3113 or 843/893-7483 Email:lhuggin@lowcountry.com **Facilities:** 4 stalls, pasture, lighted riding area, camper parking w/elec & water and apt/sleeps 5 w/washer-dryer, cable TV, refrigerator & microwave.

WALTERBORO, 29488

★ **Mt. Carmel Farm Bed & Breakfast**
3610 Mt. Carmel Rd. (3.6 m. off I-95, exits 57 or 62)
Ph. 843/538-5770 **Facilities:** 8 stalls, paddocks, turnout and Bed & Breakfast - 2 rooms w/private bath. Also, above ground pool. Convenient parking/loading/unloading. Pets OK - outside. Reservations req

One Horse Gap, Genie Stewart-Spears on Fancy Photo by: Kris Robards

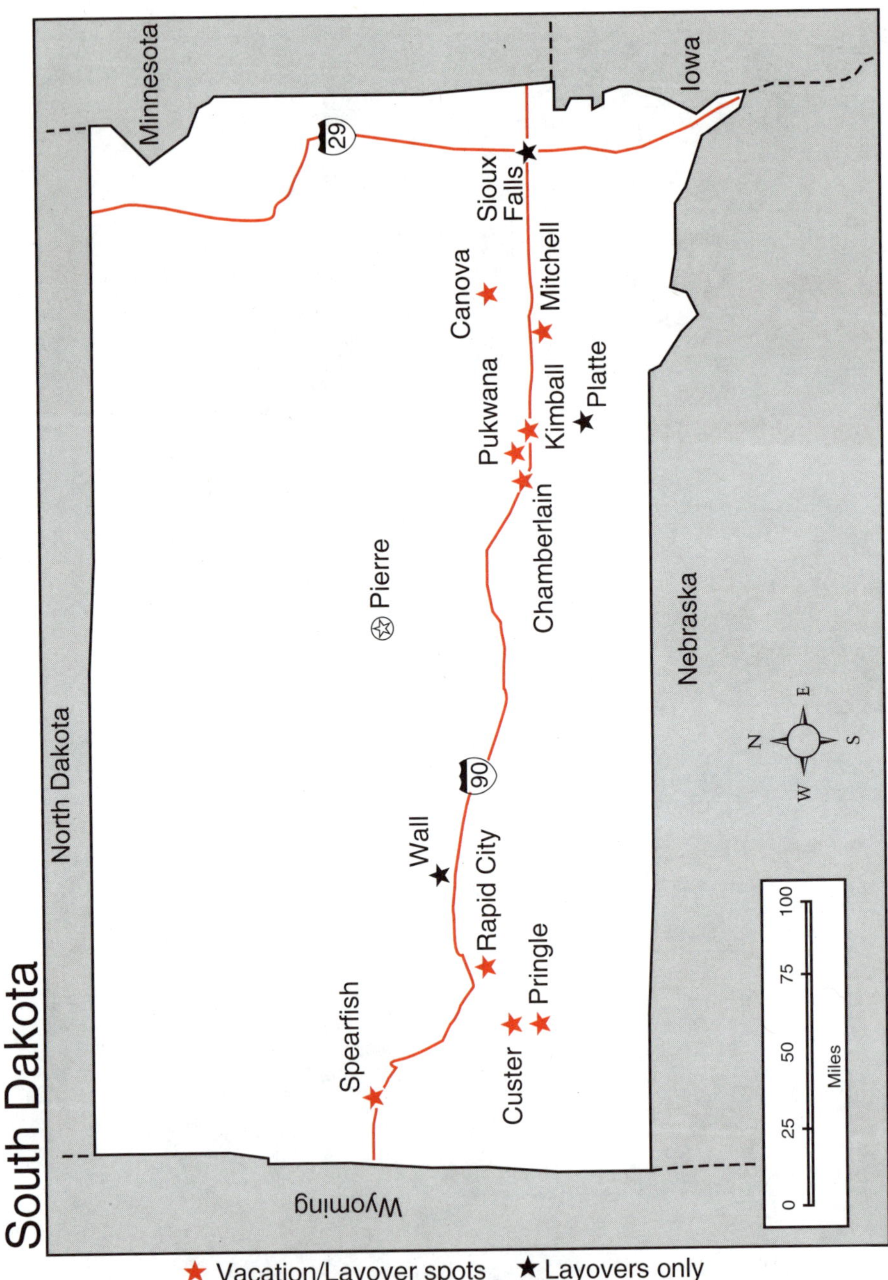
South Dakota
Minnesota
Iowa
North Dakota
Nebraska
Wyoming
29
90
Sioux Falls
Canova
Mitchell
Pukwana
Kimball
Platte
Chamberlain
Pierre
Wall
Rapid City
Spearfish
Custer
Pringle
N
E
S
W
0
25
50
75
100
Miles
Vacation/Layover spots
Layovers only
State Capitol
Hwy Junction cities

CURRENT NEGATIVE COGGINS, HEALTH CERTIFICATE & OWNERSHIP PAPERS REQUIRED - *see page 2 for details*

CANOVA, 57321-7316

★ **Alden & Delores Skoglund**
24375 438th Ave. (I-90, exit 364 onto Hwy 81. 9 m. N., 3 m. W., 3-1/4 m. N.) Ph. 605/247-3445 **Facilities:** Holding pens, pasture, camper hookup and Bed & Breakfast.

CHAMBERLAIN, 57325

★ **WingMasters Lodge**
24561 - 348th Ave. (I-90, exit 273 or 263. 5 min. off I-90 and the Missouri River) Ph. 605/734-6152 or 605/730-6152 Email:rickloyd@sd.cybernex.net **Facilities:** Modern lodge connecting to indoor/outdoor arenas, 10-12x12 stalls w/auto waterers & feed avail., outdoor pens, camping, dog kennels & indoor parking. Rolling pastures & trails to ride near Lewis & Clark Trail. Hunt upland game/fish walleye on Missouri River.

CUSTER, 57730

★ **Spirit Horse Escape**
11596 W. Hwy 16 (6 m. W. of Custer on Hwy 16. Mile marker 19 on N. side of Hwy. From W., 7 m. E. of Jewel Cave Nat'l Park on left)
Ph. Camp 605/673-6005 Cell 520/906-1843 Office 505/546-1115
Email:endurancevet@zianet.com Web:www.spirithorseescape.com **Facilities:** New pipe corrals, turnout, plenty of riding in the Black Hills Nat'l Forest, 6 full hookups & room for 10+ rigs w/corrals for all spots, B&B, new deluxe cabins & Tee Pee's for rent. Seasonal (May-Oct) overnight/vacation facility located in the beautiful Black Hills.

KIMBALL, 57355-6638

★ **Jim & Patsy's Bed & Breakfast**
36121 - 247th St. (5 m. from I-90, Kimball exit. Call for directions)
Ph. 605/778-6492 Email:basspatsy@hotmail.com **Facilities:** Outdoor sheltered area, holding pens, feed, if needed, and Bed & Breakfast.

KIMBALL, 57355

★ **Red Barn Inn, Dave & Barb Konechne**
25406 - 358th Ave. (I-90, exit 284 or exit 272)
Ph. 605/778-6332 **1-800/870-6332** **Facilities:** 4 stalls, 4 holding pens, 2 pastures, feed avail., 2 arenas (7 m. away), 2 camper hookups w/water & elec. and 5 rooms for Bed & Breakfast.

CURRENT NEGATIVE COGGINS, HEALTH CERTIFICATE & OWNERSHIP PAPERS REQUIRED - see page 2 for details

MITCHELL, 57301

★ **Hobby Horse Stables**
815 W. Spruce (I-90, exit 330. S. 1/4 m., E. 1/2 m.)
Ph. 605/995-1581 **Facilities:**15-12x2 indoor stalls, 12 covered runs w/paddocks, 9 holding pens, 2 pastures, hay, 60x120 indoor/125x250 outdoor arenas, round pen & parking w/elec & water. Rubber mats/ heated water/bedding avail. Home of world's only Corn Palace. Motels at exit.

PLATTE, 57309

Yellow Rose Arena
27480 N. Hwy 45 (1 m. N. of Platte)
Ph. 605/337-3022 605/337-3318 605/337-3520 **Facilities:** 40 heated stalls, 6 holding pens, feed, 100x300 arena, walker, trails & camper hookup. B&B next door. Steakhouse & lounge in Arena.

PRINGLE, 57773

★ **Plenty Star Ranch, John & Isa Kirk**
P.O. Box 106 (On US 385; 2 m. N. of Pringle; 9-1/2 m. S. of Custer. Right on Mickelson Trail - 110 m. Rails to Trails thru the entire Black Hills)
Ph. 605/673-3012 Email:isa@plentystarranch.com **Facilities:** 18-10x30 covered outdoor stalls, 4 holding pens, 30 m. marked loop trails leaving from camp, 12 camper (e/w) hookups, 3 cabins, tipis & tent sites and dump stations. Rare Spanish Mustangs. All breed trail horses for sale.

PUKWANA, 57370

★ **Crystal & Tucker Ashley**
35540 - 250th St. (I-90, Pukwana or Kimball exit)
Ph. 605/778-6885 605/730-1074 **Facilities:** 3 indoor/8-10 outdoor stalls, roping arena, elec. for campers, and Cabin & Sheepherder's wagon. Indoor roping & rodeo arena.

CURRENT NEGATIVE COGGINS, HEALTH CERTIFICATE & OWNERSHIP PAPERS REQUIRED - see page 2 for details

RAPID CITY, 57702

★ **Lightning Ridge Ranch Bed & Breakfast**
22576 Lightning Ridge Rd. (6-1/2 m. W. of Rapid City on Nemo Rd)
Ph. 605/342-6034 **Facilities:** 5 indoor/2 outdoor stalls, 2 holding pens, feed, many trails in Black Hills Nat'l Forest, Bed & Breakfast w/2 guest rooms & tent camping avail. No smoking inside/no stallions. Close to all major attractions. Brochure upon request.

SIOUX FALLS, 57103

Laura Wagner
4104 E. 36th
Ph. 605/371-0789 **Facilities:** 38 stalls & 9 paddocks. Call for holding pens.

SPEARFISH, 57783

Seven Down Arena, Jason Grubb
P.O. Box 999 Location:6623 Centennial Rd. (Off I-90, exit 17, between Spearfish & Whitewood, Hwy 85 S. 1 m.)
Ph. 605/578-3518 or 605/645-6782 Call if you have questions or to make a reservation Web:sevendown.net **Facilities:** 12x12 indoor stalls or 12x12 indoor stalls w/outdoor runs. Daily or monthly boarding avail..

SPEARFISH, 57783

★ **Two Bar T Ranch**
Mail: 6025 E. Colorado Blvd. Location: 410 Rainbow Rd. (Exits 17 & 14 off I-90)
Ph. 605/578-1012 Email:lickteig@mato.com Web:www.twobartranch.com
Facilities: 4 indoor stalls, holding pens, large corral/barn, pasture & feed possible, camper parking, trails and 2 bedroom fully furnished log cabin/sleeps 6. Minutes from Spearfish & Deadwood.

WALL, 57790

Ruland Arena LLC, Larry Ruland, Reg. Corrientes Cattle, Quarterhorse Ranch & Horse Trainers
19580 239th St. (I-90, exit 116, 6 m. SE of Wall)
Ph. 605/386-2164 - Larry, Lenora & T.J. 605/386-2165 - Shaun & Michelle Barn 605/386-4040 **Facilities:** 7 indoor heavy duty Hi Qual stalls, 6 holding pens, feed negotiable, fully-insulated 250x110 indoor sand arena w/excellent lighting in steel building, 250x120 outdoor arena & 2 camper hookups.

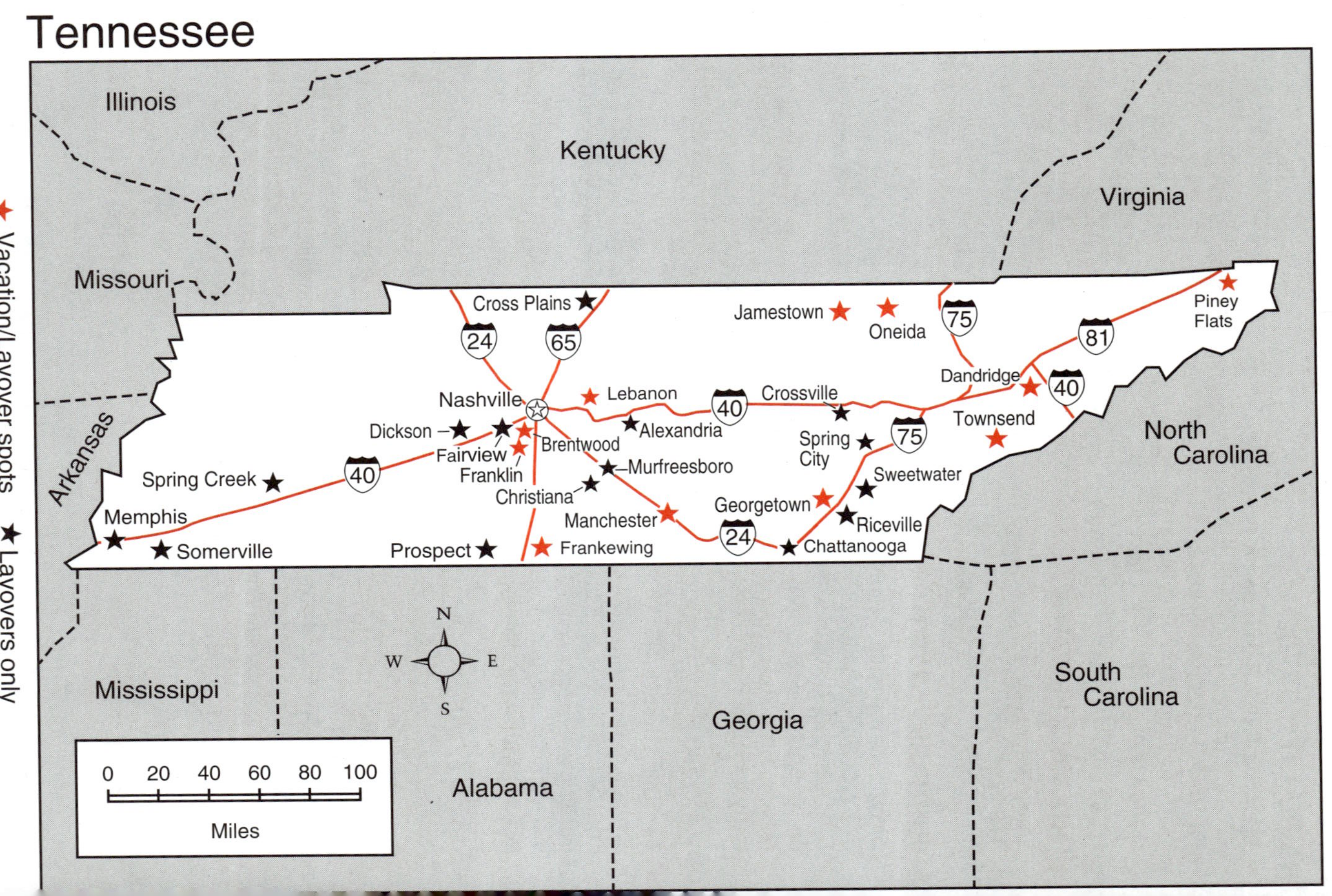
Tennessee
Illinois
Kentucky
Virginia
Missouri
Arkansas
Cross Plains
24
65
Jamestown
Oneida
75
81
Piney Flats
Nashville
Lebanon
40
Crossville
Dandridge
40
Dickson
Alexandria
Spring City
75
Townsend
North Carolina
Fairview
Brentwood
Franklin
Murfreesboro
Sweetwater
Spring Creek
40
Christiana
Georgetown
Riceville
Memphis
Manchester
24
Chattanooga
Somerville
Prospect
Frankewing
N
W
E
S
Mississippi
Georgia
South Carolina
Alabama
0 20 40 60 80 100
Miles
Vacation/Layover spots
Layovers only
State Capitol
Hwy Junction cities

CURRENT NEGATIVE COGGINS, HEALTH CERTIFICATE & OWNERSHIP PAPERS REQUIRED - see page 2 for details

ALEXANDRIA, 37012

Tom Stephens, Stephens Stables
Box 503 (20 min. off I-40, Alexandria exit/Hwy 53; 25 min. from I-40, Lebanon/Watertown exit)
Ph. 615/464-3868 Email:walkinghorseman2002@yahoo.com **Facilities:** 10 indoor stalls, 12% grain & camper hookup. 8 hour notice required.

BRENTWOOD (Nashville area), 37027-6210

★ **English Manor Bed & Breakfast and Catering**
6304 Murray Ln. (I-65, exit 74-B. 12 m. S. of Nashville)
Ph. 615/373-4627 615/373-4640 **1-800/332-4640** Fax 615/221-9666 Email:englishm@englishmanor.com Web:www.englishmanor.com **Facilities:** 3 indoor stalls, 5 acres of pasture, camper hookup & 8 rooms for Bed & Breakfast w/full baths Also, a stall for dogs. Meals available besides breakfast. Credit card to hold. Stabling for B&B lodgers only.

CHATTANOOGA, 37412

Seahorse Farms, Jerry Clark
529 Frawley Rd. (2 blks E. of I-75 at TN/GA line, exit 1)
Ph. 423/499-2648 - barn 667-0440 - mobile **Facilities:** 10 indoor stalls, round pen, pasture, feed, 40x60 indoor arena & camper hookup (call for info.) Stalls avail., if needed, at another facility about 20 min. N.

CHRISTIANA, 37037

Kanawha Farm, Janet E. Stevens & John B. Ingleson
9996 Manchester Hwy (8/10th m. off I-24, exit 89, on Hwy 41E)
Ph. 615/895-9262 **Facilities:** 3-10x10 indoor stalls, 2 holding pens w/run-ins, hay & 60' round pen.

CROSS PLAINS, 37049

Single Tree Farm, Joe & Marcia Goins
7951 Hwy 25 E. (3 m. W. of I-65, exit 112)
Ph.615/654-2636 Cell 615/218-9579 Email:singletreeversatile@worldnet.att.net **Facilities:** 7-10x10 indoor stalls, 1-20x14 mare & foal stall, 3 paddock areas, 50' round pen w/run-in shelter, 60x100 indoor arena. 7 m. to motels/restaurants. $15 per horse advance payment required for reservations - no arrivals after midnight (no-shows lose advance.)

CURRENT NEGATIVE COGGINS, HEALTH CERTIFICATE & OWNERSHIP PAPERS REQUIRED - see page 2 for details

CROSSVILLE, 38571

JWP Stables, John & Pamela Prince
503 Old Genesis Rd. (I-40, exit 320. 6 m. from interstate)
Ph. 913/456-7534 Fax 931/456-6612 Email:jwp@multipro.com **Facilities:** 3 indoor stalls & pasture, Cash only. Motels & restaurants within 10 m.

DANDRIDGE, (Knoxville area) 37725

★ **Combs Crest Farm, Hillary & L.D. Combs, Owners**
2 m. off I-40, E. of Knoxville; 15 min. E. of I-75)
Ph. 865/397-3045 - home or Barn 865/397-1212 **Facilities:** Modern block barn. 12x12 stalls, mats, shavings, paddocks, hay, arena, wash-rack, hot water & RV hookup. Deluxe suite sleeps 4, breakfast, kitchen, VCR, A/C. Please call for Reservations & Directions. Vet/farrier avail.

DICKSON, 37055

Hit-A-Lick Farm, Edison or Jason Myatt
1582 S. Bear Creek Rd. (I-40, exit 172/Dickson-Centerville. 3 m. to barn)
Ph. 615/446-9905 615/446-2858
Facilities: Stalls & turn-outs, holdng pens, pasture, feed & parking w/elec & water. No alcohol.

FAIRVIEW, 37062

"Best Little Horse House," Gennette S. Norman, hostess
7201 Cumberland Dr. (5 min. from I-40, exit 182. 25 m. SW of Nashville)
Ph. 615/799-8833 Mobile 615/500-8812 Fax 715/297-8624
Email:genettesn@aol.com **Facilities:** 6 indoor stalls, 2 holding pens & pasture. Close to fishing, camping, hiking, horse trails and Nashville attractions.

FAIRVIEW, 37062

Lazy Susan Appaloosas, Rick & Susan Morrison
7250 Northwest Hwy (3 m. off I-40W, exit 182. 20 m. W. of Nashville)
Ph. 615/799-0991 **Facilities:** 6 indoor stalls, 60' round pen, 6 acres of pasture & oats/hay.

CURRENT NEGATIVE COGGINS, HEALTH CERTIFICATE & OWNERSHIP PAPERS REQUIRED - see page 2 for details

FRANKEWING, 38459

Frankewing, Tennessee

★ **Hollow Pond Farm,**
P.O. Box 775 Location: 800 Tight Bark Rd. (2 m. off I-65, exit 14. 1 hr. S. of Nashville)
Ph. **1-800/463-0154** 931/424-8535 Fax 931/424-9918
Email:hollowpond@aol.com **Facilities:** Barn w/8 indoor stalls or pasture - no barbed wire. Reservations required.

FRANKLIN, 37064

★ **Namaste Acres Country Ranch Inn, Bill & Lisa Winters**
5436 Leipers Creek Rd. (13 m. off I-65. 1 m. off Natchez Trace Pkwy; 11 m. from Franklin. Quiet valley setting)
Ph. 615/791-0333 Web:namasteacres.com Email:namastebb@aol.com **Facilities:** Stalls, paddocks, pasture, arena, round pen & walker. Swimming/horseback riding/year round hot tub. Country home offers 3 theme privacy suites w/in-room coffee/ phone/fridge & TV/VCR. Private entrance & bath. Credit cards accepted. Call for rates & availability.

GEORGETOWN, 37336

Jerry L. Fenstermaker
11555 Hwy 58 (Exit 25 off I-75)
Ph. 423/961-2572 Cell 423/284-5872 Email:cparider@volstate.net **Facilities:** 6 indoor stalls, round pen, small pasture & elec/water for campers.

GEORGETOWN, 37336

★ **Windwood Farms, Lucy C. Austin**
8123 Smith Rd. (I-75, Cleveland exit 25, W.)
Ph. 423/326-2115 Email:lucylucypony@aol.com Web:www.windwoodfarmsdart-moors.com**Facilities:** 8 stall barn, private paddock, round pen, wash rack, 65 ac. with trails, parking for large trailers and guest quarters in barn, can accommodate 4 adults (see website.)

TENNESSEE

CURRENT NEGATIVE COGGINS, HEALTH CERTIFICATE & OWNERSHIP PAPERS REQUIRED - see page 2 for details

JAMESTOWN, 38556

★ **East Fork Stables**
3598 S. York Hwy. (27 m. N. of I-40; 25 m. S. of KY line)
Ph.931/879-1176 Fax 931/879-1179 Email:eastfork@multipro.com Web:eastforkstables.com **Facilities:** 120 covered stalls, corral panel sets, pasture, feed avail., for sale, arena, 100 m. privately owned trails & 150 campsites. 7-2/bdrm cabins, 1 apt. & 3 houses avail. All major credit cards accepted.

LEBANON, 37087

★ **J.R. & Juli Kelley, Cool Breeze Ranch**
1400 Peyton Rd. (1-1/2 m. off I-40, exit 239 West; exit 239B East)
Ph. 615/443-0347 or 615/453-8404 **Facilities:** 17 indoor stalls ($20/night), 50x125 holding pen & parking/elec/water for campers. 30 m. E. of Nashville; Cedars of Lebanon State Park, 10 m.

MANCHESTER, 37355

★ **The Barn: Bob & Mary Kraft**
287 Matlock Rd. (Off I-24. 1 hr. S. of Nashville; 15 m. to Shelbyville/ Home of the Celebration; 12 m. to Tulahoma)
Ph. 931/857-3860 **1-800/292-5807** **Facilities:** 10 indoor stalls, fenced pasture, outdoor arena, 45 acres of trails, space for campers/ trailers, private efficiency apt. & on site mgr. Near Lake Normandy/ quiet location for stop-over/vacation. Call or write for reservations/rates.

MEMPHIS, 38018

Shelby Farms Show Place Arena
105 S. Germantown Rd. (I-40, exit 16 S; I-240, exit 13 E. See map on ad.)
Ph. 901/756-7433Fax 901/756-9920 **Facilities:** 600+ stalls, bedding (60-70 lb. bags) & elec/water for campers at site, dump station on grounds. Reservations REQUIRED! - at least one week in advance of arrival. (See ad on next pg.)

CURRENT NEGATIVE COGGINS, HEALTH CERTIFICATE & OWNERSHIP PAPERS REQUIRED - see page 2 for details

MURFREESBORO, 37128

★ **Hunter's Court Stables, David Wright**
6331 Franklin Rd. (Hwy 96 W. 3-1/2 m. W. of I-24)
Ph. 615/896-4189 Email:dqwright@man.com Web:www.hunterscourt.com
Facilities: 50 stalls, holding pens, pasture, feed, large indoor ring, outdoor arenas, trails & space for campers.

MURFREESBORO, 37128

Womack Stables at Glen Oaks Farm, Rick Womack
4024 Barfield Crescent Rd. (5 m. from I-24, 35 m. SE of Nashville)
Ph. 615/896-2310 Fax 615/848-9290 Email:womackst@aol.com
Web:www.glenoaksfarms.com **Facilities:** 100 stalls.

ONEIDA, 37841

★ **Crikett Lane c/o Wilderness Resorts**
1463 Big Ridge Rd. (Off I-40 or I-75/Big South Fork exit)
Ph. 423/569-9847 **Facilities:** 8 indoor stalls. New 3 bdrm cabin/2 bath/sleeps 12 w/fireplaces & hot tub on 8 acres adjoining Big South Fork Nat'l River & Recreation Area. Hiking, riding, canoeing & fishing.

CURRENT NEGATIVE COGGINS, HEALTH CERTIFICATE & OWNERSHIP PAPERS REQUIRED - see page 2 for details

PINEY FLATS, 37686

★ **Walnut Creek Farm, Jane & Phil Elsea, D.V.M.**
2490 Enterprise Rd. (7 m. S. of I-81, exit 69. Scenic upper NE Tennessee area)
Ph. 423/538-8931 **Facilities:** 4-12x12 & 2-12x24 box stalls, turnout lot, pasture, walker, draft horse shoeing stocks, camper/ trailer space & 2 bdrm for B&B w/kitchen/screened porch/laundry area adjoining barn. Equine vet on premises. Call for availability/rates. Clean, safe facilities.

PROSPECT, 38477

Cherokee Ridge Stables, C.A. & Pam House
505 Dog Branch Rd. (I-65, exit 14/Hwy 11-TL, left to TLR beside Hilltop Mkt. Stay left 3/8 m. on left)
Ph. 931/363-3229 Fax 931/363-4660 **Facilities:** 18 indoor stalls, holding pens, pasture, feed, arena, trails, camper parking w/elec & water and Bed & Breakfast - above barn.

RICEVILLE, 37370

Twin Oaks Farm, Steve & Sherry Landers
180 Co. Rd. 726 (I-75, exit 42/Riceville)
Ph. Home 423/462-2386 Work 423/745-1683 Cell 423/506-3890 Email:slander@farmcredit.com **Facilities:** 6-12x12 indoor stalls, round pen, grass hay avail. & camp w/elec. & water. 163 acres near Cherokee Nat'l Forest. Reservations required.

SOMERVILLE, 38068

Lucky D Ranch
2950 Tomlin Rd. (Hwy 64. 30 min. from Memphis)
Ph. 901/465-2066 **Facilities:** 5 indoor stalls, 2 holding pens, 50x60 covered arena, 4-horse walker & 1 camper hookup. $20/night, bedding incl.

SPRING CITY, 38381

Mountain Echo Farm & Tack, Kirk & Pat Webb
1851 Dixie Lee Hwy. (On US 27, 6 m. N. of Spring City; 15 m. S. of I-40)
Ph. 423/365-5687 **Facilities:** 8 indoor stalls, 2 with walkout paddocks, holding pen, pasture, feed, mtn. trails, camper hookup possible & bunk house w/bath. Vet on call. Clean & good care.

SPRING CREEK, 38378

Journey's End, James & Micki Page
P.O. Box 59 Location:103 Springcreek-Law Rd./Hwy 152 (I-40, exit 93, 2 m.)
Ph. 731/935-2413 Fax 731/427-4710 Email:pages@charter.net **Facilities:** 20 stalls, 4 holding pens, 80 ac. of pasture, small indoor arena, camper hookup and rooms avail. Meals weekends only.

CURRENT NEGATIVE COGGINS, HEALTH CERTIFICATE & OWNERSHIP PAPERS REQUIRED - see page 2 for details

SWEETWATER

Sweetwater Equestrian Center, Inc.
Mail: 1065 County Rd. #316, Niota TN 37826 (3-1/2 m. off I-75, exit 60)
Ph. **1-800/662-4042** 615/337-2674 **Facilities:** 28 indoor stalls, holding pens, pasture, feed, arena, round pen, washrack w/H&C water & parking space. Motels/restaurants at exit.

TOWNSEND, 37882

★ **Lazy Horse Retreat**
938 Schoolhouse Gap Rd. (3 m. off Hwy 321 which runs thru Townsend)
Ph. 865/448-6810 Email:lazyhrse@icx.net
Web:www.thesmokies.com/lazy_horse/ **Facilities:** 12 indoor box stalls, 2-80x100 holding pens, 3 stock pens, 1/2 acre pasture, 150-175 m. of trails in immediate area (Smoky Mt. Nat'l Park - free), 3 furnished, 2-bdrm cabins and 1-bdrm furnished efficiency cabin.

TENNESSEE

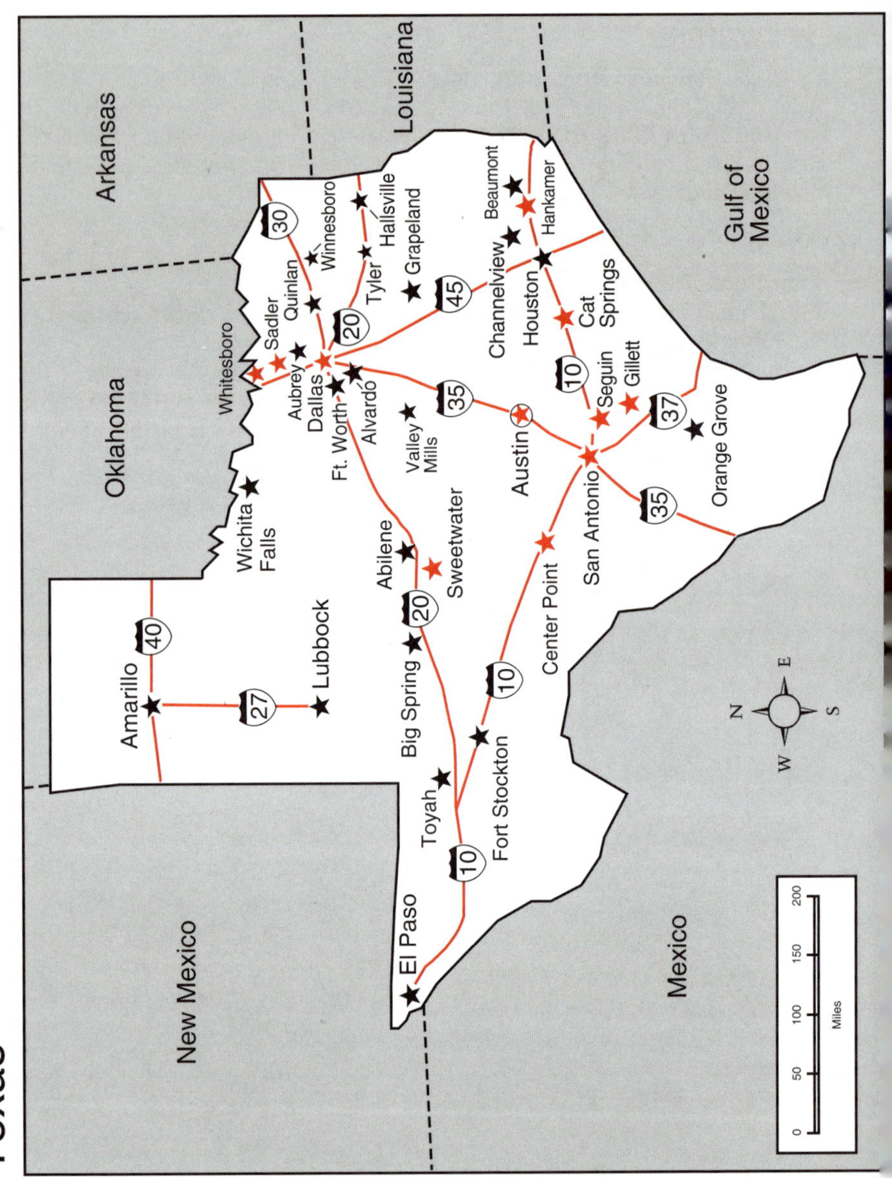

★ Vacation/Layover spots ★ Layovers only
State Capitol Hwy Junction cities

CURRENT NEGATIVE COGGINS, HEALTH CERTIFICATE & OWNERSHIP PAPERS REQUIRED - see page 2 for details

ABILENE, 79601

Blue Horse Stables, John & Janie Tucher
5709 Summerhill Rd. (1 m. N. & 2 m. W. of I-20, off FM 2404)
Ph. 915/676-1877 Email:johnjanietucher@hotmail.com Web:www.bluehorsestables.com **Facilities:** 5 indoor stalls, 5 large turnouts & 5 small turnouts - all partially covered steel pipe pens w/water & feeders, wash rack, round pen, riding areas, limited elec & water hookups & fishing. Completely fenced in w/coded front gate for security.

ABILENE, 79602

Taylor County Expo Center, Tony McMillan, Gen. Mgr.
1700 Hwy 36 (Hwy 36 & Loop 322)
Ph. 915/677-4376 **Facilities:** 750 stalls, holding pens, arenas, camper hookup & parking space. Reservations preferred.

ALVARADO, 76009

Jaynor Farm, Jan & Dayne Brenneman
P.O. Box 1247 Location: 8516 FM 3136 (20 m. S. of Ft. Worth; 30 m. SW of Dallas; 1/2 m. W. of I-35 W. Call for directions)
Ph. **1-800/216-4697** 817/790-3307 Email:jan@jaynorfarm.com
Web:www.jaynorfarm.com **Facilities:** 12x12 stalls, 3 pasturettes w/sheds, bring own feed/hay, lighted sandy arena, covered/lighted 50x50 arena, h&c wash rack, 40 ac. woods/fields to ride, elec. for trailers & efficiency apt. avail. Shavings provided. Owners live on property. Call for rates/reservations. Cash only.

AMARILLO, 79103

Double E Arena
1300 S.E. 46th (Off I-40, S. on Osage, right on 46th St. Barn at top of hill)
Ph. 806/379-8866 Email:eearena@niinet.net **Facilities:** 50 stalls available & camper hookups..

CURRENT NEGATIVE COGGINS, HEALTH CERTIFICATE & OWNERSHIP PAPERS REQUIRED - *see page 2 for details*

AMARILLO, 79106

Tascosa Stables, Inc., Jimmie & Cheryl Rhoderick

907 Broadmoor Location: 3513 N. Western St. (Between I-40 & Loop 335 on Western. 4 m. N. of I-40, Western exit and 1/2 m. S. of Loop 335 on Western)
Ph.**1-866/272-3996** Office 806/342-9061 Fax 806/374-9401 Cell 806/680-8399 Email:tascosastables@earthlink.net Web:tascosastables.com **Facilities:** 30 indoor stalls w/outdoor runs, 17 shedrow stalls w/fly spray system, holding pens, 2 round pens - 60' & 70', feed, indoor arena, 8-horse walker, trails, elec. for campers, stallion stalls, organic fly spray system, & security gates 1-bdrm apt. w/satelitte dish.

AMARILLO, 79124-2609

Happy Tracks Horse Motel

14731 Indian Hill Rd. (I-40 West, 4 m. to exit 60, turn right, then left into motel - all weather driveway)
Ph. 806/352-4031 352-9508 **Facilities:** 23 indoor box stalls, runs, outside pens, parking w/elec & water for campers and guest rooms avail.

AMARILLO, 79159

Lone Star Bed & Bale

P.O. Box 51067 Location: Apx. 8 m. E. of Amarillo (I-40, exit 87 S. on FM 2373 3-1/2 m.)
Ph. Office 806/944-5324 Mobile 806/674-8047 Email:dpoliver@arn.net
Facilities: New barn w/12x12 stalls w/bedding, holding pens, 50' round pen, furnish own feed, trailer parking & water/elec for campers. Facility enclosed w/7' fencing & auto gate entrance. Owners live on premises. Reservations preferred.

AUBREY, 76227

Bison Hollow Bed, Breakfast & Barn, Charles & Jean Burch

1149 Raymond Burch Trail (I-35 N. of Denton, exit 470/Loop 288 E. to exit Hwy 380E/377N, Ike Byrom E., Running Branch N., R Burch Tr W)
Ph. 940/365-9460 **Facilities:** 3 outdoor stalls, 3 overhangs, 3 runs, camper parking w/limited elec/water avail., parking space for trailers and 2 rooms avail. w/full country breakfast. Vet. nearby. Non-smoking facilitiy. Call for reservations/rates.

CURRENT NEGATIVE COGGINS, HEALTH CERTIFICATE & OWNERSHIP PAPERS REQUIRED - see page 2 for details

AUSTIN area

★ **Happy Horse Hotel, Hollis Wayne**
860 Pope Bend N., Cedar Creek TX 78612 (20 m. E. of Austin off Hwy 71. 12 m. W. of Bastrop)
Ph. 512/303/0589 Email:hollis@holliswayne.com
Web:www.happyhorsehotel.com **Facilities:** 8 large pens, water/elec/gravel space for 5 big rigs, firepit, furnished bungalow/sleeps 3 w/outdoor privy & hot shower. Quiet country site/owners next door. 1 m. from McKinney Roughs Eques, Park w/18 m. of dirt trails along the Colorado River.

BEAUMONT, 77713

Reins Rd. Mobil Home/RV Park & Stables, Linda C. Shackelford
2758 Reins Rd. (I-10 thru Beaumont. E. or W. take Eastex Frwy, exit at Hwy 105 W., 5.3 m. to Reins Rd. at Exxon-Mobile station)
Ph. & Fax 409/753-2787 Call before sending fax **Facilities:** 10 indoor stalls, holding pens, pasture, feed, arena, walker, trails & camper hookup. Dogs welcome. No credit cards, no personal checks.

BIG SPRING, 79720

The Pet Connection, Melanie & Randy Gambrell
4510 S. Hwy 87 (20 min. E. of Big Spring. I-20, exit 192/FM 821)
Ph. 915/267-PETS (7387) - day Nights 915/394-4251 **Facilities:** 15 outdoor stalls w/covers, 3 holding pens w/covers, 2 arenas & camper hookup. Call for reservations/rates. Must have copies of all current health papers incl. rabies, VEWT.

CAT SPRING (Houston area), 78933

★ **Rancho Texcelente IXL, Nancy Flick**
P.O. Box 55 Location: 14012 Paso Fino Rd. (I-10, 35 m. W. of Houston, exit 720; N. on 36 2 m., left on 1094 12 m.)
Ph. 979/865-3636 Fax - 979/865-1929
Email:ixl@paso.net Web:www.paso.net
Facilities: 38 indoor stalls, 4 holding pens, 250 acres of pasture, feed, 1 open/1 covered arenas, covered round pen, walker, escorted or unescorted trails, camper hookupand guest quarters. Kennels. Lease horses - Paso Finos.

TEXAS

CURRENT NEGATIVE COGGINS, HEALTH CERTIFICATE & OWNERSHIP PAPERS REQUIRED - *see page 2 for details*

CENTER POINT, 78010

★ **Canaan Acres, Clay & Lainey Clark**
P.O. Box 6 Location: 1 Elm Pass Rd. (40 m. W. of San Antonio off I-10. 25 m. from Fredricksberg; 10 m. from Kerrville)
Ph. 830/634-7066 Fax 830/634-2236 Email:canaan@hctc.net **Facilities:** 10 stalls w/paddocks, pasture, riding arena, walker, round pen & plenty of room for trailers/campers. Quiet country roads w/wide shoulders for trail rides in the scenic Texas Hill Country.

CHANNELVIEW (Houston area), 77530

Evergreen Stables, James & Nadine Helmer
1422 North Dr. Location: 1416 North Dr. (I-10, Sheldon Rd. exit, N. 2 m. E. side of Houston)
Ph. 281/452-4480 **Facilities:** 8 indoor stalls, 2 fenced pastures, lighted arena, round pen & walker. Owner lives on premises. Farrier on premises.

DALLAS, 75238

★ **Bettina Stable, Irmgard Christina Pomper, owner**
7921 Goforth Rd. at White Rock Trail (N. of White Rock Lake)
Ph. 214/343-4747 Email:pompbarn@flash.net **Facilities:** Indoor stalls.

EL PASO, 79927

The Ranch, Steve & Juanita Proffitt
12320 Gateway Blvd. East (Eastbound side of I-10. I-10 Westbound, exit 42, 2-1/2 m. on Eastbound side. I-10 Eastbound, exit 37, 2 m.E)
Ph. 915/851-3766 Fax 915/851-0530 **Facilities:** 38 indoor stalls, holding pens, arena, round pens & walker. Horse Trailer sales lot. Reservations appreciated.

EL PASO, 79932

Paul Billingsley
924 Gato Rd. (Exit 8/Artcraft Rd. off I-10; 10 min. to farm))
Ph. 915/877-2182 Email:horseshoestable@cs.com Web:www.horseshoestable.com **Facilities:** 18 indoor stalls, 10 outdoor pens & feed incl.

FORT STOCKTON, 79735

Daggett Stables - Buster & Mary Williams
1816 E. 53rd Ln. (4-1/2 m. N. of I-10 on Hwy 1053)
Ph. 915/336-0219 Fax 915/336-8105 Email:adaggett@west-tex.net **Facilities:** 5 indoor stalls w/runs, 4 outdoor stalls w/roof, holding pens, round pen, elec/water/camper parking. Furnish own feed. PLEASE call at least 3 days in advance. If unable to give advance notice, call as soon as possible and come on in.

CURRENT NEGATIVE COGGINS, HEALTH CERTIFICATE & OWNERSHIP PAPERS REQUIRED - *see page 2 for details*

FORT WORTH, 76126

ParkRidge Stables, Doug & Susan Anderson, mgrs.
6019 Hwy 377 S. (W. side of Ft. Worth. 1/2 m. off I-20. 20 min. from Will Rogers/John Justin Arena complex)
Ph. 817/705-5101 Email:cowboysu@flash.net **Facilities:** 12x12 indoor stalls, 12x24 stalls in shed row, paddocks, round pens, turnouts/pasture, indoor/outdoor arenas w/lights, indoor wash rack, walker, Park Trail riding, parking area for trailers & RV hookups next to stalls. Vet/farrier on call. Call for reservations.

GILLETT, 78116

★ **Ken & Jody Gabbert**
516 P.R. 2200 (I-10, Seguin exit. St. Hwy 119)
Ph. 830/789-4133 Email:adanal@adanalranch.com Web:www.adanalranch.com **Facilities:** 3 outdoor stalls, holding pens, pasture, arena, trails incl. for those who stay the nite. camper hookup and 4 cottages for Bed & Breakfast - pictures on web site.

GRAPELAND, 75844

Duke & Nancy Kacvinski
3510 Anderson County Rd. 174 (Just off US 287 between Palestine & Crockett)
Ph. 903/478-2112 Cell 813/220-0010 Email:nancyk_1@bigfoot.com **Facilities:** 4 indoor 12x12 pipe stalls, feed & hay avail., arena/turnout & 30-50 amp/water/sewer avail for campers. No stallions. Call first for availability.

HALLSVILLE, 75650

Triple Creek Ranch Equine Motel, Ellie & Raymond Murray
2119 FM 450 S. (50 yds. S. of I-20, exit 604/Hallsville exit, on FM 450, between Longview & Marshall)
Ph. 903/660-0139 Pager **1-800/725-5195** Email:raymond@cfeinc.com **Facilities:** 56-12x12 stalls, large turnouts w/sheds, 84x140 lighted indoor/150x300 lighted outdoor arenas, 60' round pen, equestrian jumps, walker, wash racks, elec. for trailers & large turnaround. Farrier on call. Motels 7 min.

CURRENT NEGATIVE COGGINS, HEALTH CERTIFICATE & OWNERSHIP PAPERS REQUIRED - see page 2 for details

HANKAMER, 77560

★ **T&L Enterprises, Trudy & Lee Masters**
HC 1, Box 581 (45 min. E. of Houston, 30 min. W. of Beaumont, 3 m. N. of I-10)
Ph. 409/374-2539 Fax 409/374-2875 Email:temasters@esc4.com **Facilities:** Stalls, pasture, covered round pen & ample parking for large trailers. RV hookups avail. Cabin w/kitchen/accommodates 4 adults w/continental or full breakfast. Easy access to I-10.

HOUSTON, 77043

Magic Moments Stable, Granger Durdin
11214 Pecan Creek Dr. Location: 1726 Upland Dr. (I-10 & Wilcrest exit)
Ph. Mobile 281/450-2538 Barn 713/461-1228 Fax 281/357-3435 Email:gdurdin@swbell.net **Facilities:** 42 indoor stalls, 3 individual paddocks, feed avail., covered arena, 1 block from trails in Addicks Reservoir & trailer parking for up to 6-horse trailer. Vet/farrier on call. Call for reservations.

HOUSTON, 77049

Circle R. Stables, Glenda Riordan
7431 Miller Rd. #2 (I-10, Beltway 8 exit N.; E. side of Houston)
Ph. 281/452-4732 Cell 281/455-4585 **Facilities:** 40 covered stalls, holding pens, pasture, feed, outdoor arena, round pen, walker, trails in Lake Houston area and parking w/elec & water for RV's/trailers.

HOUSTON, 77090

Rocking H Farm, Pam Hocker
333 Woerner Rd. (Located in North Houston. Close to I-45. 1 m. N. of FM 1960 off of Kuykendahl)
Ph. 281/444-7633 Email:PamPonyGirl@aol.com **Facilities:** 14 very large box stalls, private paddocks, large tree covered sandy area to ride, wash rack & camper hookup avail. This is a private boarding stable, but do have stalls & paddocks avail. for traveling horses. Can care for your animals if you need this service.

HOUSTON, 77245

Foxfire Farms, Julie & Jennifer Vaughan
P.O. Box 450210 Location: 13034 S. Post Oak (SW Houston, midway between I-610 & S. Sam Houston Tollway/Beltway 8. Near Astrodome)
Ph. 713/729-8308 Fax 713/729-3220 Email:JVFoxfire@aol.com Web:foxfirefarms.cc **Facilities:** 5 indoor stalls, 3 holding pens, outdoor stall w/paddock, pastures, feed/hay/water avail., indoor/outdoor lighted arenas, round pen, washracks, locked tack storage, trails & parking for trailers. 24 hr. security/extra services avail. Hotels nearby.

CURRENT NEGATIVE COGGINS, HEALTH CERTIFICATE & OWNERSHIP PAPERS REQUIRED - see page 2 for details

LUBBOCK, 79423

Four Bar K Ranch, Chuck Kershner
2811 98th St. (2 m. W. of I-27 on 98th/city limits)
Ph. 806/789-8682 **Facilities:** 8 indoor/8 outdoor stalls, feed avail. & camper hookup avail.

ORANGE GROVE, 78372

The LUR Ranch, L.T. Umfleet
459 Co. Rd. 300 (I-37, Mathis exit. Call for directions)
Ph. 361/384-9118 Email:LTumfleet@msn.com **Facilities:** 6 indoor stalls, 16 ac. of pasture, coastal hay provided, 1-100x100/1-130x250 arenas, 10 m. of trails & camper hookup avail.

QUINLAN, 75474

Tatum's Boarding Stable
6135 Hwy 34 S. (I-30, exit Hwy 34. 8 m. S)
Ph. Barn 903/883-0486 Voice Mail 903/883-2606 Email:davietatum@aol.com **Facilities:** 12 indoor stalls, 8 large runs, round pen, feed, indoor/outdoor arenas, wash rack & camper hookup.

SADLER, 76264

★ **Cross Country Stables - Equine B&B, Jennifer Noblin**
16830 FM 901 (Access from Hwy 82 or 377, between I-35 & US 75)
Ph. 903/523-1049 Fax 903/523-5389 Email:jen@crosscountrystables.com Webs:trax.to/stables and www.gnomehollow.net/Cross Country **Facilities:** 5 stalls w/outside access, 1 ac./2 ac./5 ac. pastures, feed avail., round pen, trails - free or w/guide, and elec & water for campers. Dogs on leash please. Hard hats if mounted on property.

SAN ANTONIO, 78245

★ **T-Slash-Bar Ranch**
13901 Hwy 90 W. (US Hwy 90 at St. Hwy 211)
Ph. 210/677-0502 Web:t-slash-barranch.com **Facilities:** 50 stalls (mix of indoor box, stalls w/runs & pens,) holding pens, pasture, feed, 150x300 lighted arena, 2 walkers, over 1500 acres of trails, Bed & Breakfast and rooms. Close to Sea World of Texas, Hyatt Resort, Historic Castroville, Kelly & Lackland AFB.

SEGUIN, 78155

★ **Buzzard Creek D, Danny & Mary Davis**
2985 Gin Rd. (Between Seguin & San Antonio. 1-1/2 m. S. of I-10, exit 559/FM 465)
Ph. 210/914-3343 **Facilities:** 5 indoor stalls, 4 holding pens/2 are stud pens. San Antonio area: The Alamo, Fiesta Texas, Sea World & horse racing at Retama Park.

CURRENT NEGATIVE COGGINS, HEALTH CERTIFICATE & OWNERSHIP PAPERS REQUIRED - see page 2 for details

SEGUIN, 78155-1509

PGL Ranch
4001 US Hwy 90E (I-10, exit 612 to US Hwy 90, 1 m. E. on right)
Ph. 830/303-4949 **Facilities:** 12 indoor/3 outdoor stalls, 3 holding pens, pasture, alfalfa/coastal hay, walker & camper hookup. Diesel, gas, repairs, motels, restaurants, RV Serv & Park, largest Farm-Ranch-Western store in TX less than 5 min. away.

SWEETWATER, 79556

★ **Ranch House Motel & Restaurant**
301 S. Georgia Ave. (I-20, exit 244)
Ph. 915/236-6341 or **1-800/622-5361** **Facilities:** 9 outdoor, covered stalls, locked & lighted. Full service Motel & Restaurant - 49 spacious rooms, cable TV, HBO & pool. Open 365 days per yr. Small pets ok. Major credit cards. Stalls avail. for motel guests only. Newly remodeled. Free full breakfast.

TOYAH, 79785

Ingram Ranch, Gary Ingram
Box 15 (I-20, exit 22. 8 blks N.)
Ph. 915/259-3951 Email:gingram@pecos.net **Facilities:** 12 indoor stalls, holding pens, pasture, feed & arena. Holding pens for cattle avail.

TYLER, 75709

Pine Lake Stables, Joanne Casmo
P.O. Box 668, Chandler TX 75758 Location: 11015 Pine Lake Blvd. (8 m. from Loop 323 W. of Tyler)
Ph. 903/592-8075 **Facilities:** 35 indoor stalls, feed avail., AQHA approved arena, walker, trails and 1 camper hookup (no pets.) Multiple hotels on Loop 323.

VALLEY MILLS, 76689

C Bar Stables, Larry & Martha Montgomery
P.O. Box 788 (Rt. 2, Hwy 56. 2 m. N. of Valley Mills on Hwy 56; 30 m. NW of Waco)
Ph. 254/934-2270 or 932-6551 Mobile 254/749-6962 Fax 254/934-2270 Email:CBarStables@hor1.net **Facilities:** 12 indoor/outdoor stalls. 5 holding pens, pasture, feed avail., lighted outdoor arena, round pen, over 1000 acres for trails and 15 camper hookups w/elec. & water. Call for reservations/rates.

WHITESBORO, 76273

4F Ranch & Arena, Tad Ferguson
566 Ferguson Rd. (6 m. N. of Hwy 82 toward TX/OK border & Lake Texoma; 72 m. N. of Dallas/Ft. Worth Metroplex)
Ph. 903/564-3414 Cell 903/814-3070 **Facilities:** 2 completely housed stables w/elec & water. Full-size arena w/chutes & working pens with access to pasture, exercise areas & close to ponds/shaded water holes. Vet/farrier on call. Hotels/2 RV parks in vicinity. Call for reservations/rates. Cattle welcome.

CURRENT NEGATIVE COGGINS, HEALTH CERTIFICATE & OWNERSHIP PAPERS REQUIRED - see page 2 for details

WHITESBORO, 76273

★ **Waldron Performance Horses**
20910 US 377 N. (2 m. N. of US Hwy 82 - right in the middle of Quarter Horse country)
Ph. 903/564-1668 or 903/271-1407 Email:jccwaldron@texoma.net **Facilities:** 29 indoor stalls, outdoor pens, hay/feed avail., lighted arena, wash rack, plenty of parking w/elec. Primarily a breeding & training operation, specializing in reining and cow horses. They have bred mares & colts for sale.

WICHITA FALLS, 76309

Turtle Creek Stables, Tambra Holcomb
2110 Turtle Creek Rd. (3 m. from Hwy 287)
Ph. 940/692-8130 Barn 940/691-6291 Cell 940/642-5807 Email:TTL@cst.net **Facilities:** 12 indoor stalls w/soft runs, 8 holding pens, 100+ acres of pasture, 2 arenas (1 lighted), walker & 6 RV hookups. 5 min. from motels. Nice newly remoded stalls.

WICHITA FALLS, 76310

Cruse Acres, Sam Cruse
(Overhead Expressway @ US 287/281[South] Interchange - take Windthorst or Midwestern Parkway exit. Min. away from J.S. Bridwell Agri Cen./Multi-Purpose Events Cen. & Coliseum)
Ph. 940/767-9284, beeper response Email:scruse@wf.net
Web:www.horsemotel.com **Facilities:** Covered stalls, shed row, stall mats, steel pens, pasture turn-out, round pen (all well lit), bedding & hay incl. @ $20 per horse. Reservations suggested. Owners live on premises w/vet on call. Expressway access & city-country location. 200 acres clean & secure.

WINNSBORO, 75494

V Ranch, Dianne Vance
541 CR 4440 (16 M. S. of I-30 at Mt. Vernon exit on 37 S.)
Ph. 903/365-7346 Email:texas_cowgirl_90@hotmail.com **Facilities:** 6-12x12 stalls, feed & bedding avail., hookups and rooms avail. Call for reservations

Utah

Idaho
15
84
Logan
Wyoming
Ogden
84
West Bountiful
Salt Lake City
80
Tooele
South Jordan
Nevada
Colorado
Salina
70
Moab
15
Cedar City
St. George
0
25
50
75
100
Miles
N
W
E
S
Arizona
New Mexico
Vacation/Layover spots
Layovers only
State Capitol
Hwy Junction cities

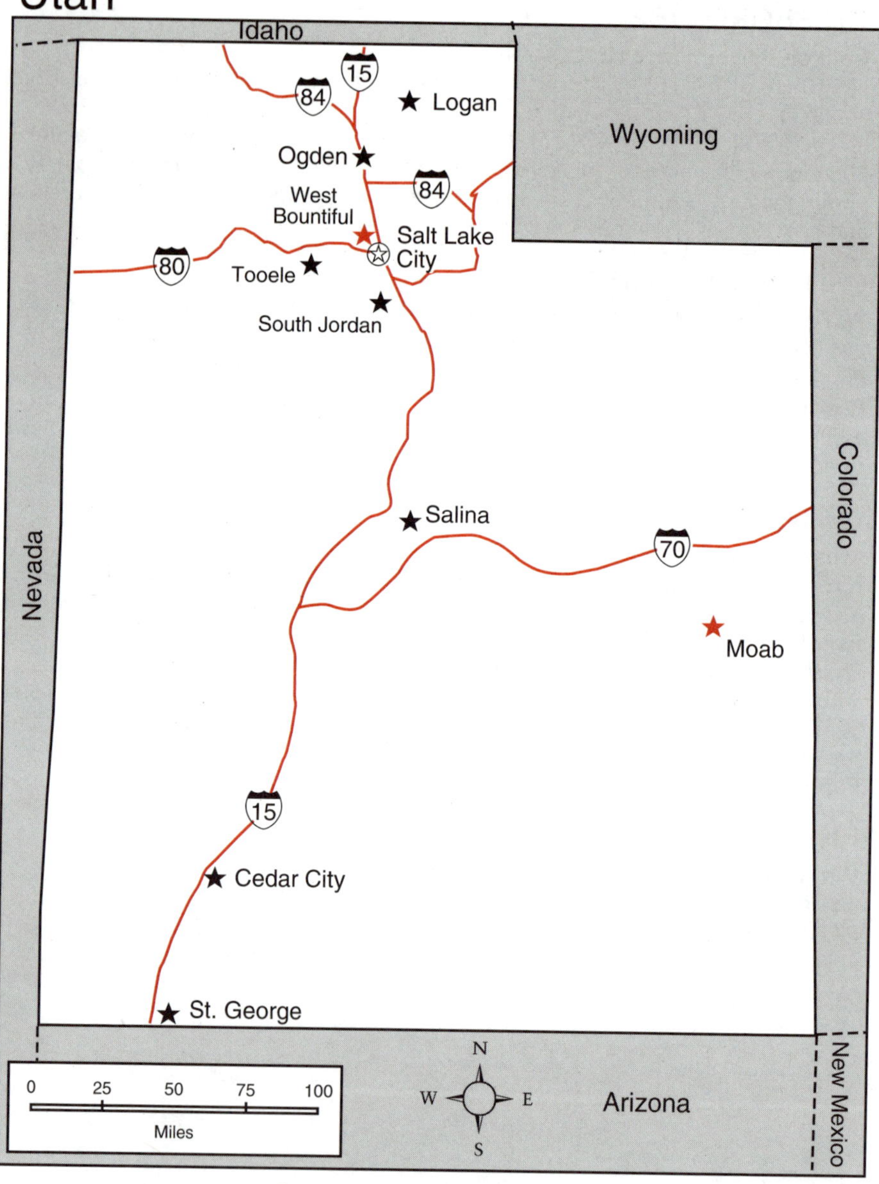

CURRENT NEGATIVE COGGINS, HEALTH CERTIFICATE & OWNERSHIP PAPERS REQUIRED - see page 2 for details

CEDAR CITY, 84720

Sundown Stables & Tack
5989 N. Minersville Hwy (4 m. N. of exit 62 off I-15 at Milepost 10 on Minersville Hwy)
Ph. 435/586-2740 **Facilities:** Indoor/outdoor stalls, holding pens, large 268x150 arena, round pen, trails and trailer parking w/elec & water. Large tack store on premises. Visa & MC accepted.

LOGAN, 84321

Triple D Stables, Dusty Davis
1880-1/2 S. Hwy 89-91 (E. of I-15/84)
Ph. 435/757-5147 Email:davisextreme@yahoo.com **Facilities:** 25-12x16 indoor stalls, 3 holding pens, 2 pastures, feed incl., outdoor arena & can trailer to trails nearby. Close to motels & RV hookup.

MOAB, 84532

★ **O.K. RV Park & Canyonlands Stables**
3310 Spanish Valley Dr. (5 m. S. of Moab on Hwy 191, exit E. at Shell Station, turn right at 4-way stop
Ph. 435/259-1400 Email:okrvpark@citlink.net Web:moab-utah.com/okrvpark/ **Facilities:** 20-20x40 covered outdoor pens, trails, complete camper hookups and apt/rooms.

OGDEN, 84404

Golden Spike Arena Events Center
1000 N. 1200 W. (I-15, exit 349; follow signs to Fairgrounds)
Ph. 801/399-8798 **1-800/44-ARENA** (2-7362) - outside Utah **Facilities:** 549 covered box stalls, holding pens & 2 indoor/1 outdoor stadiums. Call in advance for reservations. (See full page ad on next page)

OGDEN, 84404

Sleep Inn Hotel
1155 S. 1700 W. (I-15, exit 347 Downtown Ogden 4 m.; Golden Spike Arena 2 m.)
Ph. 801/731-6500 Fax 801/731-6282 Email:info@sleepinogden.com Web:www.sleepinogden.com **Facilities:** 10 outdoor stalls, locks & horse trailer parking avail. 65 rooms w/desk, dataports, VCR & direct TV. Complimentary deluxe continental breakfast & newpapers avail. in lobby. Hot tub avail. 24 hrs. Free local/800 calls. Restaurant next door. Vet 1-1/2 m.

SALINA, 84654

Best Western Shaheen's Motel
1225 South State (I-70/US 89, exit 54)
Ph. 801/529-7455 **Facilities:** 61 outdoor stalls (25 covered) and Black Hawk arena. Parking avail.

CURRENT NEGATIVE COGGINS, HEALTH CERTIFICATE & OWNERSHIP PAPERS REQUIRED - see page 2 for details

SOUTH JORDAN (SLC area), 84095

Salt Lake County Event Center & Fairgrounds, Garin Lamph
11400 S. 2200 W. (I-15 to 10600 S., W. to 2200 W., S. to 11500 S)
Ph. 801/254-0106 Fax 801/254-5113 Email:alovato@slc.ut.us
Web:www.slcoequestrian.org **Facilities:** 500 covered stalls & arenas avail. Call for reservations - credit card required to hold. County Fair.

SOUTH JORDAN, 84095

Terry Teeples Horse Stabling.
P.O. Box 95501 Location: 11040 S. 2700 W. (20 m. SW of SLC)
Ph. 801/446-8343 **Facilities:** 32 - 12 X 12 indoor/14outdoor stalls, stallion stalls, several outside runs, holding pens, feed, round ring, 3 arenas, 2 walkers, trails & truck/trailer parking. Short distance to all new motels at I-15.

ST GEORGE, 84770

Harmony Horse Haven, Steve Hafen
2321 S. Washington Fields Rd. (I-15, exit 10)
Ph. 435/673-3991 Cell 435/680-2650 **Facilities:** 6 covered stalls, holding pens, pasture, feed, arena, walker, wash bay, trails & room for parking. 6 p.m. arrival or call.

TOOELE/ERDA

Horse Haven Hotel, Diane Hernandez
3779 N. 570 W., Erda UT 84074 (Easy access from I-80, exit 99, 20 m. W. of SLC, then 6-1/2 m. S. on Hwy 36)
Ph. 435/833-9321 Email:horsehvn@trilobyte.net **Facilities:** Clean, dry covered stalls, turn out area for exercise, twice daily feedings, quality alfalfa & trailer parking. Grain avail. at extra cost. Local equine vet. Experienced care. Nightly or weekly boarding. Local motels within 5 m.

CURRENT NEGATIVE COGGINS, HEALTH CERTIFICATE & OWNERSHIP PAPERS REQUIRED - *see page 2 for details*

WEST BOUNTIFUL, 84087

★ **The American Cowboy/ Universal Equestrian Center, Jed Christensen**
1450 W. 400 N. (5 min. from I-15. 1 m. W. of I-15, exit 321. 10 m. N. of Salt Lake City)
Ph. 801/295-RIDE (7433) **Facilities:** 78 indoor/30 outdoor covered stalls, 3 holding pens, enclosed bull pen, pasture, indoor/outdoor arenas & hot walker. Barn Mgr. lives on premises. Reservations req. Complete Western Store & Feed Store, open 9-7, M-F & 9-6, Sat. Close to motels/restaurants.

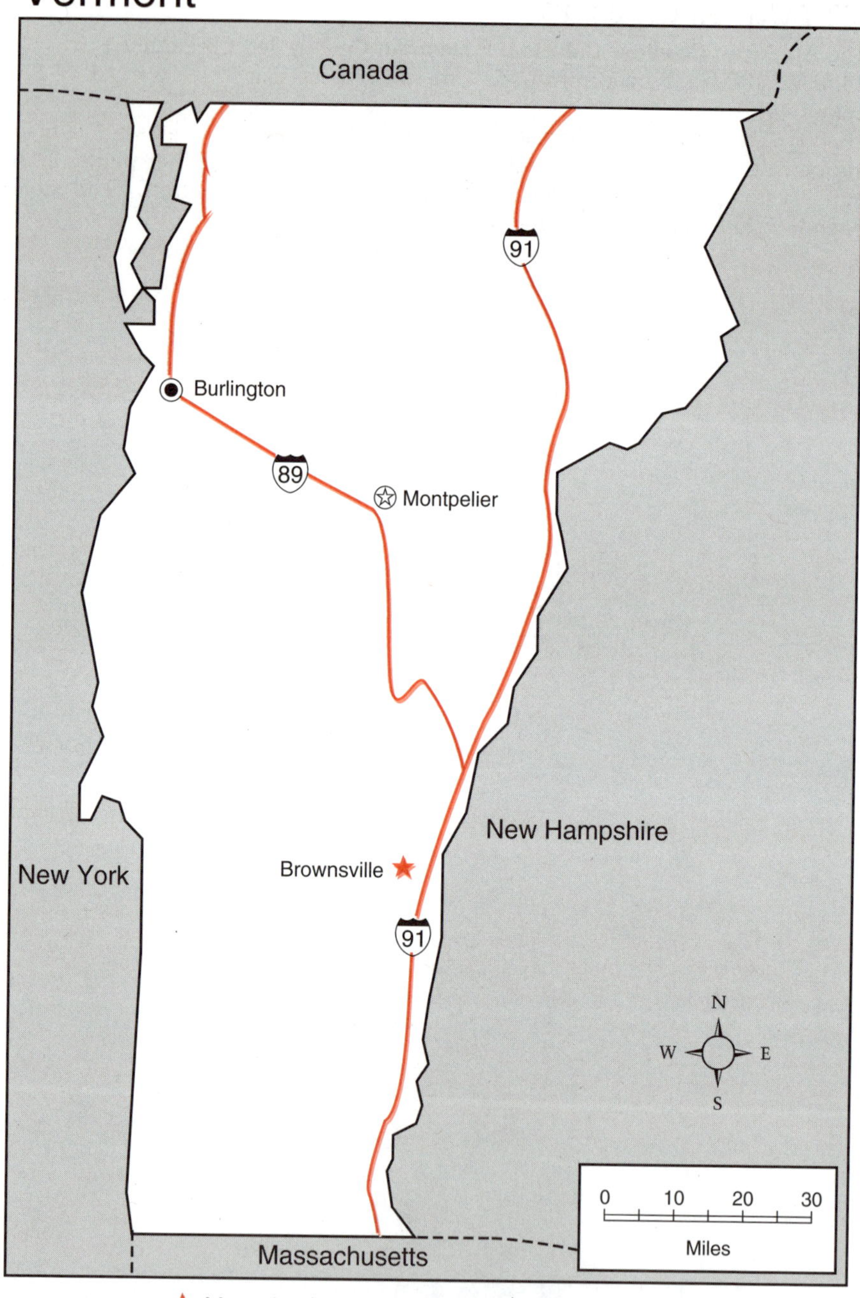
Vermont
Canada
91
Burlington
89
Montpelier
New Hampshire
New York
Brownsville
91
N
W
E
S
0
10
20
30
Miles
Massachusetts
Vacation/Layover spots
Layovers only
State Capitol
Hwy Junction cities

CURRENT NEGATIVE COGGINS, HEALTH CERTIFICATE & OWNERSHIP PAPERS REQUIRED - see page 2 for details

BROWNSVILLE, 05037

★ **Pond House Inn, Gretel Schuck**
P.O. Box 234 Location: 325 Shattuck Hill Rd. (15 min. from I-91,exit 8)
Ph. 802/484-0011 Email:pondhouse0011@yahoo.com Web:pondhouseinn.com
Facilities: Box stalls & turnout and springfed pond. Dinner (5 course N. Italian(& breakfast are included for Inn guests (all rooms w/queen-size beds/private bath.) No camping. Reservations are required. Near GMHA and miles of dirt roads & trails for recreational riding.

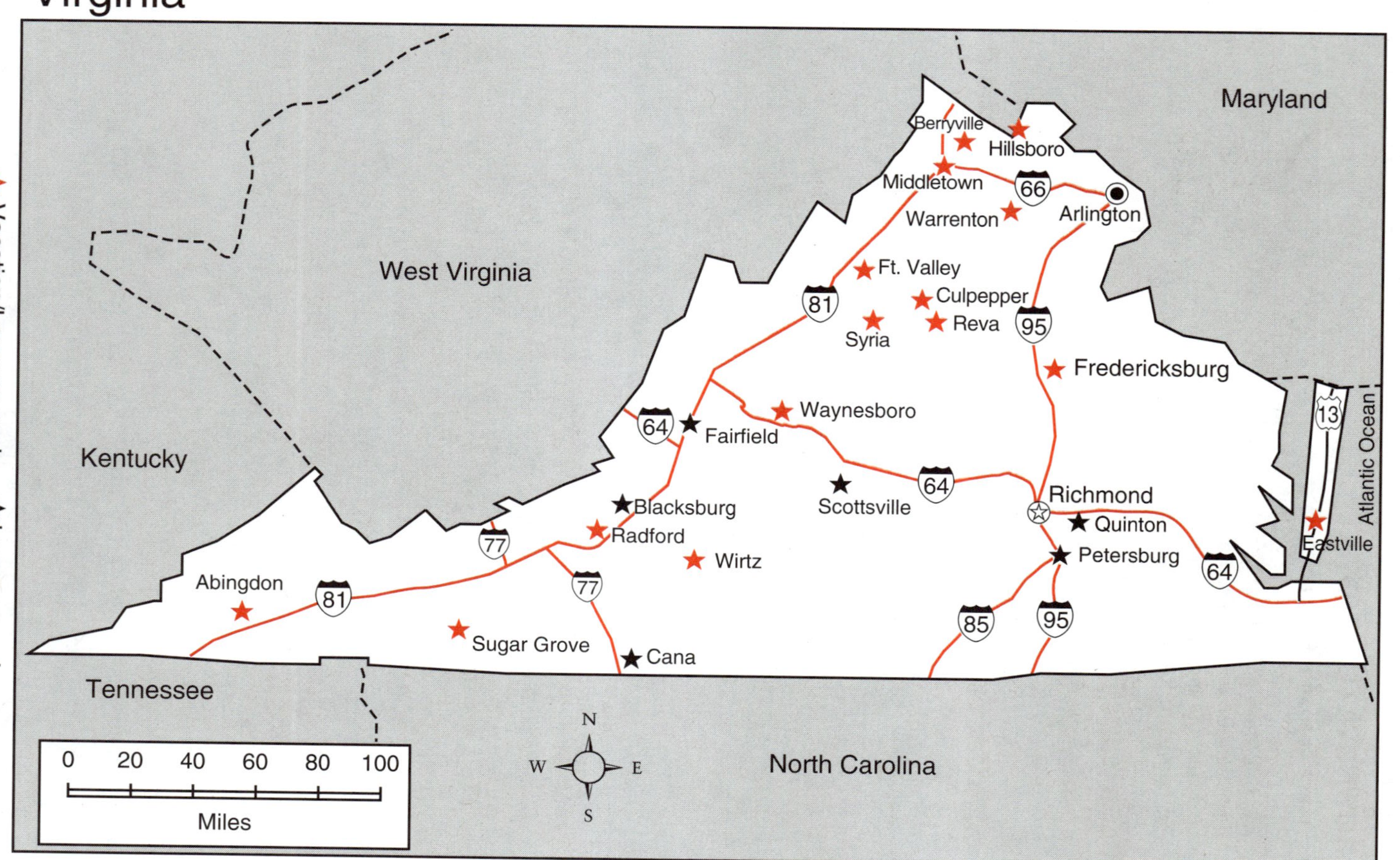
Virginia
Maryland
West Virginia
Kentucky
Tennessee
North Carolina
Atlantic Ocean
Berryville
Hillsboro
Middletown
66
Arlington
Warrenton
Ft. Valley
81
Culpepper
Syria
Reva
95
Fredericksburg
Waynesboro
13
64
Fairfield
Scottsville
Richmond
Quinton
Eastville
Blacksburg
Radford
Wirtz
Petersburg
77
Abingdon
85
Sugar Grove
Cana
N
W
E
S
0 20 40 60 80 100
Miles
Vacation/Layover spots
Layovers only
State Capitol
Hwy Junction cities

CURRENT NEGATIVE COGGINS, HEALTH CERTIFICATE & OWNERSHIP PAPERS REQUIRED - see page 2 for details

ABINGDON, 24211

★ **Black's Fort Stable, Inc., Cindy & Jimmy Patterson**
410 Green Spring Rd. (Less than 1 m. from I-81, exit 17)
Ph. 276/628-6263 Email:cpatterson@naxs.net **Facilities:** 12-12x12 indoor stalls, pasture, feed/hay avail., riding arena, wash rack w/cold water, near Virginia Creeper Trail, trailer parking and 3 rooms for Bed & Breakfast plus an efficiency apt. Reservation required.

BERRYVILLE, 22611

★ **The JBit Ranch, Barbara Johnson**
1674 Summit Point Rd. (15 min. from I-81 in Winchester VA. In Virginia horse country/beautiful Clark County)
Ph.& Fax 540/955-4099 Email:thejbit@earthlink.net Web:www.thejbitranch.com **Facilities:** 14 stalls, 5 paddocks, holding pen, feed (incl. senior & specialty), grass hay, pastures, 100x225 riding arena, 8 wash racks w/h&c water; 80 acres for trail riding, trailer/RV parking and Bed & Breakfast, 2 rooms w/private entrance/bath/dish TV. Pets welcome

BLACKSBURG, 24060

Dori-Del Hills & Training Stables, Del, Doris & Debbie Dyer
4180 Dori-Del Hills. (9 m. W. of I-81 on US 460; 2.7 m. on St. 624. N. side of Blacksburg)
Ph. 540/552-0085 or 540/951-8545 **Facilities:** 34 box stalls, 3 holding pens, pasture, feed, indoor/outdoor arenas, walker, trails, elec/parking for campers and Bed & Breakfast for up to 4. Training Facility. Motels within 4-6 m.

CANA, 24317

Tanbark Acres, L.L.C., Carlton & Dee Everhart
240 Tanbark Trail (1-1/10 m. from Hwy 52 or 6 m. from I-77. Call for directions)
Ph. 276/755-5191 Fax 276/755-2739 Email:deverhart@aisva.net Web:tanbarkacres.com **Facilities:** 10 indoor stalls, 4 paddocks, 15 ac. pasture & hay/grain. B&B next door, call 276/755-4900 for prices/reservations. Will direct to trails nearby. Call for reservations. Motel 3 m., will direct or make reservations.

CULPEPER, 22701-7531

★ **Andora Farm & Stables**
17275 Germanna Hwy (Rt. 3, 3 m. E. of Rt. 29/Culpepper)
Ph. & Fax 540/829-9555 Email:andora5seay@netscape.com **Facilities:** 6 indoor stalls, 8 indoor holding pens, lighted show arena, bathroom & shower w/arena, 300 acres for riding, parking & elec/water hookup.

CURRENT NEGATIVE COGGINS, HEALTH CERTIFICATE & OWNERSHIP PAPERS REQUIRED - see page 2 for details

EASTVILLE, 23347

★ **Windrush Farm B&B, Eleanor Gordon**
P.O. Box 1076 Location: 5350 Willow Oak Rd. (Right off Rt. 13, a major N/S Hwy. 20 min. N. of Chesapeake Bay Bridge-Tunnel. 1 hr. N. of Norfolk VA & 2 hr. S. of Salisbury MD)
Ph.757/678-7725 Fax 757/678-5577 Email:lcgordon@esva.net **Facilities:** Big, old barn w/5 box stalls & wash rack, paddocks & pasture avail., bring own feed/hay, miles of farm trails, incl. Chesapeake Bay beaches. Mid-19th century farmhouse B&B w/2 rooms & shared bath, central A/C. Guest pets welcome.

FAIRFIELD, 24435

Dream Away Farms, Carol Lange
P.O. Box 124 Location: 70 Jennifer Dr. (I-81, exit 200. 1.6 m. from Interstate)
Ph. 540/348-2273 **Facilities:** 10 new indoor stalls w/shavings, 8 holding pens, 4-board fencing, pastures, h&c wash rack & tractor trailer parking.. Rooms avail. Come and stay in the heart of the beautiful Shenandoah Valley. 10 m. from the V.A. Horse Center

FORT VALLEY, 22652

★ **Fort Valley Stable/Campground, Richard Deschenes**
299 S. Fort Valley Rd. (I-81, exit 279. Rt. 675 E. to Rt. 678 S))
Ph. 540/933-6633 **1-888/754-5771** Email:fvs@fortvalleystable.com
Web :www.fortvalleystable.com **Facilities:** 8 barn stalls, 3 -90x90 paddocks, 22-12x16 holding pens, 3 cabins w/kitchen & bath. 18 RV sites w/water & elec., 12 RV sites w/no hookups, 16 tent sites, 80 m. of mtn. trails, camp store, tack sales, fishing & dogs on leash.

FREDERICKSBURG, 22407

★ **Redfield Farm, Kathryn Dennis**
7506 Chancellor Rd. (5 m. W. of I-95. Located 50 m. S. of Washington D.C. in historic Fredericksburg)
Ph. 540/786-6453 or 540/786-2875 Email:kdennis@erols.com **Facilities:** 14 stalls, 3 paddocks, 3 large pastures, lots of parking & easy access for tractor trailers/large rigs and apt. avail. for overnight stays. Lots of restaurants/hotels nearby.

HILLSBORO

★ **Buckskin Manor, Gail & Jeff Bogert**
Rt. 671, 13452 Harpers Ferry Rd., Purcellville VA 20132 (10 m. E. of Rt. 340 @ Harpers Ferry WV. 10 m. W. of Rt. 7 @ Leesburg VA)
Ph.**1-888/668-7056** Email:innkeeper@buckskinmanor.com
Web:www.buckskinmanor.com **Facilities:** Barn w/4 indoor stalls, 2 paddocks, pasture, parking space for trailers, Bed & Breakfast - 3 rooms w/private baths, and 1 cottage. C&O Canal and W&OD riding trails nearby. Call for rates & reservations. Buckskin Manor started in the 1750's as a tavern.

CURRENT NEGATIVE COGGINS, HEALTH CERTIFICATE & OWNERSHIP PAPERS REQUIRED - *see page 2 for details*

MIDDLETOWN, 22645

★ **Monte Vista Stable**
8183 Valley Pike (I-81, exit 302. Near I-66 & I-81 intersection)
Ph. 540/869-4621 Fax 540/869-0979 **Facilities:** 5 indoor stalls, 2 holding pens, hay provided w/stabling and B&B on site avail. - call for rates. Reservations required/call for directions. Victorian estate w/renovated barn - on Nat'l Historic Registry. On major Civil War battlefield near Nat'l Forest trailheads.

PETERSBURG, 23805

Idle Moment Farm, Garry & Bobbie Moretz
7724 Vaughan Rd. (3 m. S. of Petersburg; 3-4 m. from I-85/I-95/I-295/ Rt. 460)
Ph. 804/862-4463 **Facilities:** 11 indoor stalls, 1 run-in shelter, paddock, pasture, feed/hay, outdoor dressage arena, trails & limited elec/water for campers. Facilities can be arranged for other animals.

QUINTON, 23141

The Winged Horse (formerly Crazy R), David M. Ruslander
2949 Pocahontas Trail (1-1/2 m. E. of the Bottoms Bridge exit/exit 205 on 64 E., which is just past the I-295 interchange. 15 m. E. of Richmond & 30 min. from Colonial Williamsburg)
Ph. 804/932-9285 Email:daveruslander@yahoo.com **Facilities:** 4 stall barn, includes h&c water, holding pens, 3-rail fenced pastures, washrack, infared heat, rubber mats, ceiling fans and clothes washer & dryer. 2 rooms each w/private bath and 1-bdrm apt w/kitchen & full bath. In ground heated pool. Call for rates.

RADFORD, 24143

★ **Rebecca Thompson, Bedlam Manor Farm Stables**
Box 3425 (10 min. N. of I-81, exit 109. Call for directions)
Ph. 540/639-4150 540/639-9756 **Facilities:** Box stalls, turnout paddocks & feed/hay avail. for purchase. Home of Highlands Pony Club.

REVA, 22735

★ **The Funny Farm Inn, Kathy & Samantha Williams**
2437 Funny Farm Rd. (5-1/2 m. off US Rt. 29, to the W. 1/2 way between Warrenton & Charlottesville)
Ph. 540/547-3481 - leave message Email:dutchsparrow@erols.com
Web:www.bbonline.com/va/funnyfarm **Facilities:** 4-6 indoor stalls, individual paddocks, 50 acres of pasture, feed/hay incl., all-weather outdoor arena, miles & miles of trails on farm, camper/trailer parking & 4 complete, fully-equipped houses. Only 10 m. to Blue Ridge mtn. trails. Pool, AC, Cable TV.

SCOTTSVILLE, 24590

Hidden Hill Arabians, Frank L. Cowles, Jr.
9313 Greenfields Farm (23 m. S. of Charlottesville; Rt. 20, #626 4-1/2 m)
Ph. 804/286-4700 **Facilities:** 47 indoor stalls, 6 holding pens, feed, indoor/outdoor arenas, walker & extensive trails. B&B off premises.

CURRENT NEGATIVE COGGINS, HEALTH CERTIFICATE & OWNERSHIP PAPERS REQUIRED - see page 2 for details

SUGAR GROVE, 24375

★ **Kissing Rock Camp, Annie Malone**
1224 Horne Hollow Rd. (Central Mt Rogers Nat'l Recreation Area. 10 m. S. of Marion; 2 m. E. of Sugar Grove)
Ph. 276/677-3851 Email:kissingrock@area-net.com **Facilities:** 2-10x10 stalls, 2-10x20 stalls, 6 board fence paddocks, feed, direct access to VA Highlands Horse Trail & rustic cabin. Rig shuttle & ground support avail. for remote camping.

SYRIA, 22743

★ **Graves' Mountain Arena**
Rt. 670 (Near Rt. 29. 1/2 way between Charlottesville & Warrenton, close to Culpeper)
Ph. & Fax 540/829-9555 Web:www.gravesmountain.com **Facilities:** 15 indoor stalls, 10 holding pens, paddocks, 55 m. of trails and 50 rooms w/meals. Access to the Nat'l Park, swimming pool, tennis courts, fishing and golf course under construction this fall.

WARRENTON

★ **Bleu Rock Farms & Bleu Rock Inn, Restaurant & Pub**
12567 Lee Hwy., Washington VA 22747 (20 m. W. of Warrenton on Hwy 211 & apx. 70 m. from Washington D.C.)
Ph. 540/987-3190 Fax 540/987-3193 Barn 540/987-9522 Email:therock@monumental.com Web:www.BleuRockInn.com **Facilities:** Full service facility. 20 stalls, 2 holding pens, 4 pastures, 2 outdoor arenas, exercise track, feed/hay on request, vet/farrier on call & parking space. Other animals welcome. Call for reservations/rates. Bleu Rock Inn, Restaurant, Pub & Vineyard.

WAYNESBORO, 22980

★ **Evans Sporthorses at Waynesboro Stables**
333 Madrid Rd. (5 m. from I-81, exit 225)
Ph. 540/363-4540 Web:www.evanssporthorses.com **Facilities:** Up to 15-12x12 box stalls, h&c wash racks, pastures, arenas & cross-country jumps. Hotel accommodations at exit 225.

WIRTZ, 24184

★ **Shadow Ridge Stables, Michelle Gilbert**
P.O. Box 459 Location: 10120 Booker T. Washington Hwy (Located at Smith Mtn Lake VA at foothills of the Blue Ridge Mtns & within driving distance of the VA Horse Center)
Ph. 540/721-5120 Email:shadowdreamer@neocom.net **Facilities:** New 4300 sq. ft. barn includes 13 stalls w/private runs, lighting & fans, 180x100 riding arena, 2 wash bays w/h&c water, secure tack room w/frig & microwave, restroom, office (all rooms have heat/ac.) and ample trailer parking & turnaround space..

PRODUCT & SERVICES USAGE SURVEY

SURVEY PROFILE

A survey card was sent to 479 current users of the Nationwide Overnight Stabling Directory & Equestrian Vacation Guide, selected at random from every state. The survey card was postage paid for return to ETA. Returns came from 44 states plus APO addresses, Washington D.C., and Canada. There was a 44% return from our users, with 64% of the respondents making comments - 79% made comments of praise, 17% made constructive suggestions and 4% made comments of a negative nature.

USERS PURCHASING PROFILE

81% of our Users make purchases by mail and by phone.

95% of our Users own their own trucks.
Ford - 41%, Dodge - 16%, Chevrolet - 14%, GMC - 10%, Others - 19%.

96% of our Users own their own horse trailers.
14% own 2-horse trailers; 15% own 3-horse trailers; 15% own 4-horse trailers; 2.5% own 5-horse trailers; 4% own 6-horse trailers; 18% own 8-horse trailers; and 31.5% all others. 7% own trailers w/living quarters.

100% of our Users purchase horse-related products.
85% purchase vet & health products; 81% purchase grooming products; 67% purchase Western or English apparel; 57% purchase boots; 54% purchase saddles; 49% purchase stall equipment; 45% purchase trailer equipment; 44% purchase hats; 32% purchase portable stalls and automatic waterers.

58% of our Users plan on making major expenditures for:
Fencing, 63%; Stables/barns, 54%; Farm fixtures, 33%; Arenas, 30%; and Tractors/loaders, 19%.

76% of our Users have horse or stable insurance or are interested in purchasing such insurance.

90% of our Users do their own hauling and 10% use commercial haulers, with many doing both.

48% of our Users would like to see advertising for quality products and services for horse owners in the Directory.

23% of our Users would be interested in ETA souvenirs available through the Directory.

44% of our Users have already used the Directory for an equine vacation, while 46% plan to do so.

ETA USERS COMMENTS:

"It's been terrific as we haul horses to Colorado in May and back to Texas in October. We also camp and go to vacation spots with them."

"Very good - would be improved with advertising. I am alone and own one horse - sometimes you just don't know where to look for safest, most economical items."

"ETA's Directory has been extremely helpful for me moving several times in the last 5 years. Thanks."

"Could not travel without it."

"Outstanding, and you do attempt to be responsible in serving the traveler - some don't."

"Advertising? Services yes. These services should be relevant to the person traveling with horses."

"Great Directory - brings me much business."

"I'm a traveling nurse and take my horse all over the country with me. I couldn't do it without my Directory. Thanks a lot."

"Advertising is usually distracting. If it were in it's own section, it would be okay." (We have such a section in the Directory called ***Equine Alley***.)

"Nothing but praise for usefulness of Directory to horse transients. Best return for advertising dollars for subscribers."

"I use it . . . active duty military. Transferred every 3 years. Couldn't get across country without it."

"It's excellent and I have had many calls from it. All of the guests have been extremely nice."

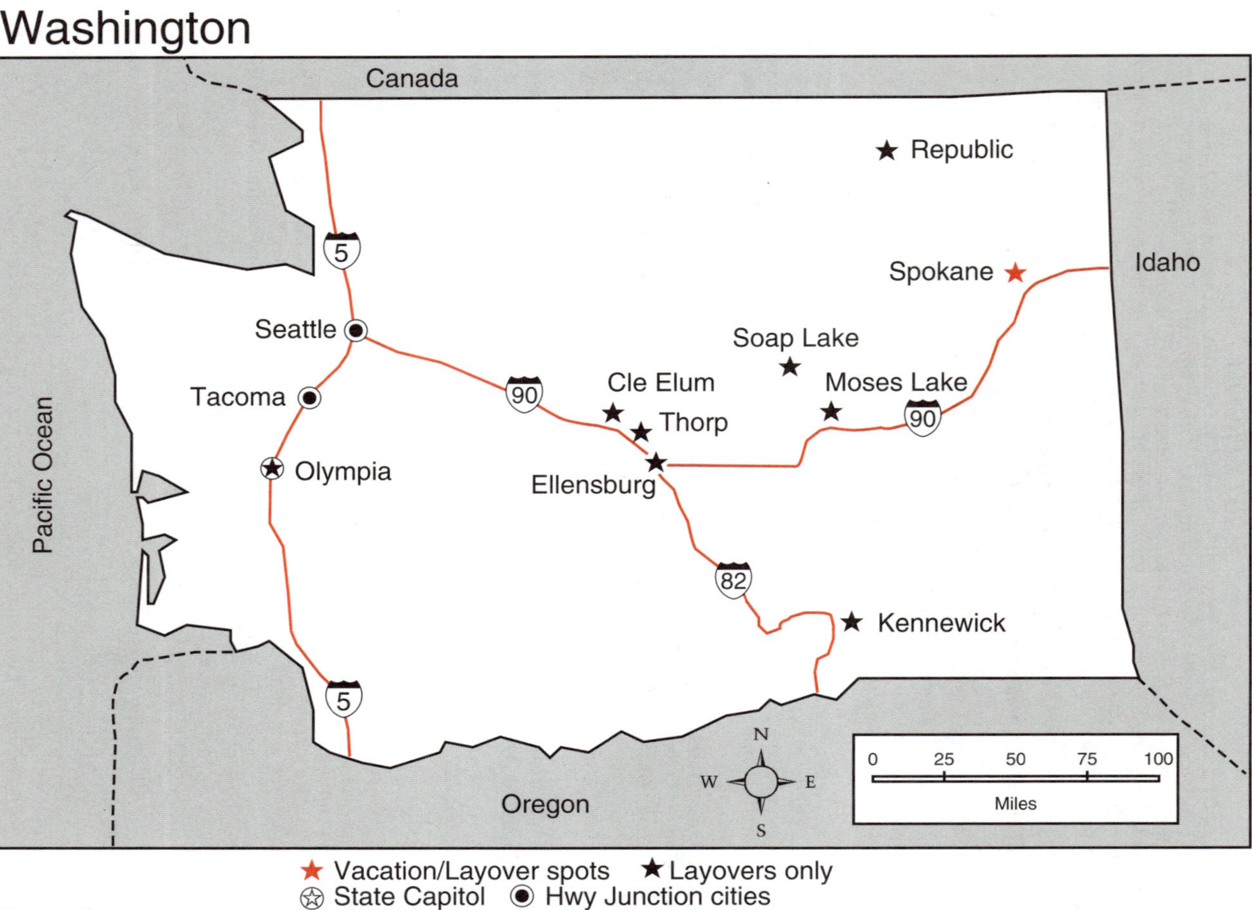
Washington
Canada
Republic
Idaho
Spokane
Seattle
Soap Lake
Tacoma
Cle Elum
Moses Lake
Thorp
Olympia
Ellensburg
Kennewick
Pacific Ocean
Oregon
5
90
82
5
90
N
W
E
S
0
25
50
75
100
Miles
Vacation/Layover spots
Layovers only
State Capitol
Hwy Junction cities

CURRENT NEGATIVE COGGINS, HEALTH CERTIFICATE & OWNERSHIP PAPERS REQUIRED - see page 2 for details

CLE ELUM, 98922

Shadow Ranch
P.O. Box 193 Location: 2851 Airport Rd. (I-90, exit 85)
Ph. 509/674-4399 206/991-6648 **Facilities:** Stalls, holding pens, pasture, feed, 60' round pen, miles of trail riding & trailer parking. Multiple motels nearby. Close & easy access from I-90.

ELLENSBURG, 98926

Kittitas County Fairgrounds, Kathryn Anderson, Adm. Sec.
512 N. Poplar (Ellensburg is at junction of I-90 & I-82)
Ph. **1-800/426-5340** 509/962-7639 **Facilities:** 120 stalls, holding pens, indoor/outdoor arenas, trails and full hookups from Apr.-Oct., power only from Nov.-Mar. Reservations req. Open 9 to 5 or call for late arrival.

KENNEWICK, 99337

Rocking J Stables
227210 E. Game Farm Rd. (I-82, exit 395/Kennewick)
Ph. 509/582-4384 **Facilities:** 19-16x20 stalls, 30 paddocks, 3 pastures, riding arena & exercise track..

MOSES LAKE, 98837

Grant County Fairgrounds, Al or Marilyn
3953 Airway Dr. NE (I-90, exit Hwy 17, between Spokane & Ellensburg)
Ph. 509/765-3581 Web:www.grantcountyfair.com **Facilities:** Covered stalls, 1 indoor/3 outdoor arenas, 187 acres for riding & camper hookups.

OLYMPIA, 98512

Miari Stables, Kari McClain
3619 49th Ave. SW Location: 3625 49th Ave. SW (I-5, exit 102, W. on Trosper Rd.)
Ph. Barn 360/786-1628 - let it ring Fax 360/943-7067 Email:miari@juno.com Web:www.miaristables.com **Facilities:** 27-12x12 rubber matted stalls, turnout paddocks, wash rack, indoor/outdoor arenas, elec & water hookup avail. Stallions accepted. Call for reservations/rates. Motels & services 5 min. away.

REPUBLIC, 99116

Horse Motel
P.O. Box 289 Location: 3374 Hwy 20 W. (30 m. S. of Canadian border)
Ph. 509/775-0624 **Facilities:** Pipe corrals, stock wire pens, round pen, water & trailer parking. Stallions accepted. Accommodations 7 m.

CURRENT NEGATIVE COGGINS, HEALTH CERTIFICATE & OWNERSHIP PAPERS REQUIRED - see page 2 for details

SOAP LAKE, 98851

Double Dream Stable, Layover and Boarding Facility, Derik & Lindee Kaiser
1551 Rd. 19 N.W. (Just outside of Ephrata. Hwy 28 N. apx. 4 m., W. on Rd. 19, S. side of road)
Ph. 509/246-8212 Email:arabtrainer@hotmail.com **Facilities:** 7 paddocks/stalls, 2 stallion pens, 1 small/1 large round pens, arena & several larger pens for groups. All paddocks & stalls have some cover. Close to lodging, fishing, camping & plenty of riding area.

SPOKANE, 99224

★ **Spokane Sport Horse Farm**
10710 S. Sherman Rd. (Close to I-90, off Hwy 195)
Ph. Cell 509/993-6786 or Message 509/448-5064
Email:ccarlson@spokanesporthorse.com
Web:www.spokanesporthorse.com
Facilities: 60-12x12 indoor stalls w/attached 60' runs, feed avail., 122x216 indoor/150x250 outdoor arenas/2 other outdoor arenas, miles of trails (many on grounds), and elec. & water for campers avail. Multiple motels nearby. Have arrrangement with Ramada Inn Airport for "farm rate."

THORP, 98946

Wheeler Performance Horses, Aimee Wheeler
261 Watt Canyon Rd. (9 m. W. of Ellensburg, with easy on/off access from I-90)
Ph. 509/964-2270 Email:rodeogal21@eburg.com Web:www.wheelerperformancehorses.com **Facilities:** Large indoor stalls (at least 12x14) some with paddocks, 12x24 outdoor pens w/loafing sheds, 70' round pen, outdoor arena (soon to be covered), and backed by some of the best trails in Kittitas Co. Hotels/KOA 10 min. away.

NOTES

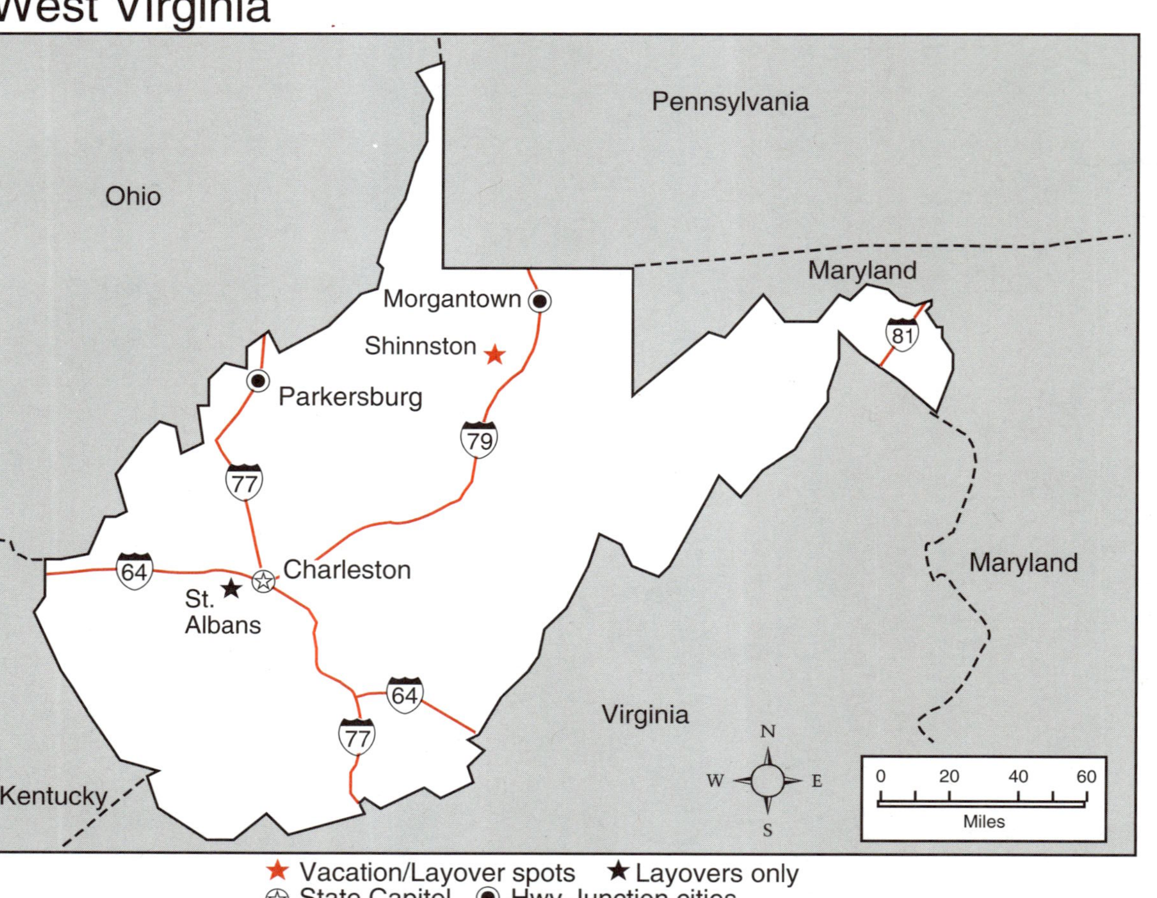
West Virginia
Ohio
Pennsylvania
Maryland
Maryland
Virginia
Kentucky
Morgantown
Shinnston
Parkersburg
Charleston
St. Albans
81
79
77
77
64
64
N
W
E
S
0
20
40
60
Miles
Vacation/Layover spots
Layovers only
State Capitol
Hwy Junction cities

CURRENT NEGATIVE COGGINS, HEALTH CERTIFICATE & OWNERSHIP PAPERS REQUIRED - *see page 2 for details*

ST. ALBANS (Charleston area), 25177

Sunday Stables, Susan Sunday
1 Twilight Ln. (6 m. from I-64)
Ph. 304/722-4630 or 304/722-4600 Email:ssunday@access.k12.wv.us or christypauley@yahoo.com **Facilities:** Indoor stalls, number varies, feed/hay, arena, camper hookup and Bed & Breakfast.

SHINNSTON, 26431-1154

★ **Gillum House Bed & Breakfast, Kathleen A. Panek**
35 Walnut St. (7 m. W. of I-79, exit 124/Jerry Dove Dr)
Ph. **1-888/592-0177** Fax 304/592-1882 Email:stabling@gillumhouse.com Web:www.gillumhouse.com **Facilities:** 2-1/2 m. from house - 6 stall stable w/wash rack, paddock w/training ring & open field. 3 guest rooms w/shared bath for B&B, incl. full breakfast. Low fat/low cholesterol/made from scratch.

Wisconsin

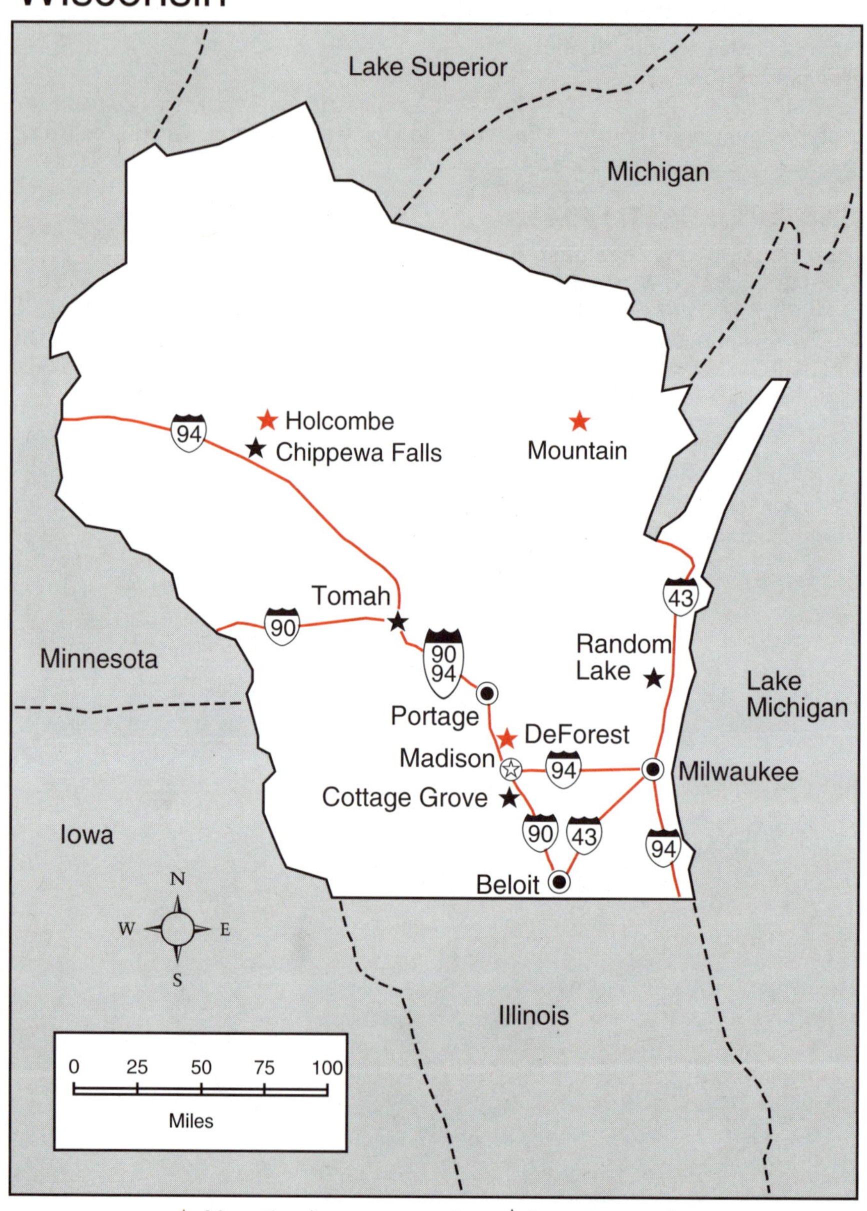

★ Vacation/Layover spots ★ Layovers only
State Capitol Hwy Junction cities

CURRENT NEGATIVE COGGINS, HEALTH CERTIFICATE & OWNERSHIP PAPERS REQUIRED - see page 2 for details

CHIPPEWA FALLS, 54729-6412

Amber Farm, Inc., Spencer & Kathy Jerome
18798-70th Ave. (From I-94W, exit 70; from I-94E, exit 59 to Hwy 53N, Chippewa Falls)
Ph. Barn 715/723-7050 Home 715/723-9513 Fax 715/726-0517
Email:dhrsldy@aol.com **Facilities:** 12x12 box stalls in barn, turnout paddocks, hay/grain, indoor/outdoor arenas, trails in nearby Lake Wissota State Park. Pine Harbor Campground,715/723-9865. Vet, 715/723-3655. Motels nearby. Owners live on premises.

COTTAGE GROVE, 53527

Lazy L Ranch & Horse Co.
2189 Rinden Rd. (1.5 m. off I-90, exit 147. 10 m. from Madison)
Ph. 608/873-6725 **Facilities:** 30 indoor stalls, paddocks, 60x120 indoor/2-lighted outdoor arenas & round pen. Vet on call/mgr on premises. Convenient access to motels/restaurants/Dane Co. Expo Center/Univ of WI Vet School. Call for reservations.

WISCONSIN

DeFOREST, 53532

★ **JBearJ Ranch, Jay & Julie Cashmore**
3037 Skaar Rd. (8 m. E. of DeForest off I-90/94)
Ph. 608/846-1301 Email:jbearj314@hotmail.com **Facilities:** 2 stalls or a round pen/pasture avail. There's plenty of room for parking and a tent or camper can be set up. One room avail. w/kg-sized bed and private bath w/jacuzzi.

HOLCOMBE, 54745

★ **Merrimount Stables/The Happy Horse B&B, Alan & Sandra Ricker**
24469 St. Hwy 27 (25 m. NE of Chippewa Falls)
Ph. 715/239-6158 - stables & 239-0707 - B&B. Email: happyhorsebb @centuryinter.net **Facilities:** 4 indoor stalls, 4 pastures, hay, indoor arena, trails on 160 acre farm and 4 rooms.

MOUNTAIN, 54149

★ **Spur of the Moment Ranch, LLC, Skip & Ann Maletzke**
14221 Helen Ln. (Hwy 32 N. to Nat'l Forest Rd. 2071, W. to West Shore Dr., S. 1 blk to Helen Ln)

Ph. 715/276-3726 **1-800/644-8783** Web:www.spurofthemomentranch.org
Facilities: Barn w/20 stalls, 100x170 turnout, round pen, 4 rustic cabins/sleeps 2-6 and modern bath house. Ranch lies in the heart of the Nicolet Nat'l Forest - miles of riding & driving pleasure await you. Call for reservations.

CURRENT NEGATIVE COGGINS, HEALTH CERTIFICATE & OWNERSHIP PAPERS REQUIRED - *see page 2 for details*

RANDOM LAKE, 53075

Drs. Bushard & Hanrahan - Care Facility
N239 Hwy D.E. (3/4 m. S. of Hwy 144 on Co. Rd. D.E.)
Ph. 920/994-4909 24 hr. answering 262/338-1838 **Facilities:** 7 indoor stalls, outdoor paddocks, limited pasture, feed avail. & limited space for campers. 10 m. from Horseman's Park in the Northern Kettle Moraine State Forest, which has over 75 m. of horse trails.

TOMAH, 54660

Twin Oaks, Douglas & Mary Maas
28720 Hwy ET Location: 28316 Hwy ET (West Central WI, 3 m. from I-90/94)
Ph. 608/372-4929 or 608/374-4466 Fax 608/374-4467
Email:mattmaas@mwt.net **Facilities:** Newly remodeled barn w/10x12 or 12x12 stalls, turn-out areas, large parking area, clean & well kept facility.

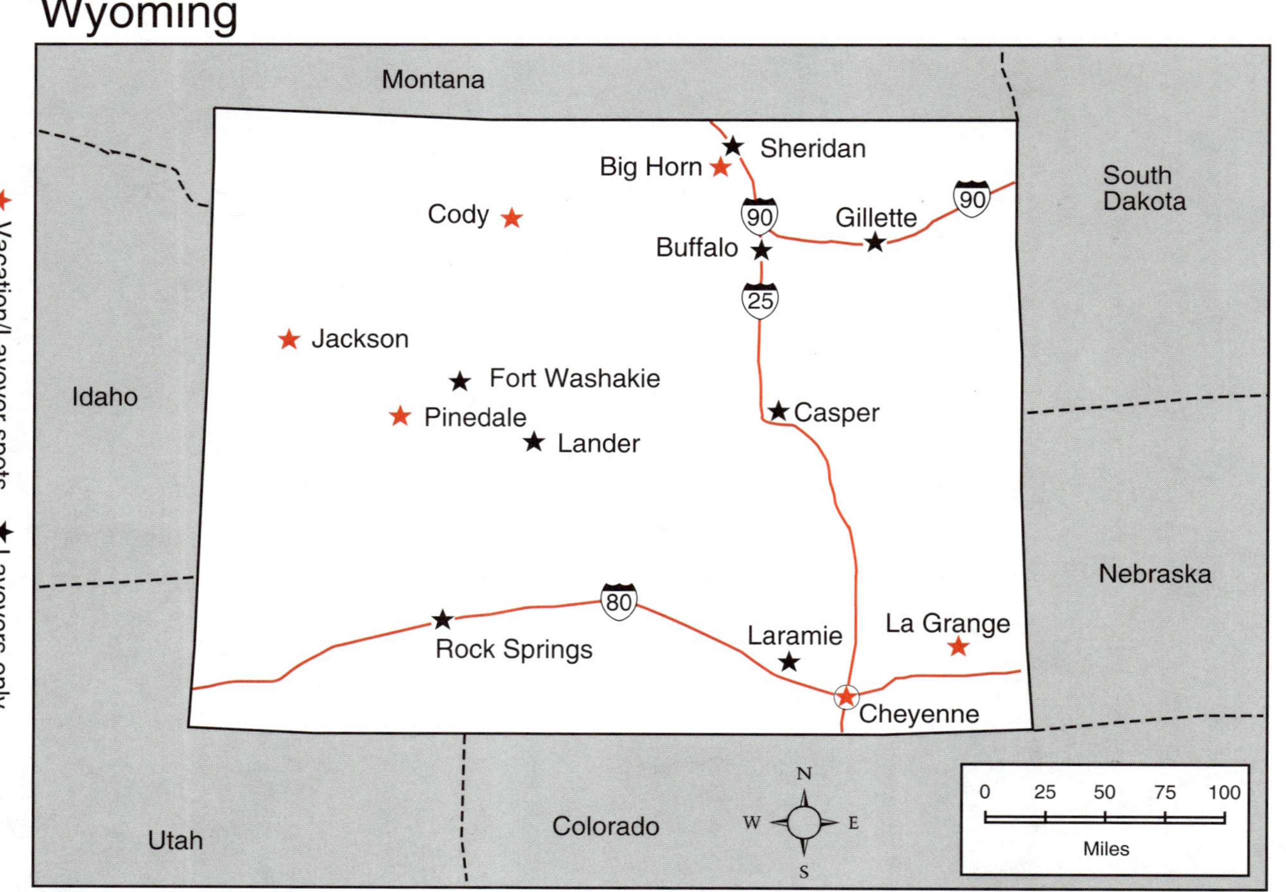

★ Vacation/Layover spots ★ Layovers only
State Capitol Hwy Junction cities

CURRENT NEGATIVE COGGINS, HEALTH CERTIFICATE & OWNERSHIP PAPERS REQUIRED - *see page 2 for details*

BIG HORN, 82833

★ **Spear Ranch Bed & Breakfast, Lonnie & Pam Wright**
P.O. Box 607 Location: 170 Brinton Rd. (I-90, exit 25 to Hwy 87 & 335. Hwy 335 to Big Horn)
Ph. 307/673-0079 Fax 307/673-0279 Web:www.spearranch.com **Facilities:** 3 indoor stalls, 5 holding pens, 2 pasture (not avail. in hay season), hay per bale and 5 rooms & 2 cottages for Bed & Breakfast. Cottages require 3 night minimum stay. Call for reservations & rates.

BUFFALO, 82834

Johnson County Fair Board
P.O. Box 911 Location: 18 Fairgrounds Rd. (I-90, exit 56A from N.; I-90, exit 58 from E.; I-25, exit 299 from S.)
Ph. Caretaker - 307/684/7357 Ph. & Fax 307/684-7869 - bookkeeping (call before faxing) **Facilities:** 80 indoor/96 outdoor stalls & camper hookup.

CASPER, 82604

Central Wyoming Fairgrounds
1700 Fairgrounds Rd. (Off Hwy 220)
Ph. 307/235-5775 Fax 307/266-4224 Email:cwfr@centralwyomingfair.com Web:www.centralwyomingfair.com/ **Facilities:** 500 outdoor stalls, holding pens, indoor/outdoor arenas & camper hookup w/booked events.

CHEYENNE & LARAMIE

★ **A. Drummond's Ranch Bed & Breakfast**
399 Happy Jack Rd., Cheyenne WY 82007 (Hwy 210. Access from I-80 on scenic St. Hwy. 210, between Cheyenne & Laramie)
Ph. & Fax 307/634-6042 Email:adrummond@juno.com **Facilities:** 4 indoor stalls w/rubber mats/bedding, 4 holding pens, indoor arena, 55,000 acres in Nat'l Forest and 4 Bed & Breakfast rooms w/outdoor hottubs & dinner avail. NO SMOKING. RESERVATIONS REQUIRED. No dogs in rooms or off leash.

CHEYENNE, 82007

★ **Cheyenne Stockyard - Cattle & Horse Motel, Tony Edwards**
350 Southwest Dr. (Easy on, easy off of I-25, exit 9/Lincolnway) 7 min. from CHEYENNE FRONTIER DAYS, "Daddy of 'em All
Ph. 307/634-7333 **1-888/634-7333** Fax 307/637-4868
Email:StockyardOffice@aol.com **Facilities:** 21-20x25, 16-20x40 indoor stalls, 7-40x70 outdoor pens & parking. Open 24 hours. Vet/farrier/groomer on call. Within walking distance of restaurants, hotels, gas station & truck stop. Can accommodate all types of livestock.

WYOMING

CURRENT NEGATIVE COGGINS, HEALTH CERTIFICATE & OWNERSHIP PAPERS REQUIRED - see page 2 for details

CHEYENNE, 82007

★ **7XL Stables at Terry Bison Ranch, Dan Thiel**
51 I-25 Service Rd. E. (I-25, at WY-CO border, take WY exit 2 to Terry Ranch Rd., 2 m. S)
Ph. 307/634-4171 **Facilities:** 16 indoor/12 outdoor stalls, outdoor pens, feed/hay, trail rides & trailer parking. Overnight & monthly stabling on 27,000 acre bison ranch. Guest ranch w/horseback riding, wagon tours, fishing, RV park, cabins, bunkhouse, restaurant & saloon.

CHEYENNE, 82009

Adventurers' Country Bed & Breakfast and Horse Motel, Chuck & Fern White
3803 I-80 S. Service Rd. (15 m. E. of Cheyenne, off I-80, exit 377)
Ph.& Fax 307/632-4087 Web:www.bbonline.com/wy/adventurers/
Email:fwhite1@juno.com **Facilities:** 4 indoor box stalls, 2 paneled outdoor stalls w/roof, large fenced pasture, $6 bale hay, hookups & parking, and Bed & Breakfast w/4 guest rooms & 1-3 room suite/sleeps up to 5. Evening desserts & home-cooked breakfast. Non-smoking. Reservations required.

CHEYENNE, 82009

Cheyenne Riding Club, Inc., Martin Wissner, owner
9409 Michigan St. (Easy access from I-80, exit 16. Minutes away from Frontier Park "Cheyenne Frontier Days." Close to motels, restaurants, truck stop, gas station, 2 major equine vet facilities)
Ph.307/634-5162 on-site mgrs Bob Fox & Jamie Allen or 307/649-2430, owner Email:sunsprit@worldnett.att.net Web:www.cheyenneridingclub.com **Facilities:** 12x12 indoor stalls in motel barn, 12x12 & 12x10 indoor stalls in main barn, 20x50 & 12x50 outdoor corrals, 12x16 outdoor pens, indoor riding/2 outdoor arenas & trailer parking. Bedding provided/feed avail. on request. Reservations appreciated.

CHEYENNE, 82009

Singletree Stable
4715 Thomas Rd. (E. Lincolnway/I-80, exit 364, N. on College, right on Thomas)
Ph. **1-800/336-0287** 307/635-6010 **Facilities:** Indoor stalls w/sawdust & waterers, feed on request & exercise arena.

CODY, 82414

★ **Heart 2 Heart Bed-Barn-Breakfast**
483 RD 2AB
Ph. 307/587-2906 **Facilities:** 4 holding pens, 3 pastures, feed, camper parking w/elec., and 2 rooms w/shared bath for Bed & full Breakfast. Pen avail. for dogs/cats.

CURRENT NEGATIVE COGGINS, HEALTH CERTIFICATE & OWNERSHIP PAPERS REQUIRED - see page 2 for details

CODY, 82414

★ **Horse Whisper Ranch Horse Hotel, R.J. & Jia Ludwick**
19 Bartlett Ln. (Hwy 14/16/20 to Yellowstone Park. 7 m. from Cody on Southfork Hwy)
Ph. 307/587-6637 Cell 307/899-6637 **Facilities:** 3 indoor/6 outdoor stalls, 2 holding pens, 2 pastures, feed, trails & parking for self-contained units. Can set up ride in Yellowstone Park. Daily, weekly or monthly stay.

FORT WASHAKIE, 82514

Fish Hunter Ranch, Ellen Clark & Harry Elyea
P.O. Box 585 Location: 90 South Fork Rd. (Between Lander & Dubois on US 287)
Ph. 307/335-9132 Email:harry651@onewest.net **Facilities:** 4 stalls w/runs, 2 paddocks, large pastures, certified hay avail., 30 amp elec. hookups, water hookups and cabin/sleeps 4 w/washer, dryer, stove, fridge & full bath.

GILLETTE, 82717

Timber Creek Stables & Arena, Jess & Marilyn Ewing
Mail: P.O. Box 3422 Location: #76 Timber Creek Rd. (From W: I-90, exit Wyo-Dak/132. From E: I-90, exit Rozet/141)
Ph. 307/682-6817 **Facilities:** 10 indoor stalls w/runs, 2-PVC fenced holding pens, hay & cubes avail., indoor arena & trails. 10 motels nearby.

JACKSON, 83001

★ **Valar - Dugan Horse Boarding & Transport, Kenny Dugan & Pia Valar Dugan**
P.O. Box 3365 Location:1770 E. River Dr. Hoback Junction (12 m. S. of Jackson at the junction of 26/89 & 189/191)
Ph.& Fax 307/733-2733 Email:kpduganbt@aol.com **Facilities:** 6 indoor stalls, 8 holding pens, feed avail., 40' round pen, access to Nat'l Forest trails, 1 camper hookup & trailer parking. All animals welcome. Vet/farrier on call. 5 min. walk to Hoback River Resort - hotel/motel & cabins. 10 min. walk to campground.

LaGRANGE, 82221

★ **Bear Mountain Riding Ranch, Sherri Lovercheck**
RR 77, Box 133 (50 m. NE of Cheyenne on Hwy 85)
Ph. 307/834-2492 Fax 307/834-2443 Email:bear@prairieweb.com Web:www.wyobearmountain.com **Facilities:** 11 outdoor panneled stalls, 2 holding pens, camper parking & a guest house/sleeps 14. Meals optional. Hay/wagon rides to BBQ's by reservation. Massage on site by appointment. Offering guests 8,000 acres of private ranch land with varied terrain for riding.

LANDER, 82520-9114

Sandstone Ranch Equine Motel, LLC, Kathryn A. Kulcher
2529 Sinks Canyon Rd. (St. Hwy 131)
Ph. 307/332-2177 Fax 307/335-9535 **Facilities:** 4 outdoor sheds w/runs, grass hay/alfalfa avail., round pen & State Park/Nat'l Forest 5 m. No hookups-motels & trailer hookups in town..

CURRENT NEGATIVE COGGINS, HEALTH CERTIFICATE & OWNERSHIP PAPERS REQUIRED - see page 2 for details

LARAMIE, 82070

On a String Ranch, Mernie C. Younger
900 Howe Rd. (2 m. S. of I-80, exit 313. Call for directions)
Ph. 307/742-4723 Email: onastring9@aol.com Web: www.onastring.com **Facilities:** 28 indoor stalls, 12 paddocks, 640 acres of pasture, feed incl., 60x120 indoor arena & parking space. Holiday Inn, Motel 6 and others nearby.

PINEDALE, 82941

★ **Pole Creek Ranch Bed & Breakfast, Dexter Smith**
P.O. Box 278 (Hwy 191, turn right on Pole Creek Rd 2.44 m.)
Ph. 307/367-4433 Email:polecreekranch@wyoming.com **Facilities:** 4 indoor stalls, 1 indoor/outdoor stall, holding pens, 7 acre pasture, feed, 1 camper hookup and Bed & Breakfast/3 rooms. No alcohol. Smoking on porches. We cater to families.

ROCK SPRINGS, 82901

Old #6 Corrals
5000 Springs Dr. (Located right in town, 2 blks off I-80, exit 104 at Elk St.) Mail: HC 67, Box 7, Lonetree WY 82936
Ph. 307/782-7912 - Lance/owner Caretaker/Jerry 307/382-7099
Cell 307/389-0333 **Facilities:** 42 individual pole & post corrals w/shelter, hay avail., small outdoor exercise arena, round pen, unlimited open range riding & extensive parking w/limited elec. & water for overnight camping. Motels/restaurants/gas stations/truck stops within walking distance.

ROCK SPRINGS, 82901

Sweetwater County Events Complex
3320 Yellowstone Rd. (Take Elk St. exit & go N.; Yellowstone forks to left - located on right side 2 m.)
307/352-6789 307/352-06786 - John Keller, Caretaker **Facilities:** All stalls individually assigned. Reservations/pmt. for stalls are to be arranged through the Complex office prior to stabling of animals. For weekends/after hours, contact Caretaker. No stalling of horses from July 20 thru Aug. 12 yearly.

ROCK SPRINGS, 82902

Last Nickel Ranch, Sara Gates & Bob Snook
P.O. Box 31 Location:506 Yellowstone Rd. (8 m. from I-80)
Ph. 307/362-9705 Cell 307/389-9953 Fax 307/362-9484
Email:saragates@earthlink.net **Facilities:** 4 indoor stalls w/matts, round pen, small indoor/large outdoor arenas, numerous trails & camper hookup. Vet/farrier on call. Other animals okay.

SHERIDAN, 82801

King Bros. Ranch
3102 Hwy 87 (8 m. S. of town)
Ph. 307/672-5354 **Facilities:** Indoor stalls w/outside runs, 5 holding pens, indoor/outdoor arenas, walker & feed. For overnight layover, you must CALL one day in advance & must arrive before 8 p.m. or call. No camping.

Moon Set Photo by: Jehnet Carlson

CURRENT NEGATIVE COGGINS, HEALTH CERTIFICATE & OWNERSHIP PAPERS REQUIRED - *see page 2 for details*

AIRDRIE, T4B 2A3

Rusty Acres Equine Bed & Bale, Barry & Karen Rustad

Site 4, Box 5, RR 1 (Located minutes N. of Calgary) Ph. 403/948-4199 Email:yourhost@overnightstables.com Web:overnightstables.com **Facilities:** For up to 6 horses: 10x12 box stalls or private 1/2 ac. grass paddocks w/8x16 shelters, alfalfa/grass hay, clean water, 70x160 indoor arena. Overnight/short term accommodations. Experienced/around-the-clock supervision. Motels/ B&B's 10 min. drive. Coggins test mandatory.

CALGARY (Priddis area),

★ **Hilltop Ranch Bale, Bed & Breakfast, Gary & Barbara Zorn**

Mail: Box 54, Priddis AB TOL 1WO (20 km/12 m. W. on 22X from Hwy 2. 12 m.SW of Calgary)
Ph. **1-800/801-0451** 403/931-3744 Fax 403/931-3426
Email:gary@hilltopranch.net Web:www.hilltopranch.net **Facilities:** 2 barns, 11 box stalls, pasture, feed, parking for campers and **Bed & Breakfast**. Mountain equestrian trails only 10 m. away in the Rocky Mountains.

GRANDE PRAIRIE, T8V 5N3

★ **A River Road Bed & Breakfast, Rod & Charlotte Young**

RR 3, Site 2, Box 15 (Hwy #40, 5 min. S. of Grande Prairie)
Ph. 780/538-1204 Fax 780/538-3420 Email:riverrd@telusplanet.net
Web:www.ariverroad.com **Facilities:** 2 outdoor stalls, holding pens, 6.9 ac. of pasture, trails, camper parking with/or without hookup, and Bed & Breakfast w/shared or private bath. No G.S. TorHotel tax. 5 min. to vet or anything needed. Horse owners: facilities to be used at own risk

CURRENT NEGATIVE COGGINS, HEALTH CERTIFICATE & OWNERSHIP PAPERS REQUIRED - see page 2 for details

LANSDOWNE, K0E 1L0

Jailin Ranch, Lynn & Jay Sargent
2414 Outlet Rd. (Exit 659 off 401 Hwy; 6 m. from I-81, Hill Island border crossing)
Ph. 613.659-4087 Cell 613/329-8718 Email:jailinsaddlery@hotmail.com
Web:www.cyberweb.ca/jailinranch
Facilities: 9-13x13 box stalls, 2 holding pens, 100 acres of pasture, hay/grain provided, outdoor sand 120x250 arena and 1000 island parkway trails.

MT. BRYDGES, N0L 1WO

Falconbrydge Farm, Dr. J.F. Gough
22329 Troops Rd., RR #1 (15 m. W. of London ONT, 1 m. from Hwy 402 at Mt. Brydges exit) Ph. 519/472-6889 **Facilities:** 4 stalls, pasture, camper hookup and Bed & Breakfast.

YUKON, Y1A 3V4

★ **Bear Creek Lodge (Kluane), Bryant & Gail Jeeves, Owners**
Mile 1002 Alaska Hwy. (6 m. N. of Haines Junction)
Ph. 867/634-2301 Fax 867/634-2302
Facilities: Holding pens, feed avail., full service restaurant & lounge. RV park, and motel. Located adjacent to Kluane Nat'l Park.

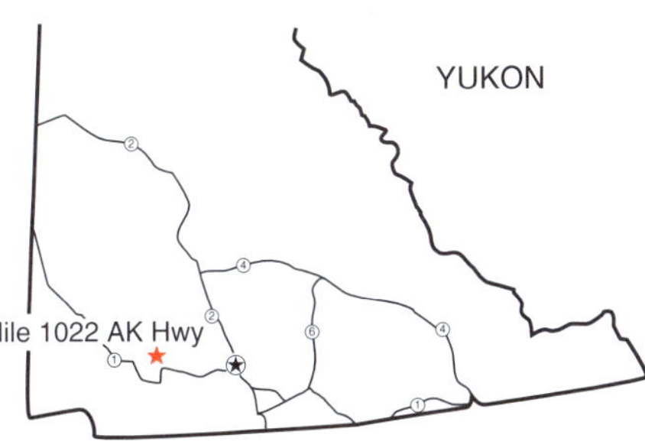

CANADA

AMERICAN HORSE
PUBLICATIONS

Make A Difference In Their Health
"At the heart of our research is the horse. With The Horseman's Card® Visa® Credit Card, you can truly make a difference"
Dr. Peter J. Timoney, Director
Maxwell H. Gluck Equine Research Center
THE HORSEMAN'S CARD®
Call today and apply for yours
800-780-5561. Mention priority code GHP6.

Now just $20.96
for the classic horse training
manual

**"True Horsemanship
Through Feel"**

by
Bill Dorrance & Leslie Desmond

750 photos/386 pages
www.lesliedesmond.com

Do You Know...

- where snow polo is played?
- where you can learn to play polo?
- how to locate a polo artist or photographer?
- where to buy the finest polo equipment in the world?
- where the first game of the millennium will be played?

Photo: David Lominska

We Do!

The Chukker Collection's
(since 1992)

2002 International Polo Calendar and Directory

The Chukker Collection invites you to join us on our annual journey around the world, through the beauty and the excitement of polo. Over 100 pages of full color photos bring to life the talent of the players, the horses and the care givers. Share in the exhilaration of the world's most exciting sport. The 2002 edition contains detailed polo information and national holidays from over 60 countries. Days and months are listed in eight languages.

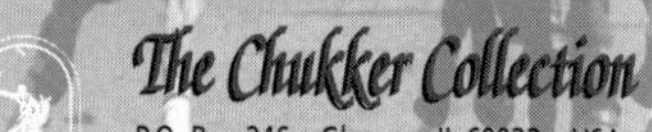

P.O. Box 246 • Glencoe, IL 60022 • USA
Tel: 1 847 835-0180 Fax: 1 847 835-0181
www.thechukkercollection.com

Photo: Shelley Heatley

Services

Western Store

DANDALES

WESTERN STORE

CLOTHING • BOOTS • HATS • TACK
• LARGE SELECTION •

Hours: M-F 10-9, Sat. 10-7, Sun. 12-6

Exit 50 off I-35, 1m. E. on Hwy 54

10929 E. Kellog — 316/683-8231
Wichita, KS. 67207 — 1-800/367-5194

Nation-Wide Horse Transportation - see ad, inside front cover

ADVERTISERS INDEX

RETAILERS INDEX

The Nationwide Overnight Stabling Directory & Equestrian Vacation Guide can be purchased at the following establishments.

ARKANSAS
Clarksville - Standridge Circle S Rance .479/754-8299

ARIZONA
Flagstaff - Flying Heart Barn .928/526-2788
Phoenix - Greenway Saddlery .602/971-8203
Phoenix - Western Ranchman Store .602/992-3410

CALIFORNIA
Bakersfield - End of the Road Ranch .661/845-3013
Baldwin Park - Broken Horn .818/337-4088
Barstow - Pan McCue Ranch .760/254-2184
Cupertino - Christensen's . 408/255-3761
Del Mar - Mary's Tack .619/755-2015
Fremont - Two Horse Enterprises .510/657-5239
Indio - Desert Feed Bag .619/342-6602
Norco - Wild West Trailers .909/737-7600
Vacaville - Ranchotel Tack Barn .707/451-8225

COLORADO
Aurora - Lancaster's Western Wear .**1-800/348-0318**, 303/343-0318
Breckenridge - Weber's Books .970/453-4723
Brighton - Brighton Feed Store .303/659-0721
Burlington - The Horse Motel .719/346-8217
Lake George - Mule Creek Outfitters/M Lazy C Ranch . **1-800/289-4868**, 719/748-3398
Larkspur - Spring Canyon Ranch .303/681-3237
Palisade/Grand Junction - Alamar Stables .970/523-1445

FLORIDA
Homosassa - Country Feed & Supply .352/628-2716
Lake Worth - John & Catey Stomski/Horse Trailer Sales .407/968-3508
Marianna - Circle D Ranch & Western Shop .904/352-4882, 904/352-4324
Ocala - Haylo Trailer Sales .352/732-3455
Ocala - Midwest Hay, Inc .352/351-8008
Ocala - Nelson's Trailer Sales .352/732-8908
Odessa - J C Saddlery .813/720-3587
Pensacola - Pine Forest Saddlery .904/944-0196
Royal Palm Beach - Discount Vet Supply .561/793-6697
West Palm Beach - The Tackeria .561/793-6422

GEORGIA
Alpharetta - Atlanta Saddlery .**1-800/356-7203**, 770/475-1967
Tyrone - Trickum Creek Rance .770/487-2146

ILLINOIS
Libertyville - Libertyville Saddle Shop, Inc. .847/362-0570
Princeton Bureau County Fairgrounds .815/875-1003
Richmond - Richmond Saddlery .815/678-6055

KANSAS
Colby - Tin Acres Quarter Horses .785/462-7525, 785/462-3600
Salina - Hunters Leigh B&B .**1-800/889-6750**, 785/823-6750
Wichita - Dandale's Western Store .**1-800/367-5194**, 316/683-8231

KENTUCKY
Lexington - Polly's Western Wear 859/229-6742
Lexington - U.S. Pony Club Bookstore 606/254-7669
Shelbyville - Sanorosa Farm 502/647-3324

LOUISIANA
Slidell - Lewis Stables 504/643-8025

MICHIGAN
Ann Arbor - Karol King 734/426-6113

MINNESOTA
Bloomington - The Brown Cow Saddle Blanket Co . .507/263-7013 - Diane, 952/854-4255

MISSISSIPPI
Gulfport - Shady Oaks Stable 228/832-0435, 228/452-2646
Utica - Big Sand Campgrounds, Inc. 601/885-8068

MISSOURI
Bland - Mules and More 573/646-3934
Excelsior Springs - Dar-B-Ann Stables 816/630-3332
Eureka - Golden Horseshoe Tack, Inc. 314/938-4309
Pineville - Ponderosa Trails & RV Park **1-888/644-6773**, 417/223-4081
Rolla - Green Acres Stables, Arena & Tack Shop 573/341-3004

MONTANA
Big Timber - Carriage House Ranch 406/932-5339
Deer Lodge - Mountain View Arena 406/846-1989

NEBRASKA
Bayard - Flying Bee Beefmaster Ranch LLC **1-888/534-2341**

NEVADA
Las Vegas - Horse "N" Around Too 702/646-1859
Reno - D Bar Western Store 775/329-9107

NEW JERSEY
Woodstown - Cow Town Cowboy Outfitters 609/769-1761

NEW MEXICO
Albuquerque - Dan's Boots & Saddles 505/345-2220

NORTH CAROLINA
Carthage - McNeill Feed 910/949-0404

OKLAHOMA
Oklahoma City - Ridgecrest Equestrian Center 405/478-1166

OREGON
Columbia River Equestrian Center 1-**888/922-TACK**. 541/922-3704

PENNSYLVANIA
Darlington - Creighton Feed and Supply 412/847-4994

RHODE ISLAND
North Scitaute - Tourbillion Trailer Sales, Inc. 401/934-2221

SOUTH CAROLINA
Aiken - Town & Country Inn 803/642-0270

SOUTH DAKOTA
Mitchell - Hobby Horse Stables 605/995-1581

TENNESSEE
Cross Plains - Single Tree Farm 615/654-2636

TEXAS
Amarillo - Equestrian Equipper 806/379-8866
Amarillo - Happy Tracks Horse Motel 806/352-4031
Amarillo - Quarter Horse Outfitters/Museum Store **1-888209-8322**
Cat Spring - Rancho Texcelente IXL 979/865-3636
Houston - Horse TV 713/868-1186
Karnack - The Josey Enterprises 903/935-5358
Millsap - Capp's Radio Ranch 940/682-2020
Weatherford - Tona Blake Studio 817/596-9546

UTAH
Salt Lake City - AA Callister Corporation **1-800/606-7058**, 801/973-7058
St. George - Harmony Horse Haven 435/673-3991
Sandy - Sagebrush Ranch 801/562-4318
West Bountiful - The American Cowboy/Universal Equestrian Center 801/295-RIDE

VIRGINIA
Fort Valley -Fort Valley Stables **1-888/992-6634**, 540/933-6634
Sugar Grove - Kissing Rock Camp 276/677-3851

WISCONSIN
Mountain - Spur of the Moment Ranch **1-800/644-8783**, 715/276-3726

WYOMING
Cheyenne - Cheyenne Stockyard **1-888/634-7333**, 307/634-7333
Jackson - Valar - Dugan Horse Boarding 307/733-2733
Landers - Main Street Books 307/332-7661

CHANGE OF ADDRESS

Ph. 620/442-8131 Fax 620/442-8215 Email:eta@hit.net Web:www.overnightstabling.com

ETA Membership or Service Access No.____________________

Name____________________

Old Address ____________________

City____________ State ________ Zip________

New Address ____________________

City____________ State ________ Zip________

New Phone____________________

2003

INFORMATION REQUEST & ORDER FORM

Ph. 620/442-8131 Fax 620/442-8215 Email:eta@hit.net Web:www.overnightstabling.com

Please check choices:

___ Directory only - $29.45 incl hdlg

___ Information Service - $19.95 yearly

___ ETA Membership (Dir & Ser) $42.45 incl hdlg

___ Please send information/rates for display advertising

___ List facilities in Dir & on Ser - $20; please send information & order form. Listing deadline Sept 15

___ List facilities & receive Directory - $39.45 incl hdlg

___ Check here to be designated as vacation spot

Name ____________________

Mailing Address ____________________

City ____________ State ________ Zip ________

Phone ____________________

To Charge to Credit Card:

Visa ❑ MasterCard ❑ American Express ❑ Discover ❑

Card No. ____________________ Ex. Date ________

Signature ____________________

2003

DIRECTORY & VACATION GUIDE USERS:

Please let us have your comments about your trip. We'd like to know what pleased you and what didn't. We are interested in your experiences using our directory/guide.

NO POSTAGE
NECESSARY
IF MAILED
IN THE
UNITED STATES

BUSINESS REPLY MAIL

FIRST-CLASS MAIL PERMIT NO. 8 ARKANSAS CITY KS

POSTAGE WILL BE PAID BY ADDRESSEE

EQUINE TRAVELERS OF AMERICA INC
PO BOX 322
ARKANSAS CITY KS 67005-9962

NO POSTAGE
NECESSARY
IF MAILED
IN THE
UNITED STATES

BUSINESS REPLY MAIL

FIRST-CLASS MAIL PERMIT NO. 8 ARKANSAS CITY KS

POSTAGE WILL BE PAID BY ADDRESSEE

EQUINE TRAVELERS OF AMERICA INC
PO BOX 322
ARKANSAS CITY KS 67005-9962